Great Lakes Books Series

A complete listing of the books in this series
can be found online at wsupress.wayne.edu.

Editor

Thomas Klug
Sterling Heights, Michigan

Detroit's Wayne State University Law School

*Future Leaders in the
Legal Community*

Alan Schenk

WAYNE STATE UNIVERSITY PRESS
DETROIT

ISBN 978-0-8143-4761-4 (hardback)
ISBN 978-0-8143-4762-1 (e-book)

Library of Congress Control Number: 2021951000

Wayne State University Press rests on Waawiyaataanong, also referred to as Detroit, the ancestral and contemporary homeland of the Three Fires Confederacy. These sovereign lands were granted by the Ojibwe, Odawa, Potawatomi, and Wyandot Nations, in 1807, through the Treaty of Detroit. Wayne State University Press affirms Indigenous sovereignty and honors all tribes with a connection to Detroit. With our Native neighbors, the press works to advance educational equity and promote a better future for the earth and all people.

Wayne State University Press
Leonard N. Simons Building
4809 Woodward Avenue
Detroit, Michigan 48201-1309

Visit us online at wsupress.wayne.edu.

To Vanessa and Ella

*To my students at Wayne Law who made
teaching over fifty years so rewarding*

Contents

Preface

I started my teaching career at Wayne State University Law School in July 1966. In the fall of 2014, my wife, Betty Schenk, asked me if I was the longest-serving member of the faculty in the history of the law school. When I determined that I was, I started reminiscing about my years at Wayne, my students, my colleagues, and the law school administration. I taught at almost a dozen law schools and I always returned to Wayne—for two important reasons. First, I was treated well at Wayne and there is a tendency to return to a place that treats you well. Second, and more importantly, Wayne students were special. I enjoyed teaching them more than the students I taught at the other law schools.

I asked four influential alumni whom I know and respect for their views about the desirability of a history of their alma mater. Eugene Driker, William and the Honorable Nancy Edmunds, and Board of Governor (and Michigan Supreme Court Justice) Marilyn Kelly encouraged me to pursue this project. I had the honor of being appointed a Distinguished Professor and, with that honor, President M. Roy Wilson and former president Irvin Reid provided research funds for this project. Dean Jocelyn Benson was very enthusiastic about the book and not only encouraged me but provided some supplementary research funds. I decided to expand the project to include the videotaped interviews with dozens of alumni, a few deans, and some current and emeriti colleagues to serve as additional background for the book and to become part of a video archive of the law school.

I approached this history in the same dispassionate manner that I approached my other scholarly work. I am not a historian and I may not be able to be completely objective when I have been in residence for over half of the school's history.

I appreciate the strong support of Wayne State University Press. Director Stephanie Williams and Editor in Chief Annie Martin worked with me through the application process. Kathryn Wildfong assisted in the early stage of this project. Thanks, too, to Kristin Harpster, editorial, design, and production manager, copyeditor Jennifer Backer, and indexer Rachel Lyon. Dr. Sandra VanBurkleo, my colleague and friend in Wayne's history department, provided essential guidance in helping a non-historian convert an earlier draft into what I hope is a more coherent story. I am grateful for the assistance of the staff at Wayne's Reuther Archives, the director of the law library, Virginia Thomas, and Kathryn Polgar and Michael Samson in locating records from the law school's early years. Julia Westblade of the library staff helped me create Appendix A, the list of Wayne Law professors.

For help in tracking down law school data, I am grateful for the assistance (always with a smile) of the law school registrar Rebecca Hollancid. Ana Campo, Zainab Sabbagh Hazimi, and Catherine Ferguson provided valuable research assistance, wading through the records of the law school Student Board of Governors and its predecessor student organizations. Virginia Thomas helped me navigate the Reuther Archives. Denise Thomas and Rob McGregor gave me access to historical data that was stuffed into cramped file cabinets. I am grateful to Kaylee Place for locating photographs and other documents and assisting with videography sessions. Michelle Alter located and sent documents when I could not obtain them in person. I am grateful for the help provided by innumerable alumni whom I called upon for information, and almost without exception they graciously gave of their time and their memories. Most importantly, thanks to Betty Schenk for her motivation to embark on this project and for her generosity as a sounding board to discuss the historical information uncovered about the law school and its students.

A Note on the Sources

In the research for this history, I conducted almost one hundred videotaped interviews, and hundreds of in-person discussions and telephone conversations with alumni, students during their legal education, and former and current law school deans and faculty colleagues. I discussed the school with many more to paint the pictures of the students, their legal education, and their school.

The student publications *The Gavel* in 1952–53 and its successor *Wayne Law Journal* in 1953–54, as well as the Student Board of Governors meeting minutes, gave me insights into the students' hopes and concerns and their significant, direct roles in expanding their educational opportunities with the student journals, the Free Legal Aid Clinic, Moot Court, and skills-based clinical programs.

Introduction

This is not a typical history of an American law school. A law school history usually discusses the establishment of the school as independent or as part of a broader university institution, the leadership of the deans, the noted faculty, the influence of their scholarship, and how the school's programs and reputation may have been influenced by the financial support it received from within the university and from its alumni and outside sources.

In researching Wayne Law's history, I dug into the written records from the school's archives, including the faculty and student meeting minutes. Over a five-year period, I videotaped interviews with a broad cross-section of graduates, as well as a number of the school's deans and professors. I found that, starting in the mid-1950s, Wayne students and alumni had an outsized impact on the school's development and reputation. This book focuses on the students.

The Detroit City Law School (predecessor of Wayne State University Law School) was established in 1927 as Detroit hosted the revolution in transportation and manufacturing. The cultural cross-currents were pulling the country between a glorious past and progress toward the future, especially through technology.[1] The American economy expanded by 42 percent in the 1920s and the Michigan economy was thriving, prompted by the modern automobile industry.

---

1. Charles J. Shindo, *1927 and the Rise of Modern America* (University of Kansas Press, 2010).

Ford Motor Company's massive River Rouge complex was completed in 1927.[2] Ford shut down its factories for six months to retool from the Model T to the Model A that was unveiled on December 2, 1927. Ford was facing increased competition from General Motors, which was growing by acquiring other automotive companies. In 1927, GM introduced the "stylish" Cadillac LaSalle, a change from marketing automobiles mainly as a means of transportation.

In terms of population growth, Detroit added approximately 50,000 people per year during the mid-1920s, reaching an estimated 1,290,000 by 1926.[3] In the 1920s, immigrants largely from Canada and western Europe were drawn to the urban centers. Homeless White sharecroppers and Black tenant farmers[4] were leaving the flooding lower Mississippi valley.[5] This natural disaster increased the ongoing migration of African Americans to the American North and West,[6] contributing to the dramatic growth in Detroit's population. Companies in Detroit and outlying cities like Flint offered these new residents blue-collar jobs.[7]

Detroit attracted national attention in the mid-1920s with two high-profile trials. In the first one, African American Dr. Ossian Sweet and ten others were on trial for murder in 1925. After hundreds of people had gathered

---

2. Thomas Sugrue, "Automobile in American Life and Society; From Motor City to Motor Metropolis: How the Automobile Industry Reshaped Urban America," *http://www.autolife.umd.umich.edu/Race/R_Overview/R_Overview.htm*.

3. Table 39, "Population: Midyear Estimates for Cities Having in 1920 over 50,000 Inhabitants," https://www2.census.gov/library/publications/1927/compendia/statab/49ed/1926-02.pdf.

4. The refugee camps for the displaced, separated by race, left African Americans in camps more resembling prisons than way stations until they could locate replacement housing.

5. The expanded role of radio in reporting on the flood coincided with the creation of the NBC and CBS national radio networks in 1926 and 1927, respectively (Shindo, *1927 and the Rise of Modern America*, 178).

6. The migration started around 1916, when America's entrance into World War I increased the need for industrial workers in the northern factories.

7. See Niles Carpenter, *Immigrants and Their Children 1920: A Study Based on Census Statistics Relative to the Foreign Born and the Native White of Foreign or Mixed Parentage* (Washington, D.C., 1927). Detroit's population was 29.3 percent foreign born, although it had declined from 33.8 percent in 1900 and 46.8 percent in 1860 (24–26).

outside the house that Sweet lived in with his family, in a White neighborhood, one person was killed with a bullet that came from inside the house. The well-known lawyers Clarence Darrow and Arthur Garfield Hays and some local lawyers defended them. Judge Frank Murphy,[8] later a U.S. Supreme Court Justice, heard the case.[9] The defendants ultimately were acquitted.

The second, the notorious *Sapiro v. Ford* trial, began on March 15, 1927. Henry Ford had accused Aaron Sapiro, a Jewish lawyer, of conspiring to control agriculture in the United States. Sapiro sued Ford for libel, claiming that he had defamed him in articles published in his anti-Semitic periodical, the *Detroit Independent*. Notwithstanding a battery of Ford lawyers, including a sitting U.S. senator, the case ended in a mistrial. In settling, Ford publicly apologized to Sapiro.

The 1920s witnessed the movement to increase the educational background of practicing lawyers. In 1921, the American Bar Association (ABA) established the Standards of Legal Education[10] and began accrediting law schools. The ABA wanted law school applicants to complete more college education before beginning their legal education. The ABA recommended that law schools require applicants to have a minimum of two years of college.[11]

---

8. Murphy later also served as Detroit mayor and Michigan governor.

9. See Edward J. Littlejohn and Donald L. Hobson, *Black Lawyers, Law Practice, and Bar Associations—1844 to 1970: A Michigan History* (Wolverine Bar Association, 1988), expanded from the original in *Wayne Law Review* 33 (1987): 1625. See also Kevin Boyle, *Arc of Justice: A Saga of Race, Civil Rights, and Murder in the Jazz Age* (Henry Holt, 2004).

10. The ABA defines "an approved law school as one with the following characteristics: an entrance requirement of two years of college education; a three-year course in the case of a full-time school or a four-year course for a part-time school, i.e., one where classes are held in the late afternoon or evening; an adequate library, which has been interpreted to mean one of not less than 7,500 usable volumes; a minimum of at least three full-time teachers or one for every one hundred students; an adequate physical plant for carrying on law school work; operation as a non-profit educational institution on a non-commercial basis; reasonably adequate facilities and maintenance of a sound educational policy" (*Wayne State Bulletin*, March 15, 1945, 12).

11. At its 1921 annual meeting, "the ABA adopts a report by a special committee, chaired by Elihu Root, of the Section of Legal Education and Admissions to the Bar. The Association recommends standards requiring students to have completed two

In the mid-1920s, the University of Michigan, the only public law school and the only ABA-accredited law school in the state, required three years of college education.

In Detroit and a few other large American cities in the early twentieth century, the boards of education that provided public elementary and secondary education extended their missions to offer junior or four-year liberal arts colleges, colleges of education, and, in some cities, colleges offering professional degrees. In 1927, the Detroit Board of Education was expanding the public school system to accommodate Detroit's exploding population. It also operated several colleges, including a medical school.

Allan Campbell, a prominent Detroit lawyer who taught part-time at the Detroit College of Law, also served on the Detroit Board of Education. He spoke publicly about the need for a better-educated Michigan bar. The two other law schools in Michigan, both located in Detroit, were the Jesuit University of Detroit and the YMCA's Detroit College of Law. They admitted students with less than two years of college study.

Along with a judge and two of his adjunct colleagues at the Detroit College of Law, Campbell lobbied the board to add a public law school in Detroit. They asked the board to provide an office and classrooms, and secure authority from the state to issue law degrees. The student tuition and fees would fund the school. Campbell thought that with pressure from two Michigan public law schools, the Michigan legislature could be persuaded to require applicants for the Michigan bar examination to have more pre-law college education.

The Detroit City Law School (DCLS) opened in the fall of 1927 under the auspices of the school board but not an official college of the board. In its first decade, DCLS offered an evening-only program for working adults who wanted a legal education in order to qualify to take the Michigan bar examination.

---

years of college, graduate from a three-year law school course of study or its equivalent and pass an examination 'by public authority' as conditions of admission to the bar." *http://www.americanbar.org/about_the_aba/timeline.html*. In 1923, there were 39 law schools on the A list of schools approved by the ABA. See "Law Schools Meet Association Standards," *ABA Journal* (November 1923): 728.

DCLS enrolled a surprisingly large and multicultural group of entering first-year students and an almost equal number of students who transferred from other law schools.

The new public law school was located within commuting distance for Detroiters and charged tuition lower than other Michigan law schools. Many students were raised in communities underrepresented in the legal profession. Some could not afford a legal education away from home at the University of Michigan or comparable law schools.

DCLS welcomed all applicants with the requisite college credits without regard to gender, race, or ethnicity. The law school provided access to the legal profession and thereby access to America's power structure to students from blue-collar and immigrant families, students of color, and women.

The elite law schools did not admit women or severely limited the number admitted. DCLS, however, enrolled many women. In addition, a large number of Jewish students, limited by quotas at many elite schools, transferred to or started their legal education at DCLS. A sprinkling of African American students enrolled in the early years.

Despite its large enrollment in the early years, the Detroit City Law School almost closed. The student enrollment was decimated by the Great Depression and then by the loss of college-age men to the military for World War II. After the war, however, the school had to limit acceptances of out-of-state applicants. Qualified Michigan applicants, especially returning veterans with GI education benefits, exceeded the school's capacity.

Part-time dean Arthur Neef administered the law school in the two decades after World War II, while also serving as university provost. In those years, Neef concentrated his efforts on university administration, underestimated the quality of the law students, and deprived the law school of essential resources.

Beginning in the mid-1950s, the Wayne law students took the lead and pressed the dean and faculty to add programs available at the elite schools. Student pressure led to the establishment of law journals run by students to enable them to hone their legal research and writing skills. In the mid-1960s, without the school's support, students organized the innovative Free Legal Aid Clinic to represent clients in communities underserved by practicing lawyers.

In 1967, Wayne's new president, William Rae Keast, recognized the need for a change in law school leadership and hired Charles Joiner, who was serving as the associate dean at the University of Michigan Law School. He was a nationally recognized legal educator, schooled in how to administer a leading law school. He was well known within the Michigan bar and the two law school accrediting agencies, the ABA and the Association of American Law Schools. In fact, during his Wayne deanship, Joiner served as president of the State Bar of Michigan.

Joiner accepted the Wayne deanship as the law school was attracting talented men and women, many with credentials comparable to those of students admitted by the University of Michigan. The University of Michigan drew its student body from across the country and limited the percentage of Michigan residents that it admitted. Thus many Michigan residents not admitted to the University of Michigan enrolled at Wayne.

Dean Joiner was showered with resources he needed to accomplish his lofty goals. He remade Wayne into a law school filled with teacher-scholars and a curriculum that mirrored the legal education offered at the elite schools. Charles Joiner radically changed the conversation about the quality of Wayne Law and its graduates within the legal academy and with leaders in the national and local legal communities.

In the pre-Joiner years, the Michigan law firms that represented large businesses and wealthy individuals rarely hired or even interviewed Wayne Law graduates. Wayne-trained lawyers had to fend for themselves, largely practicing alone or in small partnerships representing individuals in areas like family law, estates and wills, bankruptcy, litigation, and criminal defense. Some represented owners of small businesses.

Starting in the late 1960s, the large national law firms experienced significant growth in their practices and absorbed an increasing number of graduates from the elite schools. The established Michigan law firms also were experiencing a growth in their legal practices and were not attracting the number of associates they needed from among the previously available graduates of the elite law schools.

Dean Joiner opened doors, first for men and then for women, for employment with those Michigan law firms that represented major corporations and wealthy individuals. Beginning in 1970, women received offers upon graduation that were not available to the most talented female graduates even six years earlier. These Wayne graduates with grit and an enviable work ethic proved valuable to those firms and, in the process, enhanced the reputation of the school. Their successors competed with graduates of the elite schools for those coveted jobs. Wayne Law alumni soon populated the firms' hiring committees. Michigan Law and Wayne Law became the two major sources of legal talent for the Michigan firms.

With Joiner's leadership and the success of the students who graduated during his tenure, Wayne Law was positioned to become the law school of choice for many Michigan residents who sought a legal education and were not admitted to the University of Michigan Law School or who, for other reasons, wanted to obtain their legal education in Detroit. For example, students required to work their way through law school had ready access to law-related, part-time work in Detroit. Many Wayne Law professors who came from similar blue-collar and immigrant families could identify with the career aspirations of a large swath of the student body.

In 1995, the Detroit College of Law affiliated with Michigan State University, which meant that Wayne Law now had to compete with both MSU and the University of Michigan for highly credentialed students. Applicants who previously might have chosen Wayne over the non-public law schools in Michigan now had the Big 10 campus in East Lansing as an option as well.

When Michigan voters in 2006 banned affirmative action in admissions to Michigan's public universities, Wayne Law maintained its efforts to enroll a highly credentialed, racially diverse student body. Back in 1968, the ABA and the U.S. Congress adopted programs designed to produce a more racially diverse legal profession. Starting in 1969, Wayne Law sponsored a summer program to expand access to a legal education for African Americans and

Hispanic Americans. The effort, especially in the early years, provided opportunities and significant challenges.

The decline in law school applications due to the 1982 recession and the 2008 financial crisis coincided with a decline in the number of available legal jobs for graduates. The Michigan legislature, strapped for revenue, reduced its support for Michigan's universities. The resulting spike in law school tuition increased the pressure on law schools to offer better scholarships in order to attract highly credentialed applicants.

In the twenty-first century, Wayne Law has amplified its social justice mission and capitalized on its Detroit location with enhanced clinical and experiential learning opportunities. Graduates continue to receive offers for coveted jobs.

The students drawn largely from the melting pot of metropolitan Detroit and outstate Michigan, relying on their talent, education, and work ethic, became leaders in the legal community. The students inspired this book and serve as the lens though which I explored Wayne Law's history.

Plan of the Book

Chapter 1 discusses the origin of the law school under the umbrella of the Detroit Board of Education. Within a few months after the board approved the law school, a law school office was constructed, a curriculum was developed, students enrolled, and a part-time faculty was enlisted to teach an evening-only law school program.

Chapter 2 covers the two decades after World War II when students took the lead in improving their legal education as the part-time dean devoted his energies to university matters. A small faculty prepared mainly men to practice law representing individuals.

Chapter 3 explores how Dean Charles Joiner changed the perception of Wayne Law in the Michigan and national legal communities and, in the process, provided graduates with access to job opportunities previously closed to them.

Chapter 4 discusses the law school's commitment to enroll a racially diverse student body and the resulting opportunities and challenges starting in the late 1960s.

Chapter 5 explores the 1972–82 decade in which some talented faculty scholars were raided by other law schools. The law school hired more professors and the faculty trained the students for an expanding range of employment opportunities.

Chapter 6 covers the 1982 recession's beginning of the national decline in the demand for a legal education and legal talent, the start of the computer age for legal research, and the success of the graduates in a broader range of career opportunities.

Chapter 7 covers the response to the school's first competitive challenge as the Detroit College of Law affiliated with Michigan State University. It also discusses professors who were singled out by students for special praise.

Chapter 8 explores the changes in the twenty-first century, as the school capitalizes on its location in the center of Michigan's legal profession, highlights its faculty strength with the program in international legal studies and the appointment of an associate dean for research and development, and promotes its public interest and civil rights missions with two legal centers. The education mission is expanding back to undergraduate students and forward to non-lawyer working adults.

1

A Public Law School in Detroit

This chapter documents the dogged determination of Allan Campbell to establish a public law school in the City of Detroit. Campbell, a practicing lawyer, taught part-time at the Detroit College of Law (DCL) and served on the governing board of the Detroit Board of Education, including as chair.

Campbell believed that practicing lawyers lacked sufficient pre–law school education, with many completing only high school before starting to apprentice or attend law school. He wanted the Michigan legislature to mandate more pre-law education as a prerequisite before a person could take the bar examination and practice law. His dream was to have a better-educated bar with high moral and legal standards.[1] He felt that the leader of a public law school in Detroit would have the independence to press for those higher standards.

In 1920, there were approximately 122,000 lawyers in the country, with 9 percent belonging to the ABA and only about 20 percent belonging to state and local bar associations. The ABA was becoming an independent professional organization, transitioning from an amalgamation of members of state and local bar associations. The ABA began accrediting law schools in 1921, and law schools wanted that imprimatur. The ABA accredited 41 schools that first

---

1. "A better educated Bar," he wrote, "is a Bar of higher moral, as well as legal standards, and of course, that is what public opinion is today demanding." Allan Campbell, "The Problem of Legal Education," *Jurist* (1931 Yearbook).

year; all of them were, like the University of Michigan, university-associated law schools. In 1922, an ABA-sponsored Conference of Bar Association Delegates endorsed the ABA position that every person fit to practice law should be required to graduate from a law school and pass a bar examination administered by a public authority.

Campbell's aim to have better-educated Michigan lawyers was consistent with the goals of the law school accrediting agencies—the ABA and the Association of American Law Schools (AALS).[2] The ABA in particular was working to toughen law school entrance requirements by raising the standards a law school had to meet to receive and retain ABA accreditation. By 1927, a resolution of the ABA's Section on Legal Education deemed that "all applicants for admission to the bar [should have] two years of college work before the beginning of the study of law." The AALS member law schools also required applicants to have completed half of the course work toward a bachelor's degree.[3] Since the tuition cost for any college prerequisite might be a financial barrier for some prospective law students, the ABA resolution added that each state should establish "opportunities for a collegiate training, free or at moderate cost . . . [to] obtain an adequate preliminary education."[4]

In 1920, the seven largest U.S. cities by population did not have a public law school. New York City, Chicago, Philadelphia, Detroit, Cleveland, St. Louis, and Boston had only private or faith-based law schools. Among the twelve largest cities, the University of Maryland, Baltimore, the University of Pittsburgh, and the University of California-Hastings School of Law in San Francisco operated state-supported, public law schools.[5]

---

2. To be accredited by the ABA, law schools had to meet the requirements laid out by the Section of Legal Education and Admission to the Bar. The AALS treats as "member schools" the law schools that meet the standards in its articles and resolutions.

3. The AALS provided exceptions for up to 10 percent of the average number of students admitted during the preceding two years.

4. Alfred Reed, ed., *A Review of Legal Education* (Carnegie Foundation for the Advancement of Teaching, 1926–27), 9.

5. Among other large cities, Minneapolis, Kansas City, and Seattle had state-funded public law schools.

In the mid-1920s, in New York City (the largest U.S. city),[6] Chicago (second largest city), and Detroit (fourth largest city), the Boards of Education were providing public education beyond high school, but none offered a legal education. Cincinnati, the sixteenth largest city, operated the municipally funded University of Cincinnati Law School.

At the time, there were three law schools in Michigan, two of which were in Detroit. The University of Michigan Law Department, the oldest and only public law school, was established in 1859 as a full-time day program in Ann Arbor.[7] The University of Detroit Law School, a Jesuit school with both a day and an evening program, admitted its first class in 1912. The Detroit College of Law (DCL), which offered daytime and evening law classes to working-class students, started its program in 1891[8] and in 1926 became affiliated with the Young Men's Christian Association.[9]

DCL's history in the dozen years leading up to 1927 influenced the establishment of what became Wayne State University Law School. It was not uncommon during that period for proprietary law schools to be operated by individual lawyers or law firms. Until 1915, DCL (established as a private corporation) was operated by "Malcolm McGregor and William C. Wetherbee." In 1915, during John Bills's interim deanship, DCL was transferred to the YMCA. In 1917, William Krichbaum became dean and, in the ensuing years, the law

---

6. City College of New York (CCNY), largely funded by the city, was founded in 1847 by the state Board of Education as the first free public institution of higher education in the United States (originally named the Free Academy). In 1926, New York City created a separate Board of Higher Education to oversee public college education in the city. See Tahir Butt, "Free Tuition and Expansion in New York Public Higher Education," *Theory, Research, and Action in Urban Education* 3, no. 1 (2014).

7. The University of Michigan moved from Detroit to Ann Arbor in 1837. See Byron D. Cooper, "Legal Education in Michigan," in *The History of Michigan Law*, ed. Paul Finkelman and Martin J. Hershock (Ohio University Press, 2006), 257, 260, 262.

8. Gwenn Bashara Samuel, *The First Hundred Years Are the Hardest: A Centennial History of the Detroit College of Law* (Detroit College of Law, 1992), 45–51.

9. http://www.americanbar.org/groups/legal_education/resources/aba_approved_law _schools. The University of Detroit Law School received accreditation in 1933, the Detroit City Law School in 1937, and DCL in 1941.

school experienced financial difficulty.[10] In 1924, the law school moved and shared space with the other programs operated by the Y.

In 1926, Campbell and several of his part-time DCL colleagues proposed to the Detroit Board of Education that it absorb DCL.[11] Campbell and a few other popular DCL adjunct professors were concerned that the YMCA was not devoting adequate financial resources to the law program. In addition, DCL students complained about the school's inadequate and poorly ventilated classrooms. The Board of Education operated a teacher's college to supply teachers for the city's elementary and secondary schools. It also operated a medical and pharmacy school and a liberal arts college that had expanded from a two-year junior college.[12] Detroit's population grew by almost 60 percent between 1920 and 1930,[13] attributable in part to the influx of workers drawn to jobs in the automobile industry. With the arrival of these workers and their families, the Detroit Board of Education needed to serve an expanding elementary and secondary school population.

Some members of the board opposed the proposal to acquire DCL. They wanted the board to focus its resources on its elementary and secondary schools and its teacher's college. The proposal was defeated, but possibly in deference to Campbell's position on the board, it included $25,000 in its upcoming

---

10. Samuel, *The First Hundred Years Are the Hardest*, 45, 51.

11. "It is my belief that the school will fare better under public administration by the Detroit school board than under the more or less financially restricted supervision of the Y.M.C.A." (*Detroit News*, April 8, 1926), cited in James Ross Irwin, "Wayne University—A History" (Ed.D. diss., Wayne State University, 1952), 201.

12. The Detroit College of Medicine and Surgery was established in 1868; the university traces its origin to that date. The College of Pharmacy was established in 1924. The Detroit Normal Training School, the forerunner of the College of Education, was established in 1881 and changed its name in 1920. The Detroit Junior College founded in 1917 became the College of the City of Detroit and then the College of Liberal Arts in 1923. See wayne.edu/about/history.

13. The population grew in the 1920s from approximately 993,000 to 1,568,000. Detroit, Michigan, Population History 1840–2019, https://www.biggestuscities.com/city/detroit-michigan.

budget as the estimated cost of offering some law courses through its liberal arts–oriented College of the City of Detroit.[14]

Undeterred, in early 1927, a group led by Campbell[15] approached the board again, but this time proposing that the board establish its own law school. Campbell's idea was controversial within the board, in the Detroit legal community, and on the Detroit City Council. Detroit Councilman Phillip A. Callahan thought that spending money on a third law school in Detroit was not a good use of the board's resources. Board member John Hall thought that the proposal was being discussed without giving the board the required notice.[16] Some practicing lawyers, perhaps concerned about increased competition from more lawyers, opposed a third law school in the city.[17]

Campbell, having served on the board since 1921, knew how to frame his group's request so that they could secure three affirmative votes out of six on the Board (his would be the fourth). The school would pay the salaries for the predominantly part-time faculty of practicing lawyers and judges entirely from student fees. The group would pledge its credit "to buy a $10,000 law library."[18] This cost also would be repaid out of future student fees.[19] Campbell and his colleagues asked the board to make only two commitments:

---

14. Irwin, "Wayne University—A History," 202.

15. The others were Fred G. Dewey, John Bills, William S. Sayers, and Judge Ira W. Jayne. Ibid., 104.

16. Dr. Hall claimed that the proposal violated Art. 13 of the bylaws of the board that required a proposal to be noticed at a meeting and then voted on at the next meeting. "Law School Intrigue Scored by Dr. Hall," Law School File—Clippings, Undated to 1965, University Archives, Wayne State University, Detroit, cited in Paul Finkelman and Martin J. Herstock, *The History of Michigan Law* (Ohio University Press, 2006), 274n58.

17. According to Callahan, "We have plenty of law schools now. If the Board of Education has any money to spare, why not spend it on something that is useful." "History of Wayne State Law School," *Wayne Lawyer* (Fall 1987): 6. In 1927, there were approximately 135,000 licensed lawyers in the United States.

18. Ray Pearson, "The Power That Erring Men Call Chance: The Seventeenth and Last of a Series of Sunday Articles on Detroit Men-Today-Dr. Arthur F. Neef," *Detroit Free Press*, March 3, 1940.

19. Arthur Neef, "Wayne University Law School," *Michigan State Bar Journal*, October 1948, 15, cited in Irwin, "Wayne University—A History," 203.

1. Obtain authority from the state to issue diplomas so that the law school graduates could qualify to take the Michigan bar examination.[20]
2. Provide some classroom and administrative space in Old Main, where the board's other colleges held their classes.

On June 9, 1927,[21] by a vote of 4 to 2, the board approved "The Detroit City Law School [DCLS] as a part of the Educational System of the City of Detroit."[22] Campbell, the chair, cast one of the four positive votes.

The law school had to be financially self-sustaining,[23] while committed to providing a quality legal education to its mainly "self-supporting students."[24] The law school was to operate under the board's auspices, but it was not included in its budget.

The board had two strategic reasons for not including the new law school as a formal part of its colleges. The board's budget had to be approved by the Detroit City Council, and if the law school were included in the budget, the council

---

20. Authority to issue diplomas was obtained in May 1927, pursuant to Public Acts of Michigan, No. 193 of 1927. At the time, a person preparing to practice law by clerking with a law firm could also sit for the bar examination if the person were certified by the mentoring firm. See Irwin, "Wayne University—A History," 203, referring to Kelly and Elliott, Provisions in the General School Laws, Part I, Ch. 8, Districts of the First Class, Originally, Public Acts of Michigan, 1927, No. 193.

21. The approval came as there was growing public attention to the role of law in society. On April 9, 1927, Nicola Sacco and Bartolomeo Vanzetti received their death sentence in what was viewed as a flawed trial in which they were charged with murder in connection with a shoe factory robbery. Shindo, *1927 and the Rise of Modern America*, 30. Felix Frankfurter wrote a scathing article in the March 1927 issue of *Atlantic Monthly*, criticizing the decision and urging a new trial.

22. Minutes of the Regular Meeting of the Board of Education, Detroit, Michigan, June 9, 1927, 615, Detroit Board of Education Proceedings, WSU002724, vol. 1926–1927, Reuther Archives, Wayne State University, Detroit (hereafter Reuther Archives).

23. The law school operated under this "Internal Accounting System" until it became part of the regular Board of Education budget in 1929. See Minutes of the Regular Meeting of the Board of Education, Detroit, Michigan, November 12, 1929, 268, Detroit Board of Education Proceedings, WSU002724, vol. 1929–1930, Reuther Archives.

24. See Detroit City Law School, Catalog and Announcements 1934–1935, published by the Authority of the Board of Education, City of Detroit, 1934, law school archives.

could delete that budget item and thereby prevent the school from opening. In addition, for the board to maintain accreditation for its colleges, the colleges had to meet the standards of the North Central Association of College and Universities. The new law school would not meet the North Central standards. The school's initial library would be inadequate and the school would not be hiring the required minimum number of full-time faculty. The law school would also not be accredited by the legal education professional organizations, the ABA and AALS.

Campbell resigned from the board just before the beginning of its next meeting on July 1, 1927. Later in the same meeting, the board appointed Campbell as the law school's first dean.[25]

Organizing a Law School and Attracting Students

Dean Campbell had two and a half months from his July 1 appointment until the September 14 start of fall classes to organize the law school and attract and register students. His first job was to secure classrooms and administrative offices. Campbell knew that the DCL students' major criticism was that the school had inadequate classrooms with poor ventilation. The Board of Education had been using part of the Central High School building on Cass and Warren in Detroit for some of its college classes, and when the board built a new Central High School campus, it used that entire building, which became known as Old Main, for its colleges.

The law school classes were held entirely at night, so the board agreed to find space in Old Main. The Old Main classrooms were well ventilated and well suited to professional instruction, but the law school also needed its own

25. Board of Education Annual and Regular Meeting, July 1, 1927, 1, 5, Detroit Board of Education Proceedings, WSU0002724, vol. 1927–1928, Reuther Archives. While two members of the board opposed his appointment, a motion to approve him passed by a vote of 5–2. See also Irwin, "Wayne University—A History," 213. Campbell was described years later as "a dignified, erudite gentleman fit to head any law school." Ira W. Jayne, "Reminiscences of a Law School Professor," *Michigan State Bar Journal* 27 (1948): 14.

administrative offices. Over the summer of 1927, the administrative offices were carved out of two rooms near the southeast corner of Old Main's second floor. According to the renovation order, "Room 213. There is a coat room and an unused girls' toilet connected here. . . . A door should be cut through from the corridor to the toilet, and the toilets removed."[26]

In one of his early acts as dean, Campbell hired Arthur Neef as part-time secretary to handle the day-to-day administration of the school. Neef, an associate in Campbell's law office, graduated from the University of Michigan "with high grades and a flair for administrative detail."[27] Together, Campbell and

Old Main, where the law school administration occupied the second-floor office with the window on the far left above the Stop sign. (With permission of the law school)

26. Leslie L. Hanawalt, *A Place of Light: The History of Wayne State University* (Wayne State University Press, 1968), 281.
27. Jayne, "Reminiscences of a Law School Professor," 14.

Neef established admission standards and other academic requirements so that graduates would qualify to take the Michigan bar examination.[28]

In organizing the law school curriculum, Campbell and Neef had the freedom to innovate with a course of study that differed from that offered at the other Detroit law schools. For almost fifty years up to 1927, the standard law school curriculum was based on the "case method" under which students examined the parameters of individual cases in order to learn general principles governing a particular area of law. At that time, there was a debate within the legal academy about the nature of a legal education. Should law schools provide the professional training (skills) needed to represent clients in basic areas of practice, or should they expose students to philosophical approaches to judicial decision making?

The Columbia Law School faculty were debating this very issue. One group of professors thought that law schools should approach law as a vehicle for social change, looking at the relationship between law and the other social sciences. They viewed the law school as a center for legal research, a community of scholars who focused on "the non-professional study of law, in order that the functions of law may be comprehended, its results evaluated, and its development kept more nearly in step with the complex development of modern life."[29] Columbia Law School had the resources to examine the relationship between law and the social sciences. Professors from other parts of the university could serve as resources and teach students in the fields of public law, international law, philosophy, finance, and economics. The schism fractured the Columbia law faculty and the press for realism shifted to Yale Law School.[30]

---

28. A person could take the Michigan bar examination if he or she received a Bachelor of Laws (LL.B.) degree or a certificate of completion of legal studies. DCLS could issue that certificate to a student who failed to meet the law school's degree requirements, such as the GPA required for graduation.
29. Staff of the Foundation for Research in Legal History, *A History of the School of Law Columbia University* (Columbia University Press, 1955), 301.
30. Laura Kalman, *Yale Law School and the Sixties: Revolt and Reverberations* (University of North Carolina Press, 2005), 16.

The new Detroit City Law School could not adopt Columbia's discussed interdisciplinary approach to the study of law in the summer of 1927. The fledgling law school did not have the luxury of Columbia Law's support from a large university of scholars. It had to finance the school solely from the tuition and fees paid by the law students and therefore had to staff its part-time faculty with practicing lawyers and judges who taught at the other Detroit law schools.[31]

The law school's curriculum, therefore, followed the traditional case method in basic courses like contracts, torts, criminal law and procedure, and real and personal property, as well as in advanced courses such as corporate law. In the school's first year, Campbell and Neef taught five courses. Practicing lawyers and judges taught the other thirty-five courses.[32]

The Board of Education publicized the opening of the new law school. By limiting costs, DCLS set tuition for men lower than that at the other law schools in Michigan: $110 for Michigan residents ($150 for non-residents). Tuition at DCL was $115, at the University of Detroit it was $191, and resident tuition at the University of Michigan was $118 for men and $109 for women.[33]

Pre-Law Education and ABA Accreditation

In the school's formative years, Dean Campbell took a number of steps designed to improve the quality of Michigan lawyers, particularly those who graduated from DCLS. Campbell lobbied the Michigan legislature to require the Michigan bar examination applicants to have more pre-law college education. DCLS imposed strict class attendance requirements, and offered practice skills courses.

---

31. In addition to Campbell and Neef, the faculty included seventeen practicing lawyers, a master in chancery, and three judges (Irwin, "Wayne University—A History," 204).
32. Brochure, Detroit City Law School, Preliminary Announcements, July 1927, published by authority of the Board of Education, City of Detroit, 1927, law school archives.
33. Cooper, "Legal Education in Michigan," 264.

Campbell wanted all law schools in the State of Michigan to follow the ABA's admission standard—two years of undergraduate education. The University of Michigan Law School, with the strictest pre-law education standards, required applicants to have a minimum of three years of undergraduate education. DCL and the University of Detroit required one year of college work. The new school decided not to adopt the ABA's two-year college requirement but students applying for their first year of law school had to have "a full high school course and, in addition, one or more years of college work in an approved college or university."[34]

Campbell, Dean Henry Bates of the Michigan law school, Carl Essary of the Detroit Bar Association, and a few others sought legislation to require all applicants for the Michigan bar examination to have more pre-law education.[35] The legislature, instead, placed the onus on the law schools. Under a 1929 law, the law schools in Michigan had to adopt admission standards that required applicants to have completed at least two years of college (or the equivalent).[36]

By 1930, the Detroit City Law School encouraged but did not require its applicants to have completed at least three years of college study.[37] As an incentive, DCLS law students with three years of pre-law study could earn two degrees: a Bachelor of Arts, Science, or Engineering after they satisfactorily completed their first full year of law studies,[38] and an LL.B. when they completed law school.

---

34. Detroit City Law School, Annual Announcement, 1927–1928 (Board of Education, Detroit, 1927), 5, law school archives.

35. "Report of Committee on Legal Education and Admission to the Bar, 1929," *Michigan State Bar Journal* (1929): 184, 185.

36. Irwin, "Wayne University—A History," 206. See Public Acts, 1929-No. 167, ch. 1, §53, amending the Judicature Act of 1915, §12,058 of Compiled Laws of 1915, retrieved from Hein Online 1929 456 1929, heinonline.org/HOL/Welcome.

37. In 1947, the law school increased this prerequisite for admission to three years of college work, even though the ABA standards did not require three years. Hanawalt, *A Place of Light*, 284.

38. Detroit City Law School, Annual Announcement, 1930–1931, May 1930, 6, law school archives.

DCLS imposed strict, even draconian, attendance rules. A DCLS student was required to attend classes regularly and prove that he or she had the capacity to master legal analysis. If a student was absent for more than twelve hours of class in any semester, the law school deducted one hour of credit (two credits for missing twenty-five hours of class) from the student's credits earned toward his or her LL.B. degree. If a student provided an acceptable explanation for the absences, he or she could complete some library work to avoid the loss of credit hours.[39] In addition, a DCLS professor had the authority to remove a student from his course, "even though [the] student satisfies all the formal requirements" of the course, if he "judged the student as lacking the *aptitude for the study or practice of law.*"[40] This broad power could be abused, so the faculty eventually removed this discretion.

Graduates from other law schools who joined large firms were mentored by the seasoned lawyers in their firms who taught them practical skills. Those firms did not hire DCLS graduates. To be more attractive to students likely to practice independently or in small firms lacking mentorship programs, DCLS offered law office and court practice skills courses. The ABA did not require accredited schools to offer "skills" courses until the twenty-first century.

Detroit City Law School opened with Dean Campbell and Secretary Neef teaching 40 percent of the classes, and 17 lawyers and judges teaching the remainder of the night school curriculum.

Once the law school opened, Dean Campbell focused on obtaining ABA accreditation. For DCLS, ABA accreditation was particularly important because the Detroit Board of Education required DCLS to receive at least provisional ABA accreditation before it would incorporate the law school as one of its official colleges.[41]

The road to ABA accreditation was not easy, especially for a law school financed solely from student tuition. To receive accreditation, the ABA required law schools to impose minimum admission standards, adopt an acceptable

---

39. Ibid., 8.
40. Ibid., 17, emphasis added.
41. Irwin, "Wayne University—A History," 209.

curriculum, and employ a minimum number of full-time professors. In 1935, when the ABA started requiring accredited law schools to employ at least three full-time faculty, the Detroit City Law School complied by adding H. Lee Endsley to Carl Whitchurch[42] and counting Assistant Dean Neef (who also taught) as the third. David Goldman, a law student at the time, served as the law school librarian.[43] Neef hired adjunct faculty to teach core courses not within the expertise of the full-time faculty. For example, in the 1940s, tax lawyer Edward Reid Jr. taught the federal taxation course.[44]

In 1937, while offering only an evening program and operating on a tight budget, DCLS became the second law school in the City of Detroit (after the University of Detroit) to receive at least provisional ABA accreditation.[45] With the board's conditions met, at its March 9, 1937 meeting, the board formally incorporated the law school as part of Wayne University and renamed it the Wayne University Law School.[46] When the law school received its provisional ABA accreditation in 1937, Dean Allan Campbell, who was concurrently serving as Circuit Court judge, resigned and became honorary dean. Effective July 1, 1937, Arthur Neef became the school's second dean.[47]

After being appointed dean, Neef focused on obtaining full ABA accreditation for the school. He added faculty and raised admission standards. The ABA frowned upon "night only" law schools, viewing them as diploma factories. To receive full ABA accreditation, a law school had to operate a full-time day

---

42. Whitchurch had an advanced degree in law. "Law School Keeps Pace with Community Needs," *Legal Advertiser*, November 28, 1974.
43. After graduation and while practicing law, Goldman taught at DCLS.
44. Reid practiced tax with the Miller Canfield law firm and litigated tax issues in federal court.
45. In 1946, the law school obtained membership in the AALS.
46. Board of Education Regular Meeting, March 9, 1937, 337, Detroit Board of Education Proceedings, WSR0002724, vol. 1936–1937, Reuther Archives. The Board of Governors of the university accepts 1927 as the founding year of the law school. See also Irwin, "Wayne University—A History," 200.
47. Board of Education Regular Meeting, April 13, 1937, 366.

program.[48] For the academic year 1937–38, the law school started a day program. Neef wrote that "employment was scarce or non-existent, and many . . . students could not afford to go away to school. Day classes within reach of their homes was the solution."[49] In July 1939, the ABA granted the law school full accreditation.[50]

Early DCLS Students

Most law students in the 1920s and 1930s were White men. Women were virtually absent in many law schools, while some African American men attended "Historically Black" law schools. Catholic law students found a welcoming environment at Jesuit schools like the University of Detroit. Jewish students were accepted by some law schools, although the elite law schools commonly imposed a Jewish quota. DCLS, however, accepted all applicants with passing grades in the required number of college credits.

When the Detroit City Law School opened in 1927, it enrolled a surprisingly large and diverse student body. The new public law school was filling an unmet need. According to Ernest Goodman, who transferred from the Detroit College of Law that September, he and his classmates decided to transfer to the unproven new school because "the city-run law school aspired to a higher standard of instruction and an emphasis on public service that was lacking in the commercially oriented DCL."[51]

The new law school enrolled 213 students in September 1927.[52] The 143 freshmen joined the students who transferred from other law schools,

48. Board of Education Regular Meeting, July 27, 1937, 19, Detroit Board of Education Proceedings, WSR0002724, vol. 1937–1938, Reuther Archives.

49. Neef, "Wayne University Law School," 17.

50. Office of the Provost, Arthur Neef Records, 1939–1963, Accession WSP 119, box 27, 3 N-E-3(3), Reuther Archives.

51. Steve Babson, Dave Riddle, and David Elsila, *The Color of Law: Ernie Goodman, Detroit, and the Struggle for Labor and Civil Rights* (Wayne State University Press, 2010), 24.

52. Neef, "Wayne University Law School," 19.

with more than half coming from the Detroit College of Law.[53] Classes were held five nights a week, from 6 to 8 and 7 to 9. It is not surprising that there were so many DCL transfers, since the Detroit City Law School's initial faculty included three of DCL's "most revered instructors," Allan Campbell, John C. Bills, and Fred G. Dewey. While the DCL students complained about their uncomfortable classrooms, DCLS's catalog assured applicants "adequate and well-ventilated classrooms and splendid library facilities."[54] Many Jewish men, denied membership in DCL's legal fraternities, found DCLS, with a Jewish fraternity at the board's colleges, more welcoming.[55]

Women gravitated to the city's public law school as well. DCLS enrolled women when very few sought a legal education. In the 1920s, as more women were entering the workforce and seeking independence,[56] they endured overt discrimination both in admission to many law schools and in employment after graduation. For example, Columbia Law School admitted its first woman in 1927, the same year DCLS opened. DCLS enrolled more women than the University of Michigan's law school. Women represented about 10 percent of the DCLS's enrolled students in 1927 and 1928,[57] and 25 percent in 1930.[58] In the same years, women accounted for about 3 percent of the University of Michigan Law School students.[59]

Two female transfer students received their law degrees as part of DCLS's first 34 graduates in February and June 1928.[60] These future "Portias," as female lawyers were referred to in those days, were Teresa Cable Flower and Elizabeth

---

53. The history of DCL suggests that not many of its students transferred. See Irwin, "Wayne University—A History," 204.
54. Brochure, Detroit City Law School, Preliminary Announcements, July 1927.
55. See Aimee Ergas, "Zionism in Detroit before the State: The First Fifty Years, 1898–1948," *Michigan Jewish History* 38 (November 1998): 14–15.
56. Shindo, *1927 and the Rise of Modern America*, 10.
57. In the 1928–29 academic year, women accounted for 25 of the 230 enrolled students. *The Jurist*, 1929, DCLS yearbook, law school archives.
58. The 24 women of 172 total students in 1931 and 27 women of 156 total students in 1932 represented 17 percent of the enrolled students. See *The Jurist* 1931 and *The Jurist* 1932.
59. See Brown, *Legal Education at Michigan*, 702.
60. Irwin, "Wayne University—A History," 205.

Boyers Taylor. Women distinguished themselves academically. Margaret Simmons was second in her Class of 1931 and received the Alumni Association's Silver Key.[61] Edith Hartman was second in her Class of 1932,[62] and two of the four senior officers that year were women.[63] DCLS female students also established the first women's fraternity at a law school in Michigan.

Most DCLS female graduates, even those with distinguished academic credentials, could not obtain jobs that required a license to practice law, and that situation continued for decades. There were a few exceptions. Mollie Hecker ('30) passed the bar examination in 1930 but was denied admission to practice until her twenty-first birthday. She then became the youngest female practicing lawyer in Detroit.[64] Laura Joslyn Robertson ('32) passed the bar and joined her father's law firm.[65] DCLS's part-time professors noticed the "best and brightest" female students and occasionally hired one. For example, Federal District Court Judge Arthur F. Lederle hired Ruth Riddell ('39) as his law clerk.[66]

Ernest Goodman and other Jewish students represented about one-third of the initial transfer students in 1927. Goodman was the son of immigrants from Russia and Ukraine. The Goodman family moved from the Saginaw-Bay City area to Detroit in 1911 when Ernest was five. Detroit was largely segregated by race and ethnicity, and the Goodmans lived in a Jewish neighborhood.[67]

---

61. *Jurist*, 1931.

62. A commencement program with handwritten notes lists forty-two who received degrees, three who received certificates, and one graduate, Harry Keil, had an undated diploma. That program is described as the commencement of the "Colleges of the City of Detroit." *The Jurist* 1932, p. 18.

63. Ruth Kohler was the vice president, and Anne Alpern was secretary.

64. *Griffin*, 1930, published by the senior class of the College of the City of Detroit, 138. See http://reuther.wayne.edu/files/CCD_1930_Yearbook.pdf; "The Youngest Practicing Woman Attorney," *Detroit Free Press*, May 2, 1931.

65. "Both Pass State Bar Examination," *Detroit News*, October 1, 1932, 8. Robertson's father was a former U.S. District Court referee in bankruptcy.

66. *The Gavel*, January 1953.

67. For information on Goodman's early years, see Babson, Riddle, and Elsila, *The Color of Law*.

When one of his high school tennis teammates suggested that they enroll in the Detroit College of Law's part-time evening program, establish a tennis team there, and travel around the state playing tennis, Goodman agreed.

After graduating and passing the bar exam, Goodman, Edward Stein, and Fred Collins, all editors of the 1928 DCLS Yearbook, started their own law firm. The Detroit law firms representing larger businesses (corporate firms) did not hire graduates from law schools like DCLS and DCL. Goodman started as a commercial lawyer, but in 1939 he joined an association of labor and civil rights lawyers known as the Sugar firm. Goodman became a nationally known civil rights lawyer,[68] in part on the basis of his 1953 defense of three individuals accused of being Communists in what was known as a "Little Smith Act" trial.[69]

Goodman was the first in a long line of Wayne Law graduates who became noted civil rights advocates. The Goodman, Crockett, Eden and Robb law firm, formally established in 1951, with African American lawyer George Crockett, was the first racially integrated law firm in Michigan, if not in the country.[70] In a eulogy, Judge Damon Keith described Goodman as "a voice for the hopeless, the voiceless, and the downtrodden."[71]

Depression and War

The fledgling Detroit City Law School's impressively large student enrollment in its initial years changed after the "Black Tuesday" stock market collapse on

---

68. Goodman successfully represented UAW president R. J. Thomas in a U.S. Supreme Court decision granting First Amendment rights for union organizers. *Thomas v. Collins*, 323 U.S. 516, 65 S. Ct. 315 (1946), discussed in Rashkin, "Alumni Profile" of Ernest Goodman, *Wayne Lawyer* (Spring 1982): 21. Goodman continued to be profiled in Wayne periodicals. When he died in 1997, Goodman was remembered in "The Lion Rests," *Wayne Lawyer* 15 (Winter 1997): 5–11.

69. The "Little Smith Acts" were state-level laws that made it a crime of subversion to engage in actions or advocacy that was intended to overthrow the federal or state form of government by force or violence or by unlawful means.

70. Rashkin, "Alumni Profile," 4. Goodman insisted that Crockett's name be listed second, though Eden was an earlier member of that firm.

71. Babson, Riddle, and Elsila, *The Color of Law*, 7.

Ernest Goodman. (Reprinted with permission of the law school)

October 29, 1929, triggered the Great Depression. Many Michigan families lacked the resources to adequately feed and house their family, let alone tuition for a child to attend law school. The 143 students who enrolled in DCLS's four-year night program in September 1927 were still in school that October 1929. Almost 50 percent dropped out. Fifty-seven received law degrees and seven received certificates of completion of law studies.[72]

From 1936 to 1943, the law school was moved off campus to the Board of Education's High School of Commerce. In his 1941 annual report to Dr. David D. Henry, the executive vice president of the colleges, Dean Neef complained about the school's "quarters" and asked "to have the law school either return to the main campus or at least secure quarters separate from that devoted to non-collegiate education."

Law school home 1941–1943 at 5063 Cass.

---

72. A person who failed to satisfy the degree requirements but received a certificate of completion of law studies could qualify to take the bar examination.

The law school suffered a second blow to its declining enrollment when military conscription took some students for what became World War II. The 1941 U.S. declaration of war increased the need for men of college age. Some Wayne Law students volunteered, while others were conscripted. The Class of 1941 had 39 students (including four women). The Class of 1942 was smaller, with 26 graduates, including one woman. The law school was on the verge of closing.[73]

---

73. Some wartime graduates pursued successful non-legal careers. Abraham Lincoln (Monte) Korn ('41) gave investment advice on his popular *Monty's Moneytime* radio show broadcast from Detroit. Honors graduate Morton Feigenson ('40) ran the family's Faygo beverage company, known in Michigan for its flavored sodas.

2

The Postwar Years under Arthur Neef

The years 1945 to 1967 represent a period of squandered opportunities for the law school itself, but the school would have fared even worse had it not been for the students who took the lead in establishing the *Wayne Law Review* and the Free Legal Aid Clinic.

During the early 1940s the law school had just finished a period of collapsing enrollment as World War II followed the Great Depression. Arthur Neef, who operated the law school with minimal resources, helped the school survive those very lean years. In 1946, Wayne Law joined the Association of American Law Schools,[1] the professional organization serving the law schools and their professors.

From 1945 to 1965, the law school tightened admission standards,[2] yet law school enrollment increased more than sixfold: from 118 in 1945 to 768

---

1. The University of Michigan Law School was a charter member in 1900; the University of Detroit Law School became a member in 1934; and the Detroit College of Law also joined in 1946. See https://www.aals.org/about/membership.
2. The pre-law requirement was increased to three years, starting in September 1947, and the minimum undergraduate GPA was raised to 0.2 above C (or 0.3 above C on the applicant's third-year's work). See *Wayne University Bulletin*, December 12, 1946.

in 1965.[3] A large number of veterans returning home with GI Bill education benefits were pursuing professional studies that would otherwise have eluded them for economic reasons. The faculty limited student enrollment due to the size of the faculty and the capacity of the classrooms. In 1948, the faculty admitted only Michigan residents and, even so, it could not accept all qualified applicants.

The law school operated in a reconditioned luxury home at 5229 Cass that had been a commercial print shop before the university purchased and converted it to educational use. Students attended classes in austere, crowded rooms and socialized between classes in the cigarette smoke–filled basement area shared with the furnace. The garage served as the only 100-student classroom.

According to Professor Maurice Kelman ('59),[4] the law school in those years operated in a "ramshackle house on Cass" and educated its students with a "drab trade-school curriculum."[5]

While some students used the GI Bill to pay for their legal education, most worked part-time while attending law school or had assistance from their families. Federal government–backed student loans were not yet available.[6] Many students enrolled in Wayne's part-time law program that offered a full array of evening classes to accommodate students who worked day jobs.[7]

An expanding, full-time student body was attracted to Wayne's low-tuition legal education, but after graduating and passing the bar examination, most graduates still had to create their own opportunities by establishing their own practices or joining with classmates representing individuals and small

---

3. Hanawalt, *A Place of Light*, 284.

4. Maurice Kelman was the editor in chief of the *Wayne Law Review* in the 1958–59 academic year and an honors graduate of the law school.

5. See "The Wayne Law Community Remembers Dean Donald H. Gordon," March 28, 2011, https://law.wayne.edu/news/the-wayne-law-community-remembers-dean-donald-h-gordon-33326.

6. The 1958 National Defense Education Act did not apply to law school tuition.

7. See Wayne University, Midyear Commencement, January 21, 1947, "For the Degree of Bachelor of Laws," located in the Wayne State University Law School archives.

businesses. Students did not graduate with the skills demanded by law firms that represented large businesses.

In 1945, David D. Henry was elevated to president of Wayne University and expanded his administrative staff to handle the postwar enrollment boom. President Henry appointed Arthur Neef, who had a reputation within the university as an able administrator, to serve concurrently as law school dean and university provost.[8]

Dean Neef gave less attention to the law school as President Henry increased Neef's university responsibilities. He was deeply involved in the acquisition of property, meetings with architects and contractors, and reviewing contracts for the expanding university enrollment. He also worked on university budgets.[9]

Neef delegated many of his law school administrative responsibilities to June Plihal and John Glavin. Plihal, who was not a lawyer, was Neef's administrative assistant and accepted responsibility for the non-academic aspects of the law school administration. Glavin became the associate dean in charge of the academic administration of the law school.

While Neef was serving as part-time dean, students were educated primarily by professors who had received their legal education in the state of Michigan. In 1945, four of the five full-time professors (a dean and three professors) received their legal education at the University of Michigan. The fifth received his LL.B. from Wayne Law.[10] In the 1964–65 academic year, two deans and eight full-time professors made Wayne their teaching home. Seven received some or all of their legal education at the University of Michigan or Wayne.

At that time, Wayne was an urban university that focused on teaching and did not measure the value of its professors by the quality and quantity of their scholarly publications. In the law school, many part-time practitioners

---

8. Neef also served as university vice president.
9. Wayne State University, Office of the Provost, Arthur F. Neef Records, WSR000119, Reuther Archives.
10. The five full-time teachers were Deans Campbell (DCL) and Neef (Michigan) and Professors Carl Whitchurch (Michigan J.D. & S.J.D.), John Glavin (Michigan), and Boaz Siegel (Wayne).

and judges taught courses that focused on the Michigan law that their students needed for a basic legal practice. Some full-time professors engaged in scholarship, while others had law practices.

Dean Neef's multiple university appointments created an irreconcilable conflict of interest, as the deans of each college reported to the provost (Dean Neef reported to Provost Neef). The provost balanced each dean's requests for resources for existing and new programs against the overall priorities and needs of the university. Provost Neef made budgetary allocations to the law school without a pitch from an independent law school dean for additional resources to improve the school.

For the academic year 1958–59, the law school instructional cost per student credit hour ($28.26)[11] was less than that of every college in the university except for Business Administration. The College of Education budget per student credit hour was about 20 percent higher, and the School of Social Work's was almost double that of the law school.

During the years 1957–59, Wayne transitioned to a state university largely funded by the Michigan legislature. In its highly critical 1959 Reaccreditation Report on the law school, the ABA wrote that the law school had an opportunity to grow in size and stature if it would have received a larger share of the university's state funding.

In 1945 the ratio of students to full-time faculty was high. With its limited university funding, the law school relied heavily on part-time adjunct faculty and low-paid full-time professors. In addition to the part-time dean, the faculty consisted of four full-time professors. Associate Dean John Glavin split his time between teaching and law school administration.[12] Boaz Siegel, hired in 1941, was praised as an excellent classroom teacher and conducted a private practice focused on pension law. Carl Whitchurch and Harry Endsley taught full-time at the law school.

---

11. The law school had $310,000 in direct costs and $182,000 in additional allocated costs. Donations to the law school, including for scholarships, were under $5,000.
12. John Glavin taught and served as student counselor, associate dean, and head of the law school's graduate law program. Ed, as he was known to the faculty, became the director of admissions and counseling in 1947.

Law school home at 5229 Cass from 1943 to 1966. (Reproduced with permission of the law school)

Classroom at 5229 Cass, with Professor Boaz Siegel teaching. (Reproduced with permission of the law school)

As the postwar law school enrollment expanded, the law school added some full-time professors. Robert Childs, who joined the faculty in 1945, had a law practice as well. Norbert West (who emigrated from Europe) joined the law school in 1946 as the law librarian and taught legal research.[13] In 1947, the law school hired Thomas A. Cowan, a prolific scholar with an impressive academic portfolio that included both a Harvard Ph.D. and S.J.D. When the law school celebrated its twenty-fifth anniversary in 1952, seven full-time professors and the adjuncts taught the 438 enrolled students.

Although Dean Neef had obtained his legal education at the University of Michigan from full-time professors with impeccable scholarly credentials, he valued practical experience and respected his full-time professors who also maintained a law practice. In a 1948 bar journal article, Neef justified his reliance on part-time practicing lawyers and judges to teach a substantial part of the law school curriculum:

> With no reflection upon the full-time faculty, it must be conceded that a student getting his criminal law from a judge of the Recorder's Court, such as Judge W. McKay Skillman, is inclined to feel that he is getting it directly from the source. So also with Frank E. Cooper in Administrative Law, Edward S. Reid, Jr. in Taxation, or Leslie P. Young in Trial Practice. And there is the additional factor of the variety of viewpoints which an association with a large faculty produces, and which would not be possible within our budget if all of the faculty were full-time members.[14]

Dean Neef maintained tight control over faculty decisions. Contrary to the common practice on law faculties, the Wayne adjunct faculty attended faculty meetings and enjoyed the same voting rights as the full-time faculty. Neef's

---

13. In the academic year 1945–46, Dean Neef and the three full-time faculty, Siegel, Whitchurch, and Endsley, taught about 40 percent of the courses offered. See Law School Catalog Issue, *Wayne State University Bulletin*, March 15, 1945, 22–25.

14. Neef, "Wayne University Law School," 17–20.

adjunct faculty and full-time teacher/practitioners could even outvote the scholars on the faculty on policy matters. He believed that giving adjuncts voting rights in faculty matters had a "stabilizing value" on law school decisions.[15]

Neef added four full-time professors in the mid-1950s. Samuel Shuman, a teacher-scholar, replaced Cowan in 1954. Harold Marchant also joined the faculty in 1954,[16] Richard Strichartz in 1956,[17] and Benjamin Carlin and Donald Gordon in 1957.

In the author's interviews with alumni, three professors who started teaching at Wayne in the 1940s and 1950s were regularly mentioned as the most inspiring, exceptional teachers. They were Thomas A. Cowan (1947–54), Boaz Siegel (1941–72), and Donald Gordon (1957–73, 1975–90).

Thomas A. Cowan was feared, respected, and admired by students. When he left Wayne after seven years to join the Rutgers-Newark University law faculty, a student tribute read in part: "We believe that few of us will ever meet, much less be taught, by anyone surpassing his brilliance and candor. . . . And probably most important from a student's viewpoint, he taught us with a terrific warmth and understanding which inspired even the most phlegmatic of us with a desire to learn."[18]

Boaz Siegel was the school's first full-time professor who developed expertise in labor law. He was a pioneer in Michigan in establishing union health and welfare funds and became a specialist in this field. He served as law school librarian while he was starting his labor law practice. When Dean Neef asked Siegel to teach his contracts course in 1945, Siegel thus began his long career

---

15. Ibid., 20.

16. Harold Marchant, first in his 1941 evening class at Wayne, joined the faculty after working at the Chrysler Corporation and teaching at DCL. See "Meet the Faculty," *Wayne Law Journal* (November 1955): 5.

17. From 1974 to 1978, Strichartz was the executive director of the project to draft Michigan's first public health code.

18. See *The Gavel*, May 1953, Wayne State University Law School Publications, Walter P. Reuther Library, WSR002163, Wayne State University, Detroit. Professor Cowan was beloved at Rutgers as well. Rutgers's law school had a professorship in his name—the Thomas A. Cowan Distinguished Professor of Law.

at the school, teaching in four of the law school's five locations. In those early years, the law school did not have a job placement office. Siegel kept notes on student employment opportunities in his breast pocket and helped many graduates obtain legal jobs.

In 1957, Donald Gordon was hired as the school's first full-time professor with experience in taxation. Gordon had practiced with a Boston law firm and completed an LL.M. from Harvard Law School. While predominantly a tax professor, in his early years, Gordon taught an array of other courses. Unlike most of his colleagues before the mid-1960s, Gordon taught students the multidimensional process by which law was developed. Eugene Driker, Stephen Ross, and innumerable other alumni placed Gordon at the top of the teaching faculty—an inspiring teacher.

Maurice Kelman, a Gordon student in the Class of 1959 and later a Wayne Law professor, wrote a tribute on Gordon's death. He summarized what Gordon meant to his students and to the law school: this "dapper Ivy Leaguer . . . made us provincials realize that law is not static black letter but a fascinating multi-dimensional process[.] This stranger . . . combined sophistication with unpretentiousness, seriousness with charm."[19]

Eugene Driker, who took a class from Gordon in every semester in law school, considered Gordon the best teacher he ever had.[20] He had the "rare talent of making complex legal principles come alive in the classroom. . . . Don's efforts in raising the intellectual level of the School contributed significantly" to the school's progress. Gordon, especially in the 1950s and early 1960s, provided

---

19. "The Wayne Law Community Remembers Dean Donald H. Gordon," March 28, 2011, https://law.wayne.edu/news/the-wayne-law-community-remembers-dean-donald-h-gordon-33326.

20. Eugene Driker, interview by the author, Detroit, April 17, 2015. "While I may not remember what I had for lunch, I can remember what Don Gordon said under the staircase in the old law school building." There were faculty at the other extreme, like Benjamin Carlin, who seemed to delight in making students squirm. "Eugene Driker '61," *Wayne Lawyer* 6 (Summer 1987): 19. "Gordon took students behind the words in cases or statutes to the 'why' of things. We discussed motivation—why parties in the cases are acting the way they are, not what they are doing. What do the litigants really want? Gordon 'stretched our minds to the utmost' in Federal Courts and the Federal System."

students "with a wholly different understanding of our legal system than [we received] in many of our 'how-to-do-it' classes. . . . While some professors were content with teaching the 'what' of the law, Don always forced us into asking 'why.'" He invited a group of students and faculty to meet periodically in his living room "to stimulate broader and deeper thinking about legal issues."[21]

Scholarship is the vehicle for a young law professor to become better known in the academic community. Young, talented law faculty like Richard Miller and Douglass Boshkoff left the law school after only a few years. Wayne developed the reputation in academic circles as a school that hired young scholars, did not grant them tenure, and then repeated the process.[22] For example, in 1963 and again in 1966, the school had twelve full-time professors, but during that period, five professors left the law school for more prestigious schools. Some young professors were denied tenure and Professor Kelman left in protest.

Moot Court and the Law Review

From 1945 to 1967, while Dean Neef focused his energies on university administration, the Wayne law students filled the leadership gap. They established the Student Board of Governors (SBG)[23] in 1947, expanded the Moot Court program, and initiated the law review and a live-client law clinic.

In the early 1950s the law school enrolled full-time day students who were taught a no-frills curriculum based on the case method. But the students

---

21. Eugene Driker, "Remembering Donald H. Gordon," *Wayne Lawyer* 27 (Spring 2011): 34.
22. New York University's Dean Robert McKay gave the author this information when he received an offer from Wayne in 1965.
23. The Student Bar Association (SBA) held its inaugural meeting on October 27, 1947. In March 1950, the SBA adopted its constitution, with the name Student Bar Association of Wayne University Law School. The SBG sponsored dances and other social activities and added the student voice to the faculty's consideration of programs that directly impacted them. In its early years, the SBA became the vehicle to help the dean's office maintain order in the law library and enforce smoking regulations. See Minutes of the Meeting of the Board of Governors of Student Bar, November 11, 1947, SBA archives at Wayne State University Law School.

wanted more, including programs to develop their litigation skills. Sheldon Otis (who became a prominent criminal defense lawyer with high-profile clients like Angela Davis) and fellow classmate Ronald Weiner took the lead in promoting an expanded Moot Court program.[24] The students in the Moot Court program started participating in national competitions and, by 1954, the team consisting of George Downing, Erwin Ziegelman, and Roger Craig qualified for the National Moot Court Regional Competition.[25]

The Detroit law firms representing large businesses hired graduates from elite law schools who acquired research and writing skills while serving on their school's law review. Wayne Law did not have a law review and most of its graduates were denied jobs in those firms. (The outlier, Alfred Wortley Jr. ['43], joined the Bodman, Longley, Bogle, Armstrong and Dahling firm.)[26] Each of the four "top-tier" Detroit corporate firms in the 1950s had about twenty lawyers[27] and were populated with men who graduated from the University of Michigan and a few highly regarded eastern law schools.[28] In 1954, a senior partner at one of those firms spoke to Wayne Law students and, in an informal conversation following his talk, he said that his firm did not hire Wayne Law graduates. It was not boastful, just a statement of the reality at the time.

In Dean Neef's July 1940 annual report to Executive Vice President Henry,[29] he noted that the faculty had discussed a possible law review. Neef wrote that a law review was "desirable but beyond the limits of our budget." In 1947, Dean Neef proposed to the Michigan Bar Association that Wayne Law students publish in the *Michigan State Bar Journal* practitioner-focused case digests that would not be "in as scholarly and sedate a manner as law review digests."[30]

---

24. See SBG Regular Meeting Minutes, April 16, 1957, SBG archives, Wayne State University Law School. Sheldon Otis became the SBG president the following year. In practice, he and Justin Ravitz defended John Sinclair of the radical White Panther Party.
25. George Downing went on to practice labor law and teach at the law school for decades.
26. See "Alumni News Notes: 1943," *Wayne State Law* 5 (December 1956): 7.
27. Donald Shely was the twentieth lawyer at the Dykema firm when he joined in 1955.
28. There were a few University of Detroit Law School graduates among them.
29. The report is in Dean Neef's papers in the Reuther Archives but has not been catalogued.
30. The proposal was included in a letter from Milton Bachman, executive secretary of

In 1950, several high-achieving students complained that their Wayne legal education was deficient because it did not offer students the opportunity to learn the research and writing skills gained as members of a law review. They would be graduating without the credentials needed to receive even an interview with a Detroit corporate law firm.

The students could not participate in faculty meetings, so they asked their faculty advisor, Professor Boaz Siegel, to formally propose that the faculty establish a student-run law review, as was done at the University of Michigan and other elite law schools.[31] The faculty, instead, suggested that the students start an "in-house" journal to publish well-researched, high-quality student articles.[32] *The Gavel*,[33] renamed the *Wayne Law Journal*, became the students' vehicle to enhance their "intellectual growth" in researching and writing law-related articles.[34] In its first issue, the journal published second-year student Richard Barber's comment on a case, and subsequent issues published in-depth articles about noted federal judges.

In 1953, Richard Barber and classmate John Moore, who shared bus rides between their homes and school, discussed the fact that the journal did not have the prestige of a law review. Classmates Donald Shely, Irving August, Robert Goren, and George Downing were having similar conversations. Goren and Shely met with Dean Neef and asked him to fund a full-fledged, student-run law review. Dean Neef's initial reaction was strongly negative, but the students ultimately persuaded him that they could organize a law review and start publishing in the academic year 1954–55.

---

the bar association, to Michigan Supreme Court Chief Justice Leland W. Carr, January 29, 1947, Reuther Archives.

31. SBG Regular Meeting Minutes, October 23, 1950.

32. SBG Regular Meeting Minutes, February 12, 1951.

33. The first managing editor of *The Gavel* was Robert Filsinger. SBG Regular Meeting Minutes, December 18, 1952.

34. *Wayne Law Journal* (October 1953): 2. In the 1953–54 academic year, Robert Goren was editor of the journal, which included columns on legal cases and also reported on social events and other items of interest to the student body.

Richard Barber and Donald Shely were instrumental in the establishment and success of the fledgling *Wayne Law Review*. Barber was born during the Depression and raised in a Catholic neighborhood on the northwest side of Detroit devoid of families with corporate executives, doctors, or lawyers. His father was an assistant to Michigan Central Railroad's vice president. During the Depression, his mother kept a pot of soup on the stove and the kitchen door unlocked so that unemployed neighbors could help themselves to a meal. In the 1950s, families in his neighborhood contributed to their children's college education by providing them meals and a room at home. Barber's classmates had similar upbringings, including the children of immigrants from Eastern Europe, raised in Detroit's East Side working-class neighborhood.[35]

Barber chose Wayne over the University of Detroit Law School because while the latter had a good reputation, he attended parochial high school and wanted to attend Wayne's public law school: "Wayne Law served as a way out of social and economic mediocrity."

According to Barber, his classmates seemed resigned to the basic education they were receiving. The coursework and teaching focused on local areas of practice and "any hope of . . . joining one of the major law firms in Detroit had long since been abandoned, if it ever developed. . . . If you wanted to do something bigger, [it was] squelched in the midst of coursework taught by part-timers and an administration with Neef that accepted [the assumption] that there was not much money around."

Donald Shely spent his childhood in Livonia, Michigan, and attended a small elementary school with multiple grades in each classroom. He graduated from Plymouth High in 1945 and attended Albion College. Without family financial support, Shely occasionally had to leave college to work and save money to return for another year. He transferred to Wayne's College of Education to earn the credentials needed to teach school. While there, he married,

---

35. The following paragraphs rely on Richard Barber, interview by the author, Bethesda, Maryland, April 13, 2015; Donald Shely, interview by the author, August 28, 2015.

Richard Barber, *Wayne Law Review*'s first editor in chief. (Reprinted with permission of the law school)

Donald Shely, the first Wayne graduate hired by a large Detroit law firm. (Reprinted with permission of the law school)

borrowing money to start Wayne Law while his wife completed her final year of college. She then taught school to support them while he completed law school.

The June 1954 issue of the *Wayne Law Journal* announced that the "Wayne Law School for the first time in its history, will publish—on a three issue per year basis—a full scale Law Review."[36] The faculty selected the first editorial board from students with the highest first-year grades. Richard Barber, first in that class, became the editor in chief. Irving August, George Downing, and Donald Shely, who ranked second, third, and fourth, were chosen to be associate editors.[37]

Dean Neef gave the editorial board a very limited budget and left it to them to learn how to organize and operate a law review. According to Shely, Barber was the person most responsible for the review's success, shouldering the administrative details that first year.[38] With its limited budget, the law review board could not engage an experienced commercial publisher of law reviews. The *Detroit Daily Lawyer* newspaper agreed to print the law review at a price that the board could afford. The students picked the name and told Associate Dean John Glavin that the review would henceforth be called the *Wayne Law Review*.

The review's primary task was to recruit scholarly articles. The editors learned from the editors of reviews at other law schools that "when you need articles, try the faculty first." The editors heeded that advice and in the first issue, the review published articles by Wayne law and political science

---

36. Robert Goren and Gene Mossner, "A Goal Achieved," *Wayne Law Journal* (June 1954): 11.
37. The senior editors were Alex Andrews, Robert Gilliat, Fred Gregory, John Moore, Howard Rice, and Erwin Ziegelman. The managing editor was Robert Goren.
38. While serving as editor in chief of the law review in his third year, Barber also took courses focusing on fiscal and public policy in other departments of the university. Upon graduation, after serving in the military for two years, he obtained a master's degree in economics from Michigan and an LL.M. from Yale Law School. He taught for several years at a few law schools and then served on Michigan senator Phil Hart's staff and then as deputy assistant secretary in the Department of Transportation. He later began a transportation consulting firm. Barber received the Distinguished Alumnus Award from Dean Roberts in 1985 and established the Richard J. Barber Fund for Interdisciplinary Legal Research at Wayne. *Wayne Lawyer* 11 (Summer 1993): 6–8.

professors.[39] The review also published some student notes on decided cases and comments on legal issues. The first issue included Shely's "Criminal Law—Probation—Power of Federal District Court to Suspend Sentence after Defendant Has Commenced Its Service"[40] and Barber's "Personal Services and the Antitrust Laws."[41]

The faculty did not directly supervise the student operation of the review, preferring to defer to the student editorial board. The faculty appointed a faculty advisor, Samuel Shuman, who reported on the review's progress. In the journal's first year, the main issues were a lack of articles and the editors' lack of experience.[42] By the end of the review's first year, Dean Neef wrote that while the faculty was reluctant to establish the review, it was successful: "Few innovations in the law school program were approached by the faculty with as much trepidation as accompanied the inauguration of the Law Review. The task was tremendous, for none of the student editors could bring to it any experience with a similar project. But the energy and enthusiasms of the editors made up for this lack of experience, and a truly professional job was performed."[43]

Once the review was established and successfully operating, the faculty wanted to encourage top students to join. Starting in 1955, the faculty awarded the Juris Doctor (J.D.) degree rather than an LL.B. to members of the review who had earned college degrees and had high law school grades.[44] In 1957,

---

39. Professor Samuel Shuman's "Publicizing Judicial Proceedings" and the Department of Political Science Professor Max Mark's article on the natural law theorists, titled "Schiffer: The Legal Community of Mankind."

40. *Phillips v. United States*, 522 F. 2d 388 (8th Cir. 1954).

41. *Wayne Law Review* (Winter 1954): 124.

42. See Law School Minutes, Regular Meeting of the Faculty, 1954–1955, January 7, 1955, 14, Accession WSU000625, box 5, file 1, Reuther Archives.

43. "*Wayne Law Review* Enters Second Year," *Wayne Law Journal* (November 1955): 7.

44. The first J.D.s were awarded to Alex Andrews, Irving August, Richard Barber, George Downing, Robert Giliat, Robert Goren, Fred Gregory, John Moore, Howard Rice, Donald Shely, and Erwin Ziegelman. "J.D. Now Offered," *Wayne Law Journal* (November 1955): 14. In 1965 the law school expanded the eligibility to earn the J.D. degree to all graduates who had an undergraduate degree.

the review started publishing what became a tradition—the "Annual Survey of Michigan Law."

Students Establish Clinic

In the 1960s, as the civil rights movement was gathering steam and students on campuses across the country demonstrated and protested, Wayne Law attracted some of the undergraduate activists. Law schools at the time were not offering students any "hands-on" experience representing actual clients.

In 1962, the Students for a Democratic Society (SDS), active on the University of Michigan campus, issued its Port Huron Statement criticizing the U.S. political system, racial discrimination, economic inequality, big business, trade unions, and political parties.[45] The student radicals at elite colleges like Yale, UC-Berkeley, and Michigan attracted media attention, especially when they disrupted campuses.

In 1963, as the civil rights movement was gaining momentum, the federal court ordered African American student James Meredith to be admitted to the University of Mississippi.[46] The U.S. Supreme Court struck down state laws requiring the separation of the races on public transportation. The Reverend Martin Luther King Jr. delivered an earlier version of his "I have a dream" speech in Detroit's Cobo Hall on June 23, 1963, as part of the "Detroit Walk for Freedom" and then gave his famous speech of that name in August as part of the March on Washington for Jobs and Freedom.

With strong public opposition to the Vietnam conflict and the military draft, many men graduating from college sought to extend their military deferments with postgraduate education. They found a three-year legal education an attractive option, expecting the Vietnam conflict to end within those three years. These factors coalesced, and with the University of Michigan Law School

---

45. Tom Hayden, a University of Michigan student, was the SDS president.
46. *Meredith v. Fair*, 313 F.2d 532 (5th Cir. 1962).

limiting the percentage of Michigan residents that they accepted, Wayne Law attracted many highly credentialed, motivated Michigan residents.[47]

In the fall of 1963, Ronald Helveston and a group of law students who had been politically active in their college years entered their first year at Wayne Law. Near the end of their second year, on March 7, 1965, Sheriff Clark and his officers in Selma, Alabama, beat individuals who were approaching the Edmund Pettus bridge on their planned march from Selma to Montgomery to protest the lack of voting rights for African Americans. The Reverend Martin Luther King Jr. issued a public call for clergymen and others to come to Selma to join in a second attempt to march. Helveston and his second-year classmates George Edwards III, Thomas Ensign, and Stanton Walker drove to Selma to participate in that planned march for voting rights.[48]

Kenneth Cockrel, Helveston's African American classmate and inspiring orator of the civil rights movement on the Wayne campus, planned to accompany his classmates to Selma, but Cockrel's wife pleaded with him to stay home. Cockrel's decision to stay in Detroit probably saved their lives because cars on Alabama roads with both Black and White passengers were regularly targeted, with some occupants killed.

When Helveston and his classmates arrived at the bridge in Selma to join the march, the police and some White residents met them with clubs. At Reverend King's urging, the marchers turned back and dispersed. The Wayne Law students went back to Detroit and did not return to Selma for the successful march weeks later.

On July 13, 1965, a few months after the Selma to Montgomery march, the Michigan Supreme Court adopted General Court Rule 921. This authorized a law student who had completed at least twenty-eight hours of coursework with

---

47. For example, in 1967, 27 University of Michigan graduates entered Wayne Law, and in 1968, 55 Michigan graduates did so.

48. Upon law school graduation, Ron Helveston clerked for Judge George Edwards and, upon the recommendation of Judge Wade McCree, he obtained a position in Washington, D.C., with the appellate court branch of the National Labor Relations Board. After a year there, he came back to Detroit and worked for many years with the highly regarded Ted Sachs labor law firm.

passing grades to represent indigent clients if the law school dean certified that the student met the law school's academic and moral standards.

The students who went to Selma, along with a few of their classmates, met with Dean Neef and asked the law school to sponsor a legal aid clinic. They wanted students, under Rule 921 and with the supervision of a practicing lawyer, to represent individuals who could not afford to hire lawyers in lord-tenant, divorce, and other civil legal disputes.[49]

Dean Neef declined to provide a location or financial and faculty support.[50] Undeterred, the students followed in the tradition of their predecessors who took the lead to enhance their legal education. They were decades ahead of the ABA's national effort to encourage law schools to offer skills courses as part of the law school curriculum.

During the academic year 1965–66, with the assistance of local attorney James Lafferty, money from Ernest Goodman's Fund for Equal Justice, and the sponsorship of the Michigan chapter of the National Lawyer's Guild, George Matish, Stanton Walker, Ronald Helveston, John Ecclestone II, George Edwards III, William Segesta, and Charles Richards organized the student-run Free Legal Aid Clinic (FLAC).[51] FLAC was the only student-run, income tax–exempt legal aid organization in the United States.[52]

Dean Robb ('49) worked with the students to find a sponsor for a legal aid clinic.[53] FLAC became the Wayne student affiliate of the New York–based Law Students Civil Rights Research Council, Inc.[54] FLAC was incorporated in

---

49. The material on the history of the organization of the Free Legal Aid Clinic (FLAC) was obtained from the FLAC historical material and from a video interview with Helveston in the author's office at Wayne Law on November 12, 2014.

50. According to William Segesta, neither the law school nor the Detroit Bar Association was willing to provide any funds. Helveston, interview.

51. The following material about FLAC comes from the FLAC records and Helveston, interview. Ronald and Mimi Helveston hosted the FLAC annual fundraisers in their Detroit home for over thirty years. To "catch flak," or criticism, was a slang expression at the time.

52. See "Free Legal Aid Clinic Celebrates 50th Year," *Wayne Lawyer* 30 (Summer 2015): 37.

53. James Robb, interview by the author, November 3, 2014.

54. See SBG Regular Meeting Minutes, April 20, 1965.

Michigan with the goal "to aid, assist, and represent persons without sufficient means by whatever remedy available within the legal and social framework of the State of Michigan." John Ecclestone II ('66) was FLAC's first director. FLAC attracted its first clients (mainly domestic relations cases) by placing flyers around its neighborhood location.[55]

Once FLAC was organized and operating, Dean Neef agreed to certify the qualifying students so that they could represent clients under Rule 921. Two years later, under the leadership of Dean Charles Joiner, the law school formally sponsored FLAC[56] and the faculty appointed an advisor.[57] A few years later, Edward Levi, the president-designate at the University of Chicago, wrote:

The Third Street office was near the Wayne campus. (Reproduced with permission of the law school)

---

55. Those offices were located off campus in a modest storefront at 4705 W. Grand River in Detroit and then moved to 4866 Third Street in Detroit.

56. The early law school support for FLAC was from the profits of the vending machines in the law school.

57. Law School Minutes, Regular Meeting of the Faculty, 1968–69, No. 8 (October 30, 1968), Accession WSU000639, box 4, file 18, 1968–69, Reuther Archives.

"If the poor have no legal problems, or at the least no problems interesting to law students, perhaps this should be a major concern for the law schools and the profession."[58]

The American Law Student Association held its first legal aid conference in December 1966.[59] At that conference, the director of legal services for the U.S. Office of Economic Opportunity (OEO) announced that OEO would fund legal aid programs at law schools.[60] FLAC received OEO funding in 1967. FLAC became Wayne Law's commitment to render free legal services to the underserved Detroit community; FLAC celebrated its fiftieth anniversary in 2015.

FLAC officers and members celebrated its fifty years of service at the Detroit Yacht Club in 2015. (Andrew Jowett, photographer)

58. Edward H. Levi, "The University, the Professions, and the Law," *California Law Review* 56, no. 2 (1968): 251, 256.
59. *Wayne Advocate* 1 (February 1967): 4.
60. See *Wayne Advocate* 2 (November 1967): 1.

Creating Opportunities

Between 1945 and 1967, Wayne Law provided a legal education and access to the legal profession to thousands of students who might not otherwise have become lawyers. While some law schools in the postwar period limited or denied admission to students from some religious and ethnic groups, Wayne Law welcomed a culturally and racially diverse student body: Jewish and Catholic students and children of immigrants from Poland and other East European countries. They included students from underrepresented African American and Hispanic communities who had not looked to lawyers and the legal system to protect their rights. There was a sense of community among these students. They supported each other in their legal studies, and they shared their ethnic food at the lunch table in the law school basement.

Most Wayne graduates who qualified to practice law in those two postwar decades went back to their hometowns in Michigan or remained in the Detroit area to practice with a small law firm, shared office space with other lawyers, or started a solo practice. They typically represented individual clients who bought or sold a personal residence or an isolated piece of residential property to earn rental income. Some pursued their clients' personal injury claims, drafted their wills, or probated their estates. Others helped individuals organize small businesses and then represented those businesses in matters such as drafting and enforcing contracts and collecting debts from customers. Wayne graduates from racial or ethnic minority communities with limited employment opportunities established their own firms representing clients largely but not solely from those communities.

In the early postwar period, the exceptional Wayne graduate represented large businesses. Jewish students Milton Zussman and William Davidson graduated in the Class of 1949. Zussman worked while attending law school full-time and played a lot of bridge in the law school's basement "social hall." After graduation, instead of accepting a job doing criminal work that did not pay enough to raise a family ($15 a week), Zussman opened his own office.[61] Some of his clients paid

61. Milton Zussman, interview by the author, July 22, 2015. He spent much of his legal

for his legal services in stock instead of in cash; some of those equity interests worked out and some did not. After graduation, Davidson's law practice focused on acquiring and rehabilitating struggling businesses. One of those businesses was his family's company, Guardian Glass. He turned that struggling business into the global Guardian Industries.[62] In 2005, Davidson received a Doctor of Laws from the university "in recognition of his business and civic contributions to Detroit, the state of Michigan and the country as a whole."[63]

A few Wayne women in that period obtained jobs with law firms and some became judges. Women who graduated from law school and qualified to practice law were offered secretarial-level jobs.[64] The experience of Dorothy Hendricks ('45) was not atypical. She passed the Michigan bar examination and accepted the only offer she received: librarian at the Detroit Bar Library.[65]

One of the 1947 female graduates was Bronze Key honors student Marie Kamberg (Coy), who in 1955 joined with two other Wayne graduates to open an all-women law firm in Center Line, Michigan. Kamberg focused on divorce and tax law. Her partner Mildred Vlaich, a former Macomb County assistant prosecutor, handled criminal cases and Justine Orris took the personal injury cases.[66]

---

career representing an auctioneer of industrial machine tools. He served as president of at least one company and served on the board of directors of several firms. Like many alumni whose children also attended Wayne Law, Zussman's daughter Susan graduated in the Class of 1981.

62. Davidson's love of sports led to his purchase of the Detroit Pistons Basketball Club and other sports franchises. He established the William Davidson Institute at the University of Michigan, focusing on helping to develop market economies around the world. Tourists visiting the Old City in Jerusalem, Israel, are keenly aware of the Davidson Center's excavations there. See www.archpark.org.il; http://williamdavidson.org.

63. William Davidson, Doctor of Laws, Honoris Causa, *Wayne Lawyer* 23 (Spring 2006): 6.

64. Notable women lawyers from the 1950s include former U.S. Supreme Court Justice Sandra Day O'Connor, Stanford Class of 1952, and U.S. Supreme Court Justice Ruth Bader Ginsberg, Columbia Class of 1959. They could not receive offers to work for a law firm. Justice O'Connor was offered a position as a legal secretary. Cynthia Grant Bowman, "Women in the Legal Profession from the 1920s to the 1970s: What Can We Learn from Their Experience about Law and Social Change?" *Maine Law Review* 61 (2017): 1, 9.

65. Dorothy Hendricks, interview by the author, 2015.

66. See "Ladies of the Law," *Wayne Lawyer* 23 (Spring 2006): 58.

Justice Dorothy Comstock Riley. (Reprinted with permission of the law school)

Before 1960, the exceptional African American or Hispanic Wayne graduate practiced law or became a judge. Dorothy Comstock Riley ('49) established her own practice because no law firm would hire her other than to perform secretarial work.[67] In 1972, she received appointment to the Wayne County Circuit Court, in 1976 to the Michigan Court of Appeals, and in 1982 to the Michigan Supreme Court. With her 1985 election to serve another term on the Michigan Supreme Court, Justice Riley became the first Hispanic woman in the United States elected to the Supreme Court of her state. She served as Chief Justice from 1987 to 1991.[68]

To Roberta Hughes Wright, her 1950 Wayne Law degree was the third of her four university degrees. Dr. Wright was the daughter of an African American physician who emigrated from Guyana and practiced medicine in Detroit.[69] She had earned two degrees from Wayne University—a B.S. and then an M.S. in "visiting teachers." She worked as a school social worker, and after she married and started raising a family, Wright enrolled as the only African American woman in her law school class. Dr. Wright then earned a Ph.D. from the University of Michigan.

With four degrees and qualified to practice law, Wright searched for a legal position. For an African American woman in those years, the opportunities with law firms representing businesses were almost nonexistent. Like Justice Riley, she endured questions from interviewers like "Can you type?" She practiced probate law with a predominantly African American firm in Pontiac, Michigan.[70]

Judge Geraldine Bledsoe-Ford ('51) was the granddaughter of a slave who, after emancipation, graduated from college. Her father was a prominent Detroit lawyer and, after her Wayne Law graduation, Bledsoe-Ford practiced

---

67. See *Wayne Lawyer* 6 (Fall 1987), 33.

68. http://www.micourthistory.org/justices/dorothy-riley.

69. During the author's videotaped interviews, Dr. Wright discussed her mother, Barbara, who emigrated from Canada. Her father, Robert Greenich, emigrated from Guyana to become a physician, graduating from Detroit Medical College in 1915.

70. She turned her energies to writing books, which in her words was "a hobby gone wild." She wrote about Rosa Parks and Juneteenth, among other topics.

in her father's law firm. She then served as an assistant U.S. attorney and as Detroit's assistant corporation counsel. In 1966 she became the first African American woman elected to a judgeship on Detroit's Recorder's (Criminal) Court. It wasn't until 1983 that an African American woman, Claudia House Morcom ('56), was appointed to the Wayne County Circuit Court.

Before 1968, Wayne graduates were almost entirely shut out of jobs with corporate law firms that represented larger businesses and their owners.[71] Those law firms were populated largely with lawyers from more prosperous families who had graduated from the University of Michigan or elite law schools largely on the East Coast.

Starting in 1955, the inaugural *Wayne Law Review* editors decided to test the barrier Wayne Law graduates faced in attempting to acquire the coveted jobs in those firms, with federal agencies in Washington, D.C., and in academia. Donald Shely, unannounced, approached the Dykema Gossett[72] corporate law firm in Detroit and requested a job interview. Shely endured three separate sets of interviews before the firm extended an offer and, on July 5, 1955, Shely started as the twentieth lawyer in that firm.[73] Law firms that size did not sectionalize their firms into particular areas of practice such as corporate, real estate, or litigation, but Shely later established and then chaired the litigation section of the Dykema firm.

The law review credential was the minimum for a student near the top of his class to obtain an offer from a corporate law firm, but few had that opportunity. Robert Goren, the managing editor of the first issue of the *Review*, was hired by a predominantly Jewish firm that grew into Honigman, Miller, Schwartz, and Cohn. The review's second editor in chief, Hugo Edberg, was hired by Detroit's Butzel, Eaman, Long, Gust & Kennedy law firm.[74]

---

71. In addition to the corporate firms in Detroit, smaller corporate firms were established in Grand Rapids, Lansing, and a couple of other Michigan cities.

72. The Dykema, Jones & Wheat firm was established in Detroit in 1926.

73. Shely does not believe that he was hired at the Dykema firm solely because he was a *Wayne Law Review* editor. In the early twentieth century, Shely's grandfather was a self-taught lawyer and judge in a small town in central Kentucky.

74. Alumni News Notes, *Wayne State Law Journal* 5 (December 1956): 8.

A few pioneers secured jobs with federal agencies in Washington, D.C. Robert Gilliat, review editor in the Class of 1955, rose as a government lawyer to become the assistant general counsel of the Department of Defense. Ronald Helveston ('66), one of the organizers of FLAC, worked for the national office of the National Labor Relations Board. Theodore Ravas ('68) secured a legal position with a federal government agency.[75]

Wayne Law Review's first editor in chief, Richard Barber ('55), was the first graduate to teach law full-time at a school outside Detroit. After two years of military service, Barber earned a master's degree in economics from the University of Michigan and an LL.M. from Yale. He taught at several law schools before leaving academia to work on the staff of a U.S. congressional committee. He then held a high administrative position at the U.S. Department of Transportation and left government service to establish his economic consulting firm specializing in mergers in the transportation industry.

Graduates who set up their own solo practice had to carve out their own legal careers. Henry Baskin ('57) was first in his family to go to college. He developed a reputation as an entertainment lawyer, representing Detroit television personalities and Motown recording stars.[76] Later in his career, he had a family law practice.

Two members of the Class of 1961 broke those barriers. In 1961, John E. S. Scott[77] was the first graduate hired by the Dickinson Wright corporate firm in Detroit. Eugene Driker was hired into the prestigious Department of Justice's Honors Program.

Eugene Driker ('61), editor in chief of the *Wayne Law Review*, was recognized by the practicing bar, as well as law school deans and professors, for his high ethical standards and for the example he set for students at his alma mater.

---

75. His son Stephen Ravas ('05) worked in the U.S. Department of Commerce's Office of Inspector General.

76. See generally, Anne Levy, "Alumni Profile: Henry Baskin," *Wayne Lawyer* 3 (Spring 1984): 10–12. Baskin represented ABC television personalities Bill Bonds and Marilyn Turner and Motown singers Marvin Gaye and Smokey Robinson.

77. He became an award-winning trial lawyer.

Driker's father, an immigrant, who strongly supported his son's education, told him something that became a legendary quote: "You can go to any college that is on the Dexter bus line." The Dexter bus line extended from the then Dexter-Davison Jewish neighborhood of northwest Detroit past Wayne State University on its route to downtown Detroit.[78]

Driker received his B.S. degree in mathematics from Wayne after completing his first year at the law school. After graduation, while working in Washington, D.C., as a lawyer with the Antitrust Division of the U.S. Justice Department, he earned an LL.M. from George Washington University Law School.

When Driker returned to Detroit, there was a bright line between Jewish and non-Jewish firms that has all but disappeared. If you were Jewish, your opportunities to practice with a corporate law firm were basically limited to Jewish firms. He joined a Jewish firm, but after his Justice Department experience, he wanted to litigate and that firm had only a small litigation practice. Driker and a few colleagues left and organized Barris, Sott, Denn and Driker. During his early years in that new firm, he found time to teach Consumer Fraud and Commercial Law as an adjunct professor at Wayne Law.

Driker enjoyed a reputation extending beyond Michigan[79] as an exceptional business litigator, a lawyer's lawyer, and a mensch. Judge Gerald Rosen,[80] the chief mediator in the 2014–15 Detroit bankruptcy, appointed Driker as a co-mediator and, in that capacity, he helped protect the City of Detroit employee pensions and the Detroit Institute of Art's valuable art collection. Driker, who claims that he owes his professional career to Wayne Law, has given back to the law school and the university.[81]

---

78. The quotes and information in this and the following paragraph come from Eugene Driker, interview by the author, October 22, 2014.
79. Tyrone Fahner ('68), who was chairman of the Mayer Brown (Chicago) law firm's management committee, referred to Driker as "one of the best, smartest lawyers I have known." Tyrone Fahner, interview by the author, July 13, 2015.
80. Judge Rosen is not a graduate of Wayne Law but served as an adjunct professor on the faculty.
81. Driker headed the law school's fundraising effort in 2000 to expand the law school campus. He and his wife, Elaine, were recognized for their efforts by former Michigan

Eugene Driker. (Photo by M. Murawka, courtesy of Wayne State University)

Some men who graduated in 1965 became leaders in business and had distinguished careers on the bench and in law practice. They included Stephen Ross (discussed later) and his classmates Arthur Tarnow, Michael Maddin, and Michael Timmis. At his fiftieth law school reunion in 2015, Michael Maddin ('65) summarized the law school during his time there:

> [Wayne Law] wasn't a fancy place. It was a place where most people who came here either couldn't go somewhere else, couldn't afford to go somewhere else, or weren't sure what they wanted to do, and I think that that's an environment that is pretty healthy. As I look back on it, I'm pretty proud of my Wayne State University Law School experience.[82]

Arthur Tarnow taught criminal procedure as an adjunct at the University of Detroit Mercy law school and spent much of his legal career defending clients in the federal court. In 1998, he was confirmed as a federal judge on the U.S. District Court for the Eastern District of Michigan. Michael (Mickey) Maddin joined his father's practice after graduation and helped establish what became Maddin, Hauser, Roth & Heller, P. C.[83] Michael Timmis practiced law and was a principal in a company that acquired struggling businesses and helped them become financially stable.

The law school since its earliest years enrolled women in numbers above the national average. Before the 1970s, they had extremely limited opportunities to practice law with existing firms. Some obtained law-related positions, but others fashioned their own distinguished legal careers.

In the 1945–46 academic year, women accounted for about 20 percent of the student body,[84] and 5 of the 13 graduates in January 1947 were women.

---

governor George W. Romney. Driker also served on Wayne State University's Board of Governors from 2002 to 2014.

82. Video of the fiftieth anniversary celebration of the Class of 1965.

83. Maddin is a Fellow of the American Bar Foundation and member of the Real Property Law Section Council of the State Bar of Michigan. He speaks frequently and has written articles on real estate matters. See https://maddinhauser.com/people/.

84. Provost Arthur Neef, Reports to the Legislative Study Committee on Wayne University,

In 1950, 6,256 women accounted for 3.5 percent of the lawyers in the United States.[85]

In 1964, 2,056 women (4.0 percent of the total) were enrolled in all ABA-approved law schools. The burgeoning women's movement in the early 1960s, however, did not help Wayne's female graduates secure the more lucrative positions with corporate law firms. Women who graduated first in their classes in 1963 and 1964 did not receive offers from any of the established Detroit law firms. Patricia Boyle ('63) clerked for Federal District Court Judge Machrowicz. With that credential, Boyle was hired as an assistant U.S. attorney in the Detroit U.S. Attorney's office and as a Wayne County Prosecuting Attorney. Boyle was appointed to the Detroit Recorder's Court and later confirmed as a Federal District Court Judge for the Eastern District of Michigan. Justice Boyle then made an exceptional career move. She resigned from her lifetime appointment on the federal bench to accept a term appointment to the Michigan Supreme Court. In that position, she had to stand for reelection.

Barbara Klarman ('64) had atypical credentials for a Wayne Law student in the early 1960s. She graduated from Barnard College in New York City and was a teaching assistant at Barnard, while she was earning a master's degree in musicology from Columbia University. At Wayne Law, she graduated first in her class and did not receive any invitations to interview with established Detroit law firms.

After graduation, labor law professor Boaz Siegel helped Klarman secure a position with the Detroit regional office of the National Labor Relations Board. Then Federal District Court Judge Wade McCree hired her as his law clerk. When McCree was elevated to the Sixth Circuit Court of Appeals,[86] he asked Klarman to clerk for him on that court. That job would have required Klarman

---

Table 1 (June 1946), Wayne State University Office of the Vice President and Provost Arthur Neef Records, Walter P. Reuther Library, Accession WSP000119, Box 12, 3 N-W-3(3).

85. Labor Force, Employment, and Earnings, Table No. 282, Detailed Occupation of Employed Persons, by sec., 1950, in *Statistical Abstract of the United States: 1960*, 81st Annual Edition (US GPO, 1960).

86. McCree later became the U.S. solicitor general.

to work in Cincinnati, Ohio, for a few weeks every couple of months. Instead, she took a second clerkship with another Federal District Court judge, placing her family priorities over professional advancement. When her first child was born, she resigned from that clerkship and accepted freelance work. In her first freelance case, Klarman assisted civil rights lawyer Ernest Goodman in their successful representation of the president of the Chrysler Corporation, who had been fired after publicly demanding that the Detroit Athletic Club accept a Jewish owner of an auto supply company for membership. Later in her career, Klarman taught and served as an assistant dean at Wayne Law.

Talented African American graduates in the 1950s did not have access to the coveted jobs with established law firms. According to Dean Robb ('49), his African American classmate Felix Lee was "one of the smartest students in his class." Lee worked for the U.S. Post Office during law school and, upon graduation, continued to work there in a non-legal job. Most African American graduates who practiced law engaged in a solo practice or in small law partnerships, while others went into business. A few served on the local and federal benches and one served as a federal magistrate. Others enjoyed successful legal careers in law and in the corporate world.

In the early 1960s, Vernelis Kinsey Armstrong and Warfield Moore Jr. were members of the *Wayne Law Review*.[87] Armstrong ('60) was an evening student who, after graduation, practiced as a Michigan assistant attorney general before clerking for Justice Paul Adams on the Michigan Supreme Court. She tried unsuccessfully to lease an apartment in Lansing for the time the court sat there. When she responded in person to newspaper advertisements for apartment rentals, she was routinely told that the apartment had been rented. After a two-year stint in Liberia, she practiced law in Detroit before moving to Toledo and becoming a U.S. magistrate.[88]

---

87. The information about these law review students was taken from personal phone calls with them on November 24, 2019.

88. Armstrong has fond memories of her law school education and her professors there. She did not witness any evidence of racism but remembered some faculty who thought that female students were in law school to meet a husband.

Warfield Moore Jr. ('60) received his undergraduate degree from the University of Michigan and was married while attending law school full-time. His wife taught school and he worked at a Pontiac automobile factory during vacations.[89] The large downtown Detroit commercial buildings would not rent to African American lawyers, so he shared an office with other lawyers in a smaller commercial building, and represented individuals in personal injury cases, real estate transactions, and divorce cases. He then served as judge on Wayne County's Third Circuit Court.

Annice Wagner moved to the Washington, D.C., area after her 1962 graduation. She held judicial positions in the District of Columbia, including service from 1994 to 2005 as Chief Judge of the D.C. Court of Appeals.[90]

Three African American students in the Class of 1965 attended law school at night while gaining experience working full-time for the IRS. Frederick Patmon, Hallison Young, and Stanley Kirk formed a firm specializing in tax law.

Wayne Budd and Elliott Hall moved between private law practice and corporate positions.[91] Elliott Hall ('65)[92] was a partner in the Dykema Gossett corporate law firm in Detroit, served as Ford Motor Company Vice President for Dealer Development, for Civic and External Affairs and Washington Affairs, and then rejoined Dykema Gossett in its Washington, D.C., practice.

Wayne Budd ('67) was raised in Springfield, Massachusetts. His father, the first African American policeman in the city, expected his son to develop a strong work ethic, to be a reliable and honest person, and to "perform better than those of a different race in order to have an even shot."[93]

---

89. Moore worked for Pontiac Motors before and during college.

90. She received Wayne State University's Distinguished Alumni Award in 2007.

91. Wayne Budd, Elliott Hall, Judge Keith, and Congressman John Conyers were inducted into the law school's Wall of Fame.

92. See "Agent of Change: Alumnus Is a Nationally Renowned Attorney Hailed a 'Legend' and 'Legal Titan,'" https://law.wayne.edu/news/agent-of-change-alumnus-is-a-nationally -renowned-attorney-hailed-a-legend-and-legal-titan-34338.

93. Wayne Budd, interview by the author, Boston, August 10, 2016. Budd's mother worked in a factory operating machinery. One of Budd's African American friends who attended public school in Springfield was counseled to attend the city's "trade" high school, but that friend's parents insisted that their son attend the college-prep Classical High School. That friend

Budd attended Boston College (BC), where he was class president and graduated cum laude. He was accepted by the Boston College, Boston University, and Georgetown University law schools but decided to move to Detroit, work for the Ford Motor Company, and obtain a legal education in the evenings. Dean Father Drinen of BC's law school tried to persuade Budd to go directly to law school full-time but told him that if he were going to attend law school part-time in Detroit, he should go to Wayne State's law school. He started in 1963.

Budd is grateful that Wayne Law prepared him for his legal career but acknowledges that he almost left school when an African American professor told him that he did not have "what it takes to be a lawyer." Budd completed his Wayne legal education without difficulty. He returned to Massachusetts and joined the Boston Corporate Counsel's office. He and a childhood friend established what became the largest predominantly minority law firm in Massachusetts.

Looking back on his career, Budd felt that he had "a great future behind him." He was elected president of the Massachusetts Black Lawyers Association (1974–75), president of the Massachusetts Bar Association (1979), and the first African American U.S. attorney for Massachusetts (1989–92); he said the latter was "the best job I have ever had." Budd then went to Washington as an associate attorney general, the third highest-ranking official in the U.S. Department of Justice (1992–93). While there, Budd supervised the highly publicized prosecution of Los Angeles police officers for violating Rodney King's civil rights.

Budd left the Justice Department to become a partner in the Goodwin Proctor law firm. He was lured away to become president of the New England Bell Atlantic Group, and then senior executive vice president and general counsel of John Hancock Financial. In 2004, he returned to Goodwin Proctor as senior counsel. For sixteen years, Budd taught Agency and Partnership at Boston College Law School.

---

earned degrees from Columbia and Harvard law schools and served on the Massachusetts Supreme Judicial Court.

Wayne Budd. (Reproduced with permission)

Cornelius Pitts and Kenneth Cockrel changed the opportunities for African American criminal defense lawyers in Detroit. Before the mid-1960s, African Americans accused of a crime in Detroit hired or were assigned by Recorder's Court judges to predominantly White criminal defense lawyers from the "Clinton Street Bar." When African American Judge George Crockett Jr. was elected to the criminal court in 1966, he changed that paradigm by also assigning cases to African American defense lawyers.[94]

Cornelius Pitts was one of ten children. His father was a factory worker and his mother worked periodically as a day worker to keep the family afloat. Pitts started shining shoes at age eight and later "moved up" to a better job delivering local newspapers. Following his military service, he worked full-time for the Wayne County Welfare Department and the U.S. Postal Service. Pitts used the GI Bill's educational benefits to attend Wayne Law at night. He

94. George Crockett Jr. was a civil rights lawyer and partner in the first integrated law firm in Michigan.

graduated in 1964 and became a respected criminal defense lawyer in metropolitan Detroit. Through his success, he created opportunities for other African American lawyers to become criminal defense lawyers.

Kenneth Cockrel Sr. ('67) was orphaned at age twelve and lived in Detroit with relatives. A self-described Marxist-Leninist, Cockrel was a frequent inspirational speaker promoting political and economic justice on the Wayne campus during his years in college and law school. He continued his activism while engaged in his criminal defense practice. Cockrel was a leader in the League of Revolutionary Black Workers (organized in the automobile plants). He led

Cornelius Pitts. (Reproduced with permission)

protests against Detroit's police undercover STRESS unit (Stop the Robberies-Enjoy Safe Streets), and the STRESS unit was shut down.

Cockrel gained notoriety defending African Americans in a number of highly publicized cases. He defended Albert Hibbitt, who was accused of killing Detroit police officers in connection with a meeting of the Republic of New Africa (urging separate states for African Americans) at the New Bethel Baptist Church. Cockrel defended James Johnson, who was accused of killing a coworker in a Chrysler plant, and Hayward Brown, who had been arrested for killing a Detroit police officer.

Cockrel was a member of the Detroit City Council from 1978 to 1982 and then returned to private practice. He might have run for mayor of Detroit had he not died in 1989 at age fifty.

3

Transforming Wayne Law

The ABA Section of Legal Education and Admissions to the Bar inspects ABA member schools every seven years to determine whether they are in compliance with the Association of American Law Schools (AALS) and ABA standards and rules for reaccreditation. The ABA inspected Wayne Law on March 22–25, 1959, a month before it inspected the University of Michigan Law School on its 100th anniversary.[1] Michigan was a national law school with Michigan residents representing less than 50 percent of its entering classes. The differences between Michigan's two public law schools were striking. Michigan Law was in full compliance with all ABA and AALS standards. Its total enrollment was 862 (approximately 24 students per faculty member), while Wayne had a much higher student-to-faculty ratio with about 450 students and 12 full-time faculty.[2]

The ABA 1959 Reaccreditation Report on Wayne Law brought glaring law school deficiencies to the university's attention. It is not clear if the faculty had access to that report.[3] Arthur Neef was the law school administrator and then

---

1. Elizabeth Gaspar Brown with William Wirt Blume, *Legal Education at Michigan: 1859–1959* (University of Michigan Law School, 1959), 432.

2. There were 198 day students, 189 evening students, and 48 graduate students. The ABA Reaccreditation Report on Wayne Law noted that most of the faculty had significant teaching responsibilities and did not engage in productive research and scholarship.

3. In a note to Dean Neef, attached to the ABA report, June Plihal, his administrative assistant, suggested that he might not want to circulate the report too widely.

dean since the school was established in 1927. In the early years, he had to operate the school on tuition alone, and he had to struggle to keep the school open when enrollment plummeted during the Depression and World War II. In the postwar years while serving concurrently as dean and university provost, Neef continued to rely heavily on adjunct faculty and minimal university budget allocations.

In the post–World War II period, the ABA used reaccreditation reports to oppose university efforts to divert law school tuition revenue to other university purposes. The ABA position was that "a sum at least equal to that derived from tuition and fees be expended in annual law school operations—or earmarked for future law school support." That should be the minimum: "it is not to be understood . . . that under normal conditions tuition income is necessarily to be regarded as a proper measure of law school support."

The ABA's 1959 Wayne Reaccreditation Report exposed Neef's conflicts and the deficiencies in the law school program,[4] especially a part-time dean administering the school with inadequate resources, an inadequate physical plant, and poorly paid professors. The poor funding occurred while the university resources increased during the 1957–59 transition from a Detroit Board of Education–administered university to a constitutionally chartered state university.

Among the ABA's detailed findings:

1. the university allocation of resources to the law school was inadequate;
2. the law school needed full-time decanal leadership;
3. the school needed more full-time faculty with an improvement in the faculty salaries;
4. the physical plant was woefully inadequate;
5. the law library, incorporated as part of the university library, lacked specialized research tools.[5]

---

4. Dean Neef relinquished his university appointment as vice president in 1965. See "Presenting the Administration and Faculty of Wayne State University Law School," *Wayne Advocate*, Commencement, 1966.

5. Dean Ralph Kharas and Rev. Joseph Tinnelly, Evaluation Report, Wayne State University Law School, Detroit, Michigan, March 22–25, 1959, Reuther Archives.

Following the receipt of the ABA report, Dean Neef solicited donations from alumni to commission a design for a new law school campus. The university sought state funding for that project. Dean Neef did not start addressing the other deficiencies for several years.

New Law Campus

On October 22, 1966, Earl Warren, the Chief Justice of the U.S. Supreme Court, dedicated the new law school campus. In his speech, the Chief Justice said that "I would like to believe that larger numbers of the products of fine law schools such as this would heed the call of public service." In part, he added:

Chief Justice Earl Warren. (Reproduced with permission of the law school)

The true law center cannot allow itself to be solely concerned with the law as it exists. It must also direct its focus upon how the law got to be what it is and how the law must develop in the future to more adequately to serve our needs—not just the needs of a privileged few but the needs of all. The true law center must not only expound the law; it must enrich the law.[6]

Dean Arthur Neef designed the new law campus. His allocation of minimal space and resources for faculty secretaries did not encourage the newly hired professors to engage in scholarship. Some of the tenured professors were practicing law part-time, so only the few scholars on the faculty in the mid-1960s

The law library (*left*) and classroom building (*right*) in 1966. (Reproduced with permission of the law school)

---

6. The Law School Dedication Address of The Honorable Earl Warren, Chief Justice of the United States, law school dedication address, October 22, 1966, WSR000218, series II, box 1, Reuther Archives.

needed secretaries in the pre-computer era to type manuscripts for their books and law review articles. The expanded faculty starting in 1966 shared four secretaries housed in a section of the registrar's office.

New Law School Administration

Some professors had been dissatisfied with Dean Neef's leadership for many years and had asked President Clarence Hilberry, who served from 1952 to 1965, to replace Neef. Arthur Neef had been President Hilberry's provost and vice president. (Together Neef and Hilberry had lobbied the Michigan legislature in 1957 to establish Wayne as the third state university with independent constitutional status.)

The critical 1959 ABA Reaccreditation Report had not moved Hilberry to replace Dean Neef so, not surprisingly, Hilberry did not act on the law professors' request. He announced on February 27, 1964, that Neef was relinquishing his position as vice president to devote all his time to the law school deanship, but Neef continued to serve in the university administration.[7]

It would take a strong, independent Wayne State president to replace Dean Neef. In 1965, William Rae Keast became Wayne State University's fifth president. Keast was the first president who was not elevated from within the university.

President Keast's strength and independence may have emboldened some law professors to ask Keast to replace Dean Neef. They witnessed his determined refusal to disclose information about Wayne students to the Selective Service and may have thought he was the leader who could make changes. As the Vietnam War heated up in the mid-1960s and the U.S. military requested more troops, the Selective Service System tightened the rules for college students to retain their deferments. Selective Service requested Wayne State and other universities to disclose the names of their students who withdrew from the university, took a semester off to work, or were not in good standing

---

7. "Neef to Devote Major Time to Law Deanship," *Inside Wayne*, March 25, 1964, 102.

academically. Those students would be eligible for military service. President Keast refused to disclose to the Selective Service a male student's class rank or academic status, claiming in part that a large number of Wayne's working students switched between part-time and full-time status semester by semester.

During the 1965–66 academic year, in a private meeting, one or two law professors asked President Keast to change the law school's administration.[8] President Keast asked Neef to resign as dean. When Neef's resignation was not forthcoming, President Keast wrote Neef that his service as dean would end on June 30, 1967.[9] This yearlong grace period gave Neef the opportunity to serve as dean of the school that was housed in the law school complex that he helped design and shepherd through the state and university budget process-es.[10] Associate Dean John E. Glavin was appointed acting dean, effective July 1, 1967. Upon Neef's retirement from the university, the Wayne State University Board of Governors named the school's library the Arthur Neef Law Library on June 11, 1969.

President Keast appointed a committee to conduct a nationwide search for a new law school dean. Associate Dean Charles Joiner was serving as acting dean at the University of Michigan Law School while the University of Michigan engaged in a search for its next law school dean. When Joiner was not selected by the University of Michigan, the Wayne dean search committee was able to consider him. President Keast, with the approval of the Board of Governors, appointed Charles Joiner as the third dean in the law school's forty-year history, effective December 1, 1967.[11] He served at both Michigan and Wayne

8. The author learned about these private conversations with President Keast from two ten-ured law faculty familiar with those meetings. Donald Gordon is credited with helping to persuade President Keast that the law school needed new leadership.

9. President Keast accepted Arthur Neef's resignation on December 22, 1966, with an effec-tive date of June 30, 1967.

10. Arthur Neef returned to the teaching faculty until his retirement in 1969, but his eye-sight prevented him from keeping up in his field.

11. The Wayne State University Board of Governors approved his appointment upon the recom-mendation of President William Rae Keast on November 9, 1967. See announcement, *Inside Wayne*, November 27, 1967.

until June 1, 1968, when he assumed full-time duties at Wayne. In 1972, Michigan senator William Griffin (a former student of Joiner's at the Michigan Law School) recommended and President Nixon nominated Charles Joiner for an open seat on the Federal District Court for the Eastern District of Michigan. Joiner was confirmed and received his commission on June 9, 1972, ending his extraordinary deanship at Wayne Law.

Changes under Dean Joiner

The history of what became the Wayne Law School of the twenty-first century could begin with Charles Joiner's deanship. At Wayne, he improved the educational and scholarly atmosphere and the hopes and expectations of the Wayne students and faculty. The Order of the Coif is *the* nationally recognized law school academic honor that member schools can bestow on their graduates. Joiner started the application process for Wayne to secure a chapter of Coif.[12] In 1984, Wayne became the second law school in Michigan to receive a chapter of the Order of the Coif society[13] and only the fourth Coif chapter in the country that offered both a full-time day program and a part-time evening program. The faculty elected Eugene Driker as its first honorary member.[14]

Joiner supported Wayne's mission as an urban university and found the Wayne Law deanship attractive.[15] While Wayne Law was located in the City of Detroit, the faculty's connection with and involvement in the city had been

---

12. "The Order of the Coif is an honorary scholastic society designed to encourage excellence in legal education by fostering a spirit of careful study, recognizing law students who attained a high grade of scholarship, and honoring those who as lawyers, judges and teachers attained high distinction for their scholarly or professional accomplishments." http://www.orderofthecoif.org.

13. See www.orderofthecoif.org. Membership is limited to students in the top 10 percent of a graduating class who have taken "at least 75 per cent of their law studies in graded courses." "Individual Chapters may impose additional qualifications."

14. When Eugene Driker graduated, Wayne did not have a Coif chapter. See "Order of the Coif," *Wayne Lawyer* 4 (Fall 1984): 24.

15. Charles Joiner, interview by the author, Naples, Florida, November 1, 2014. He lived to age 101.

thin before Edward Wise, who taught criminal law, and a few other professors helped volunteer lawyers defend individuals arrested during the Summer of 1967 "Rebellion."

Dean Joiner knew how to lead an elite law school. He served as Wayne Law's dean for less than five years, but he had an outsized impact on the reputation of the school and on the career opportunities for Wayne Law graduates. In modestly recounting his accomplishments as dean, Joiner claimed that he merely applied at Wayne Law the skills he learned as professor and associate dean at the University of Michigan Law School.

President Keast provided Joiner with the resources he needed to enhance the school's reputation. Joiner hired more professors, but rather than recruiting faculty almost exclusively from the graduate programs and from the Association of American Law Schools' faculty recruitment conference as Neef had done in recent years, Joiner broadened the search to include individuals engaged in government service and lateral appointments of professors teaching at other law schools. Joiner increased faculty salaries. He wanted Wayne to be known as a law school that valued its faculty and paid them well.

Until Joiner's arrival, the four-person law school administration consisted of Dean Arthur Neef; his administrative assistant, June Plihal; Associate Dean and Director of the Graduate Law Program John Glavin; and Registrar May Hall. Joiner radically changed the law school administration to accomplish the goals that he set for the school. One of his first changes was selecting Donald Gordon as his associate dean. Gordon was the "inside" dean that enabled Joiner to spend his time away from his office promoting the law school, its faculty, and its students. Joiner's administration in the 1969–70 academic year, in addition to Gordon, included Anthony Vernava, assistant dean for student affairs; Paul Borman, assistant dean for urban issues; and John Glavin, director of the Graduate Program.[16]

---

16. May Hall remained as registrar, and two extraordinarily devoted women—Betty Pruzinsky (Van Goethem) and Rebecca Hollancid—succeeded her for the next fifty years. For more of Joiner's changes, see Update, Student Board of Governors' *Law School News*, February 2, 1970.

Stabilizing and Expanding the Faculty

The Wayne faculty during the Joiner deanship became the Joiner faculty. The law school started hiring more teacher-scholars in the 1960s, but most left after a few years. In 1964 Wayne hired Kenneth Callahan, who had received his LL.B. from Ohio State and LL.M. from Columbia Law in 1962. He previously taught at Texas Southern Law School. When Wayne increased its efforts to recruit and retain more students of color, the law school relied on Callahan to mentor many of those students.

The faculty hired four professors in 1965, but only two, Edward Wise and Anthony Vernava, stayed more than one year. Wise earned his undergraduate degree from the University of Chicago while a teenager. He received his J.D. from Cornell Law School and his LL.M. from New York University. When Wise joined the Wayne faculty, he was working on a law school casebook with Gerhard Mueller, New York University's preeminent comparative criminal law scholar. The faculty relied on Professor Wise to write or edit most of the faculty's significant reports. He remained on the faculty and directed the Comparative Criminal Law Project until his untimely death in 2000.

Anthony Vernava received his legal education at Harvard Law School. He joined the faculty after practicing tax law. He taught taxation course and business planning, served as Joiner's dean for student affairs, and left in 1971 to return to law practice.

In 1966, when the new law school campus opened, the faculty hired six tenure-track professors. The new hires included the law school's first female professor. They received some or all of their legal education at elite eastern law schools. The six new hires plus the three who were hired recently and remained more than one year represented over 50 percent of the full-time professors. For the first time, a majority of the Wayne Law professors were teacher-scholars.

In early July 1966, Dean Neef visited five of the six hires, all new to full-time law school teaching. He carried an 8 × 14 yellow pad and parceled out courses that he needed taught two months later. Those five were Friedrich Juenger,

Vincent Rinella Jr., Frederica (Koller) Lombard, Stephen Schulman, and Alan Schenk. Arthur Lombard joined later that summer. Five came directly after completing their J.D. or LL.M from Harvard, Yale, and New York University. Juenger, who had received his primary legal education in Europe, joined the faculty after years of law practice with a firm known for its international legal work. He was assigned to teach Comparative Law and Conflicts of Law. Vincent Rinella Jr. was hired to teach courses in the field of criminal law. He had received his J.D. from Yale a couple of months earlier. Neef assigned Rinella to teach Evidence and a course that combined Criminal Law and Criminal Procedure.[17]

Frederica Koller (Koller Lombard after she married colleague Arthur Lombard) became Wayne Law's first full-time female law professor and, in 1966, was one of only a few dozen women[18] holding tenure or tenure-track positions in all of the U.S. accredited law schools.[19] She received her J.D. degree from the University of Pennsylvania Law School, clerked for a Pennsylvania judge, and had just completed her LL.M. at Yale. Wayne hired Koller to teach family law, but she also taught Civil Procedure.[20]

In the early 1960s, female law students were not treated well, even at many elite law schools. Some "Penn" professors did not call on women to participate in classroom discussions, except on their "ladies" day. In 1961, Harvard Law

---

17. Juenger taught at Wayne until he joined the University of California-Davis faculty. Arthur Lombard thought that he was hired to teach Civil Procedure. He earned his J.D. from Harvard Law School, then clerked for Chief Judge Lumbard on the Second Circuit, and returned to Harvard as a teaching fellow for Civil Procedure. When he arrived on the Wayne campus later that month, Neef had already assigned Frederica Koller to teach Civil Procedure, so Lombard was assigned to teach Legal Process (a course he wanted to teach), along with Equity and Restitution. Lombard left Wayne after twenty-one years to become dean at the Detroit College of Law. Rinella left Wayne after two years to obtain a master's degree in psychology at Duke and had a productive career as a clinical psychologist.

18. See Herma Hill Kay, "The Future of Women Law Professors," *Iowa Law Review* 77 (1991): 5, 6. Thirteen women were on tenure track in 1959. Seventeen more were hired by 1965.

19. Nationwide, there were eight women hired in 1966. Ibid., 12.

20. Frederica Lombard spent her entire career at Wayne, teaching and serving as associate dean and acting dean, until she retired in 2007.

School increased the entering class by twenty-five in order to accommodate the twenty-five women without reducing the number of admitted men.[21]

Stephen Schulman was hired to teach Corporate Law. Schulman earned his J.D. from Columbia Law School, and he had just completed an LL.M. in Corporate and Securities Law at New York University. Schulman spent years working for the New York attorney general, examining possible securities fraud in the syndication of Broadway plays. In addition to Corporations, he was assigned to teach Administrative Law.

Alan Schenk was hired to teach Federal Income Taxation because Wayne tax professor Donald Gordon had a one-year special appointment at the United States Treasury for the 1966–67 academic year. Schenk earned his LL.B. from the University of Illinois and had just completed an LL.M. in Taxation from New York University. He was a Certified Public Accountant and previously practiced with the Arthur Andersen & Co. international accounting firm. In Schenk's meeting with Dean Neef to discuss the upcoming semester's assignments, Neef told Schenk that since he was familiar with one statute, the Internal Revenue Code, Schenk would teach the other statute, the Uniform Commercial Code (UCC). Neef did not think it important that Schenk's only background in the relatively new UCC was one course in law school two years earlier. Neef said: "That does not matter; you are smarter than our students." Schenk learned during those early years on the faculty that Neef greatly underestimated the quality of the Wayne Law students.

Dean Joiner reversed Wayne Law's reputation in the academic community as a school that routinely denied tenure to young, productive scholars. Wayne's reputation was well known in the respected graduate law programs[22] from which it more recently recruited new faculty. He attended the meetings of the tenured faculty during which the professors hired before 1968 were considered

---

21. Dean Joan Mahoney ('75) reported that in her property class in 1972–73, the professor called on women only one or two days a month.

22. At the time, Wayne Law recruited new faculty largely from Harvard, Yale, Columbia, and New York University.

for tenure. Professors who were hired without tenure no longer had to seek positions elsewhere.

During Joiner's deanship that started in 1967, the number of full-time faculty members almost doubled. Joiner was directly involved in the recruitment of professors. He wanted the Wayne Law faculty to resemble that at law schools like the University of Michigan. Joiner's goal was for Wayne to have three professors in each required first-year and upper-level course, so that there could be a lively scholarly interchange among professors in those areas.

President William Rae Keast's important focus, especially after the 1967 Detroit "Rebellion," was on urban issues. With Joiner's leadership, the faculty hired three professors with particular teaching and scholarly interests in urban issues: John Mogk, Otto Hetzel, and Paul Borman.

John Mogk grew up in the Jefferson-Chalmers neighborhood on the east side of Detroit. After graduating from Michigan's law school, he practiced law with Shearman & Sterling, a Wall Street law firm. He was attracted to Wayne because Joiner and the university were promoting an urban mission, and he moved back to his old Detroit neighborhood.

Otto Hetzel had been Chief Counsel for Model Cities and Government Relations within the U.S. Department of Housing and Urban Development. In addition to his appointment on the law faculty, Hetzel served as the associate director of Wayne's Center for Urban Studies.

Paul Borman had been an assistant U.S. attorney in the Detroit office of the U.S. Attorney. He served as special counsel to Detroit mayor Jerome Cavanagh before joining the faculty as assistant dean and associate professor.[23]

Joiner encouraged his law professors to get involved in local nonprofit organizations that were addressing the causes and consequences of the 1967 Detroit Rebellion. John Mogk became involved in New Detroit, one of the groups organized by leaders of the business community to address the issues raised by the Detroit Rebellion. He chaired a state commission on education,

---

23. Borman then served in the Eastern District of Michigan as Chief Federal Defender (1979–94) until confirmed as a United States District Judge on August 10, 1994.

was a candidate for mayor of the City of Detroit, chaired the Michigan Energy Research Recovery Administration (MERRA), and headed an electric power team delegation to China.[24] Professors Schulman and Schenk advised the Inner City Business Improvement Forum (ICBIF), a coalition designed to encourage African American Detroiters to own and operate Detroit businesses.

Joiner also encouraged the faculty to hire experienced legal academics. Joiner recruited former Tulane law professor Ralph Slovenko, who, while not a medical school–trained physician, completed psychiatric training at Tulane's Medical School and then worked for the Menninger Clinic in Kansas.[25] Joiner also lured Professor B. J. George Jr., his former colleague at the University of Michigan Law School, to Wayne Law. With a grant from the W. K. Kellogg Foundation, George established and directed the law school's Center for the Administration of Justice, which provided in-service education for Michigan judges, court employees, and prosecutors.[26]

During the Joiner years, Maurice Kelman rejoined the faculty. Kelman left Wayne Law for the Ohio State faculty in 1966 in protest over Wayne's denial of tenure to a young law school scholar. He was serving as special counsel to Mayor Jerome Cavanagh when the faculty invited him to return to the law school. The faculty hired Michael Josephson, a young entrepreneur, who, while teaching at Wayne, established a national bar review company.[27]

Under Dean Joiner's leadership, the faculty modernized the first-year curriculum,[28] emulating the trends at elite law schools. Constitutional Law became

---

24. In 2021, Mogk was appointed as one of Wayne State's first Distinguished Service Professors.

25. Slovenko developed an international reputation in the field of law and medicine. The Menninger Clinic was the first American group psychiatric practice.

26. The Center for the Administration of Justice (CAJ) performed research and conducted projects to evaluate programs. It also hosted conferences and courses to assist Michigan judges.

27. Professor Josephson established the Michigan Bar Review Center, using experts in each field to write and lecture on their topics covered on the bar exam. See Chase, "Geared to Results: New Bar Review Formed," *Wayne Advocate* 3, no. 4 (1969).

28. See "First-Year Courses Changed, Update," *Wayne State University Law School News*, April 13, 1970.

a required first-year course. A large portion of the Uniform Commercial Code (UCC) had been taught as a single upper-level course. As part of this reform, the Sales rules in the UCC were moved to the first-year contracts course.[29]

The faculty enhanced the upper-level curriculum by offering students more in-depth coverage in specific practice areas. For a real estate practice, Land Use Planning was added. For a criminal law practice, the faculty introduced two Criminal Procedure courses and a course in the Administration of Justice. To prepare students for careers as business lawyers in large corporate law firms, the faculty introduced a capstone, year-long Business Planning course.[30]

Charles Joiner was active and well known within the State Bar of Michigan, and within the law school accrediting agencies, the ABA, and the AALS. He attended ABA and AALS meetings and introduced his Wayne professors to practicing lawyers, law school deans, and professors from across the country. He recommended faculty for ABA committee membership.[31]

During one of his years as dean, Joiner served as president of the State Bar of Michigan. Joiner encouraged the faculty to participate in state and local professional organizations, and he promoted Wayne as a school with a scholarly faculty that prized teaching and maintained connections with the practicing bar. For example, Professor Stephen Schulman became active in the Business Law section of the Michigan bar, helped in the revision of the Michigan Business Corporation Act, and then, with a coauthor, wrote the definitive treatise on that Act. The practicing Detroit bar no longer considered Wayne professors

---

29. The faculty modified the first-year curriculum in 2008 with the split of at least one first-year course into small enrollment sections. See Faculty Meeting Minutes, February 27, 2008.

30. Professors Schulman and Schenk team-taught Business Planning using a transactional approach to explore planning issues ordinarily covered in the separate Corporate Taxation, Securities Regulation, and Business Planning courses, the latter inspired by Harvard professor David Herwitz. This yearlong transactional course was offered at only one other law school.

31. For example, Joiner encouraged Alan Schenk to join the ABA Section of Taxation Special Committee on Value Added Tax (VAT) and assisted him in that effort. Schenk spent the next four decades writing and speaking about VAT, two decades of which he spent drafting VAT laws for developing countries on behalf of the International Monetary Fund.

as fellow practitioners. Wayne professors, like the University of Michigan law professors, were scholars who served as resources for legal reform and teachers in the state's continuing legal education programs.

Charles Joiner increased the school's visibility and reputation nationally and locally. He capitalized on his national visibility and professional connections and, assisted by Assistant Dean Borman, the law school invited nationally known judges and political figures to Wayne. In 1971, a panel consisting of U.S. Supreme Court Justice Potter Stewart, U.S. Federal District Judge Damon Keith, and Michigan Supreme Court Judge Thomas Kavanagh judged Wayne's Moot Court Law Day program. Senator Henry Jackson from Washington state was the keynote speaker at the Wayne Law Alumni Day program.[32] Senator Phil Hart from Michigan spoke about the U.S. Senate's 1970 hearings (and ultimate rejection) of U.S. Supreme Court nominee Judge G. Harrold Carswell.

Joiner invited well-known academics to teach in the 1970 summer school program. New York University's Leroy Clark taught courses on violence, disorder, and criminal justice. Detroit councilman, future senator, and Wayne's Distinguished Legislator in Residence Carl Levin, who earlier in his career served on the Civil Rights Commission, taught a civil rights seminar. Indiana University professor Daniel Tarlock taught a course on the emerging area of law and environmental quality.[33] Another impressive group of visiting professors taught in the 1971 summer program.[34]

Joiner hired some Wayne Law graduates in his law school administration and in non–tenure track teaching positions, highlighting the confidence he had

---

32. See "Distinguished Guests," *Student Board of Governors Law School News*, April 12, 1971. In the prior year, the Moot Court team took first place in the regional round of the National Moot Court competition and represented the region in the national finals. Members of the best team were Robert Brott, Robert Nix, and Lawrence Farmer. "WSU Team Goes to Moot Court Finals," *Legal Advertiser*, November 19, 1970.

33. "Urban Law Program Set for Summer, Update," *Wayne State University Law School News*, February 23, 1970.

34. Harvard professor Lloyd Weinreb taught Criminal Procedure, and Professor Ernest Gellhorn of Virginia taught Defective Products and the Consumer. Carl Levin and his brother, Sander Levin (later a U.S. congressman), taught State and Local Government.

in Wayne students. He hired Tyrone Fahner ('68) as his special assistant, and he hired recent graduates to teach legal research and writing to Wayne's first-year students.

Improved Employment Opportunities

Wayne Law students in the Joiner years came largely from working-class and immigrant families and from communities not well represented in the legal profession. Wayne graduates started solo practices, joined with other lawyers to share offices, went back to a family business, or went into corporate management programs, but except for a few isolated cases, Wayne graduates before the Joiner deanship were denied the higher-paying jobs with the Michigan corporate law firms.

In the Charles Joiner years, the most dramatic change in new and expanding employment opportunities for Wayne graduates was the increase in offers to join Michigan's corporate law firms as business lawyers. Dean Joiner changed the conversation within the Michigan legal community about the preparedness of Wayne's graduates for a legal practice representing business. His enthusiasm about the quality of the students was well received by the leading lawyers in Michigan's corporate law firms. This was also a time when the large Michigan law firms could not attract all of the associates they needed from their usual sources: the University of Michigan and some elite eastern law schools. This opened up opportunities for Wayne Law graduates, primarily men, to practice with large and midsize Michigan corporate law firms.[35]

Some pioneering graduates during the Joiner deanship impressed their firms and the firms thus sought more Wayne-trained lawyers. Litigators Tyrone Fahner and James Robinson and transactional lawyers David Joswick and Peter Sugar were four of those graduates during the Joiner years. Two students from western Michigan, David Clanton and Jon Muth, achieved prominence

---

35. For the first time, Wayne men were also being recruited by New York and Philadelphia law firms. Some graduates during the Joiner years became judges later in their careers. For example, Donald Swank ('68) was a judge on Michigan's 33rd District Court.

in legal practices in Washington, D.C., and Grand Rapids, respectively. Some litigators practicing with smaller law firms, like Barry Waldman, received their start during the Joiner years. These graduates created opportunities for future Wayne Law students. Others, like Sam Bernstein and Michael Terry, established careers outside the mainstream of private law practices.

Tyrone Fahner ('68) and David Joswick ('69) were childhood neighbors in an ethnically diverse, blue-collar, working-class Italian and immigrant Polish and German neighborhood on the East Side of Detroit.[36] When Fahner was not admitted to the University of Michigan Law School, he decided to attend Wayne Law. "I often think that if Charles Joiner had let me into Michigan [Joiner was associate dean at Michigan when Fahner applied], I would have been a good mediocre lawyer."

Fahner and many of his law school classmates were motivated to succeed. They had something to prove. "Wayne creates opportunities," said Fahner. He appreciated the rigor of the Wayne Law classes that taught students how to apply the law that they were learning. Fahner contrasted his "nuts and bolts" legal education at Wayne with his Northwestern Law School's more policy-oriented LL.M. program in criminal law. After his LL.M., Fahner practiced as an assistant U.S. attorney in Chicago—"The best job I ever had."

Governor James Thompson (one of Fahner's professors at Northwestern) then appointed Fahner as the State of Illinois Director of Law Enforcement, and later, as Illinois attorney general. He spent most of his career practicing with the Mayer Brown law firm in Chicago, including as chairman of the firm's executive committee. He defended clients against white-collar criminal charges. He was active in civic affairs, serving on the board of the Mexican American Legal Defense and Education Fund and as president of Chicago's Civic Committee.[37]

In David Joswick's Detroit neighborhood, parents had to make difficult choices about their children's college education. Joswick's sister Trudy wanted

36. Tyrone Fahner, interview by the author, Chicago, July 13, 2015.
37. The Civic Committee of the Commercial Club of Chicago is "a private, non-profit organization of senior executives of the region's largest employers." www.civiccommittee .org. Fahner was the 2002 *Chicago Lawyer*'s Person of the Year.

Tyrone Fahner, Class of 1968. (Reprinted with permission)

David to go to college, even if it meant that the family could not continue to finance her college education. Joswick attended the University of Michigan and worked at campus jobs that paid for his meals and accommodations.

Joswick chose Wayne Law instead of the University of Michigan's MBA program because law offered a three-year military deferment in the midst of the Vietnam War. He was second in his class after his second year, and upon graduation was the first Wayne Law graduate hired by the Miller Canfield law firm in Detroit. He became a partner in a record five and a half years.

As Joswick rose at Miller Canfield, he encouraged his colleagues to hire more Wayne graduates, and that firm for years boasted the largest number of Wayne Law alumni of any law firm in Michigan. Wayne graduates, according to Joswick, worked for their promotions; they did not feel *entitled* to a firm partnership. They connected with their business clients more easily than "credentialed" colleagues from elite law schools.[38] With their "real-life backgrounds," they worked through their clients' legal issues without their egos getting in the way. Joswick also taught as an adjunct professor at Wayne, the University of Michigan, and the University of Detroit Mercy law schools.

James Robinson ('68) was raised in Grand Rapids, the son of a regional director of the UAW. Robinson and Fahner were successful partners in the regional Moot Court competition.[39] Robinson was also the editor in chief of the *Wayne Law Review*. He practiced with two Detroit law firms where he earned his reputation as a distinguished litigator. He served as the United States Attorney for the Eastern District of Michigan, was president of the State Bar of Michigan,[40] and chaired the litigation department of Detroit's Honigman law firm. In 1993, twenty-five years after graduation, he became Wayne Law's

---

38. David Joswick, interview by the author, May 11, 2016.
39. The Moot Court brief, co-authored by Fahner, won second place in the regional competition, just a fraction of a point below the first-place brief. *The Wayne Advocate* 2 (February 1968). The Wayne Moot Court program continued to excel. In 1969, the Wayne team was the only undefeated team in the Sixth Circuit competition. Raymond Winter and Thomas Geggie took the honors that year. See *The Wayne Advocate* 3 (March 1969).
40. During his presidency in 1990–91, Robinson worked to increase the pro bono work by Michigan lawyers.

David Joswick, Class of 1969. (Reprinted with permission)

seventh dean. After his deanship, President Clinton appointed Robinson as the assistant attorney general overseeing the Justice Department's Criminal Division.[41]

Peter Sugar ('70) enrolled in the law school after receiving his Wayne degree in business administration. It is not surprising, according to Sugar, that Wayne Law graduates from immigrant families pursued business after becoming lawyers. That background "drives people to fend for themselves." "It is 'industry and grit' that gives [those lawyers] the confidence to take the risks inherent in establishing a business."[42]

Sugar spent his legal career advising business clients with legal issues in fields that his law school professor Stephen Schulman taught: securities regulation and business planning. For decades, he taught the same classes as an adjunct professor. Sugar was honored as the first Wayne Law adjunct professor to receive the Donald H. Gordon Award for Excellence in Teaching.

Wayne attracted many students from the western part of Michigan's lower peninsula. After graduation, some left Michigan, some practiced in the Detroit area, and some returned to their other hometowns. In addition to Robinson, David Clanton and Jon Muth came from western Michigan.

David Clanton ('69) was raised in Berrien Springs (population 2,000).[43] He credits Dean Joiner with making positive changes in the law school during his years there, including promoting the school nationally. The Wayne

---

41. After service in the Justice Department, Robinson became a partner at the Washington, D.C., office of Cadwalader, Wickersham & Taft. He served on the Presidential Commission on Holocaust Assets and consulted for the UN Center for International Crime Prevention in Vienna.

42. In the interest of full disclosure, Peter Sugar was my former student whom I asked to team-teach the Business Planning course after my previous co-teacher in that course, Stephen Schulman, died. Sugar's Jewish family survived World War II while living in Pest, Hungary. After the war when the Soviets gained control in Hungary and closed the borders, the Sugar family walked into Austria and were housed in a Viennese refugee camp. They made their way, via Canada, to Detroit. Peter Sugar, interview by the author, May 22, 2015.

43. The material in this section comes from David Clanton, interview by the author, Washington, DC, April 14, 2015.

Law environment, according to Clanton, encouraged students to consider their legal education as a valuable tool to pursue a wide variety of career opportunities.

Clanton, an honors graduate, went job hunting in Washington, D.C., without any personal contacts or prospects there. Michigan senator Robert Griffin hired Clanton as his legislative assistant.[44] After almost a decade with Griffin, Clanton was appointed a commissioner on the Federal Trade Commission (FTC).[45] Among the major issues examined while he was at the FTC, the commission considered the advertising restrictions applicable to lawyers like Wayne graduate Sam Bernstein.[46]

Clanton applied the antitrust expertise he gained at the FTC to ultimately lead the Baker & McKenzie law firm's global antitrust practice.[47] During the years that Clanton hosted the Wayne Law alumni receptions at his firm, he witnessed more and more Wayne graduates working with government agencies in Washington, D.C., where they successfully competed against graduates from East Coast law schools.

Upon graduation, Jon Muth ('71) returned to his native Grand Rapids and practiced as a litigator.[48] Later in his career, he worked with the Kent County Bar Association to establish the Legal Assistance Center to help "unrepresented"[49] individuals in civil matters. Muth received the state bar's Roberts P. Hud-

---

44. Clanton served as Griffin's legislative assistant from 1969 to 1971; on Griffin's Commerce Committee staff (with jurisdiction over the FTC) from 1971 to 1975; and then in Griffin's leadership office (Griffin was the #2 Republican in the Senate) for about eighteen months.

45. While at the FTC, Clanton served as its acting chair.

46. See *Bates v. State Bar of Arizona*, 433 U.S. 350 (1977), in which the U.S. Supreme Court reduced professional restrictions on lawyers.

47. Baker & McKenzie was the "global law firm in the twentieth century." See http://www .bakermckenzie.com/aboutus.

48. The federal judges in the Western District of Michigan referred cases to those mediators rather than the federal court magistrates. Muth decided that he did not have the temperament to practice tax law and instead became a trial lawyer. Jon Muth, interview by the author, April 14, 2016.

49. The center serves individuals who do not qualify for legal aid but cannot afford a private attorney. See www.legalassistancecenter.org.

son award, bestowed on the member of the Michigan bar "who best exemplifies that which brings honor, esteem, and respect to the legal profession."[50] He was one of many Wayne Law alumni to serve as president of the State Bar of Michigan. Muth, while mentoring young lawyers, told them to "start thinking very early on about the kind of lawyer you want to be, the kind of reputation you want to develop, and what you want people to be saying about you at the end of your career because you don't build that overnight."[51]

Many Wayne graduates built successful personal injury practices. For Barry Waldman ('69) and others, Wayne provided access to the legal profession to children from working-class and immigrant families.[52] Waldman was representative of many children of Jewish immigrant parents who attended the law school since its opening days in 1927. Wayne educated students "from families that have had to work their way through life." "We learned the urban way to get by."[53] Waldman chose Wayne Law because it charged lower tuition and gave him access to a legal education while he worked part-time to support his wife and young son. He "got a bargain" with a high-quality legal education. As Barry's son Bryan ('92) told his father: "I was trained to come out of law school running."

Waldman joined the respected labor law firm that became Sachs Waldman. He described Wayne graduates as facile. The litigators could accept losses in their litigation practices, adapt to changing times, and kept going. When Michigan reformed its tort laws, he changed his practice.

Waldman took pride in his litigation successes that improved the lives of workers beyond his clients. For example, one of his clients, a truck driver, recovered for injuries caused by a defective truck design and the truck manufacturer redesigned its tractor-trailers. When his clients received compensation

---

50. https://www.michbar.org/programs/hudsonaward.

51. Jon Muth, interview by the author, April 14, 2016.

52. Raj Chetty, John N. Friedman, Emmanuel Saez, Nicholas Turner, and Danny Yagan, "Mobility Report Cards: The Role of Colleges in Intergenerational Mobility," www.equality -of-opportunity.org/papers/coll_mrc_paper.pdf, July 2017.

53. The material in these paragraphs comes from Barry Waldman, interview by the author, May 11, 2016.

for their brain injuries resulting from exposure to their employer's brake bonding adhesive, the adhesive manufacturer removed the product from the market.

Samuel Bernstein ('69) was a trailblazer in advertising for legal services. The Sam Bernstein Law Firm challenged the legal profession's prohibition against advertising legal services on radio and television. In 1977, the U.S. Supreme Court upheld a lawyer's right to advertise as a First Amendment "speech right."[54]

After serving as editor in chief of the *Wayne Law Review*, graduating in 1968, and earning an LL.M. at Harvard, Michael Terry joined the United States Office of Economic Opportunity (OEO) back-up organization in Atlanta and then worked with Atlanta's first African American mayor, Maynard Jackson. In 1981, he and his chef wife, Elizabeth, established the James Beard award-winning Elizabeth's on 37th in Savannah, Georgia.

Women Break Employment Barriers

Wayne Law has a long history of providing women access to a legal education.[55] Before 1971, no female Wayne Law graduates received offers to join corporate law firms or legal departments of public companies, even the top-performing students. In those years, except for the outlier, Wayne women qualified to practice law were relegated to positions within law firms rendering secretarial services or what later were described as paralegal services.

In April 1970,[56] Wayne's female students established the Women's Liberation Caucus (WLC) and promptly lobbied the faculty to deny access to the law school's placement office[57] to any Michigan law firm that refused to hire

---

54. See Susan R. Martyn, "Lawyers and Advertising," *Advocate* 8 (March 1978): 13–15.
55. According to the 1931 yearbook for the Detroit City Law School, the 24 women represented 14 percent of the 172 enrolled students. In the 1932 yearbook, the 27 women represented 17 percent of the 156 enrolled students that year.
56. See "Notices! Update," *Wayne State University Law School News*, April 13, 1970.
57. "Update," *Student Board of Governors Law School News*, May 4, 1970.

women. As part of a "Women's Teach In" on campus in 1970, with Betty Friedan and Jane Fonda participating,[58] members of the WLC discussed the effects of sex discrimination within the legal profession. WLC member Diane Middleton assisted Professor Frederica Lombard in preparing a presentation to the Association of American Law Schools convention, promoting equal employment opportunities for women in the legal profession.

In 1972, Wayne Law students pressed the faculty to admit more women.[59] Renee Siegan, a member of the law school's Admissions Committee, criticized the faculty for maintaining "criteria for admissions which tend to freeze patterns of discrimination in enrollment." According to Siegan, the law school had a duty to set admission standards so that women enrolled at Wayne reflected their numbers in the general population.[60]

The students wanted women to make up 50 percent of Wayne's first-year class in the fall of 1972. The faculty refused to grant female applicants preferential treatment in admission, but with more active recruitment of women, the faculty expected women to represent 35–50 percent[61] of the entering class by 1975. The faculty achieved that goal in 1976 when women made up 35.7 percent of the entering class. Two years later, the school's largest entering class (364 students) had 142 women (39 percent of the class).[62]

Joan Mahoney,[63] the school's eighth dean, entered Wayne Law in the fall of 1972. She was admitted to both Wayne and Michigan law schools, and she

---

58. "Update," *Student Board of Governors Law School News*, October 19, 1970.

59. Faculty Meeting Minutes, 1971–72, no. 12, March 1, 1972, p. 2. The Law School Women's Liberation Congress had given the dean a list of demands, including the "elimination of sexist stereotypes and 'jokes' from the repertoire of law school faculty members, and the encouragement of the use of non-sexist language by both students and faculty, e.g. the *reasonable* person standard." "Women's Demands," Faculty Meeting Minutes, 1971–72, no. 9, January 19, 1972, p. 1.

60. See Professor Benjamin Carlin, Chairman, Admissions Committee, to Dean Charles W. Joiner and Faculty, April 14, 1972.

61. See "Admissions," Law School Minutes, Special Meeting of the Faculty, 1971–1972, no. 15, April 17, 1972, 1–2, WSR000639, box 4, file 15, Reuther Archives.

62. "Female Enrollments Rising," 2.

63. In the interest of full disclosure, while she was a student, Mahoney was the author's

chose Wayne because it offered her a full scholarship. According to Mahoney, the 1972 entering class included many talented women who were not admitted to the University of Michigan Law School, in part because Michigan limited the admission of Michigan residents.[64]

The surge in the number of female law students in the 1970s might have abated if the women who graduated and passed the Michigan bar examination in the early 1970s were excluded from the jobs available to their male classmates. In 1971, Wayne women for the first time were offered positions to practice with Michigan's corporate law firms and in the legal departments of large Michigan corporations. The challenges facing those women were daunting as they had to integrate themselves into the male-dominated legal profession with predominantly male clients and colleagues. Those groundbreaking women who graduated during the Joiner years enhanced the reputation of Wayne-trained female graduates and thereby provided opportunities for their successors.

From the Class of 1971, the Dykema firm hired Marilyn Kelly, the Dickinson Wright firm hired Julia Darlow, and the Ford Motor Company's legal department hired Helen (Slywynsky) Petrauskas. Sarah Wildgen ('68) spent time in the Peace Corps in Venezuela before returning to Michigan to work at the Plunkett Cooney firm. The other large Detroit firms were a little slower in hiring Wayne women. In 1975, Honigman, Miller, Schwartz and Cohn hired Joan Mahoney. Sheryl Giddings ('79) joined the Bodman firm, and Cynthia Faulhaber ('82) (and Karen McCoy six months later) joined Miller Canfield.[65]

Marilyn Kelly and Helen Petrauskas ('71) both attended the law school's evening program while maintaining their day jobs.[66] Kelly was raised in a blue-collar family and attended the Detroit public schools. After earning degrees from Eastern Michigan University and Middlebury College, she taught French

---

research assistant for a book on the VAT.

64. Joan Mahoney, interview by the author, November 2, 2019. The author did not verify the reported Michigan quota.

65. Starting in the early 1970s, the Miller Canfield firm hired a few women from other law schools.

66. There were three other women who attended the law school part-time and graduated in 1971.

in public school and then at Albion College and Eastern Michigan University. In the mid-1960s at age twenty-five, she was elected to the State Board of Education. Working on the board "opened her eyes to the legal aspects of education" and she decided to pursue a legal education. She chose Wayne Law because the University of Michigan Law School would not allow her to attend part-time. Kelly found the law school welcoming to women.[67]

Kelly spent five years litigating commercial disputes. She did not find the large law firm environment welcoming for women in the early 1970s and decided that practicing alone and specializing in family law fit her better. She was active in the State Bar of Michigan, serving as chair of the Women Lawyer's section. Kelly was elected and reelected to the Michigan Court of Appeals and in 1996 was elected to the Michigan Supreme Court.

Justice Kelly found that many Michigan residents did not have ready access to Michigan courts, including those with limited financial resources, with mental and physical disabilities, with limited English proficiency, or who lived geographically distant from the Michigan courts. To address those issues, while serving as Chief Justice, Kelly created the office of coordinator of Access to Justice. When the state's age restriction prevented her from seeking another term,[68] Justice Kelly returned to her alma mater as the Wayne Law Distinguished Jurist in Residence. She was elected to the Wayne State University Board of Governors and served as chair in 2021.

Helen (Slywynsky) Petrauskas was an immigrant success story. She was three weeks old in the spring of 1944, when the Soviet army began advancing toward the family's hometown in Lvov, Ukraine. The family left by train for the southern part of Germany that was controlled by the U.S. Army. In 1947, Mary Beck,[69] a Detroiter who met the Slywynsky family in Ukraine before the war,

---

67. The information on Kelly comes from Marilyn Kelly, interview by the author, March 23, 2015. Some of her law school classmates were her former students at Albion.

68. She received the Guardian of Justice Award from the American-Arab Anti-Discrimination Committee and received lifetime achievement awards from many legal organizations.

69. Beck became the first woman elected to the Detroit City Council.

Marilyn Kelly. (Permission of WSU)

sponsored them to emigrate to Detroit. Helen's mother died when Helen was twelve and her father, who had a European law degree but could not practice law in the United States, struggled to support the family.

Petrauskas earned her bachelor's degree in mathematics from Wayne at age twenty. While socializing with the Ukrainian and Lithuanian immigrants at Mackenzie Hall's student union on campus, she met her future husband, Raymond Petrauskas. After college graduation, she worked full-time as a chemist and dated Raymond while he was studying at Wayne Law. Raymond suggested that she take the LSAT. Encouraged by her high LSAT score, but unable to afford full-time studies, Helen enrolled in Wayne's evening program.

Petrauskas received job offers to practice with corporate law firms and with the legal departments at GM and Ford. She joined the Environmental and Safety Engineering section of Ford's legal department, moved up the corporate ladder, and became the first female and youngest Ford vice president. She was responsible for automobile safety and pollution,[70] working on the Ford-U.S. government agreement requiring the installation of air bags in cars. Years later, Petrauskas wrote that "Wayne State University Law School represented a marvelous opportunity for me because there are not very many quality law schools which one can attend on a part-time basis."[71]

Julia Darlow ('71) joined Detroit's Dickinson Wright law firm and was instrumental in expanding the firm's international practice. She was a leader within the Michigan legal community. Darlow was the Reporter for the Michigan Nonprofit Corporation Act, chaired the Women Lawyers Association,[72] and in 1986 became the first woman president of the State Bar of Michigan.[73]

---

70. "Helen Petrauskas; Helped Promote Air Bags at Ford," *Washington Post*, March 12, 2006. She died on March 8, 2006.
71. "Alumni Profile: Helen O. Petrauskas," *Wayne Lawyer* 5 (Spring 1986): 11.
72. See *Wayne Lawyer* 6 (Fall 1986): 15.
73. www.michbar.org/file/generalinfo/pdfs/BOC_presidents.pdf. Nancy Diehl ('78) and Lori Buiteweg ('90) later served as presidents of the bar association. Seven men, from the following Wayne Law classes, served as State Bar of Michigan presidents. They were Eugene Mossner ('55), James K. Robinson ('68), Michael Hayes Dettmer ('71), Thomas G. Kienbaum ('68), Jon Muth ('71), Ronald D. Keefe ('72), and Brian D. Einhorn ('67).

Helen Petrauskas. (Reprinted with permission of the law school)

Julia Darlow ('71). (Photo by Dantê Nagy and reproduced with permission of the law school)

Female enrollment in law schools across the United States increased exponentially after the 1973 *Roe v. Wade* U.S. Supreme Court decision affirmed a woman's right to an abortion. Nationally women represented 10.3 percent (3,542) of entering law students in 1970 and almost tripled to 28.4 percent (11,354) by 1976.[74] The seismic shift in the gender balance continued, with women accounting for 54 percent of all entering J.D. students in 2019.[75]

---

74. ABA Section of Legal Education and Admissions to the Bar, Enrollment and Degrees Awarded 1963–2013, https://www.americanbar.org/groups/legal_education/resources/statistics/statistics-archives. From 1971–72 to 1972–73, female enrollment grew about 50 percent, from 8,567 to 11,878.

75. In 2019, the 20,690 entering women accounted for 54 percent of entering students. For Wayne Law, the 62 entering women accounted for 50 percent of the 125 entering students. See ABA Law School Data: J.D. Total First Year Class Enrollment Data, Fall, https://www.americanbar.org/groups/legal_education/resources/statistics. In 2009–10, the 68,502 women accounted for 47.2 percent of total J.D. enrollment. See American Bar Association, First Year and Total J.D. Enrollment by Gender 1947–2011, http://www.americanbar.org.

Dean Joiner's Final Changes

With the expanded student enrollment and more professors, the law school was outgrowing its relatively new campus. Joiner's vision for the future of Wayne Law required space for more student, faculty, and administrative offices and more clinical programs. At Joiner's urging, the university leased a "temporary" law school annex, available for use in the fall of 1971. The annex remained an essential facility until the law school replaced it in 2000 with a building that housed seminar rooms, student offices for the law school journals, and more faculty offices.

Joiner took a personal interest in the Wayne students and made them feel a part of the Wayne law school community. He and his wife, Anne, hosted a series of dinners and brunches for graduating students, with faculty participating.[76] At these events, Dean Joiner encouraged the students, especially the women, to speak candidly about their experiences at Wayne Law. His leadership improved the reputation of the law school, its professors within the legal academy, and its graduates among the leading lawyers in Michigan and among the highly respected national firms. Men and women who graduated during his deanship thrived in legal positions previously not open to them.

---

76. "Senior Suppers," Faculty Meeting Minutes, 1969–70, no. 9 (January 21, 1970), 3. See also *CHATTIN' with CHARLIE*, Update, *Student Board of Governors Law School News*, spring 1971.

4

A Racially Diverse Student Body

Charles Joiner promoted and sincerely believed that law schools should provide people of color more access to a legal education in order to achieve a racially diverse student body and ultimately a legal profession more reflective of the society in which lawyers practiced. This chapter documents Joiner's efforts to enable Wayne Law to provide more access to racial minorities.

The Wayne Law faculty hired African American professors at a time when they were completely absent in most law schools. The Wayne campus served as a center for Black intellectual life and a gathering place for progressive national movements. In 1959, the faculty hired its first African American law professor, Charles Quick. In 1964, when Quick was being recruited by another law school, the faculty hired a second African American professor, Kenneth Callahan. In the 1965–66 academic year, except for the Historically Black law schools, Professors Callahan[1] and Quick represented 50 percent of all of the tenured and tenure-track African American law professors in the country. It was not until 1970 that the other law schools in Michigan hired their first African American professors.[2]

---

1. Callahan came from modest means; he was born in a log cabin in Ohio, the youngest of ten children.
2. In 1970, the University of Michigan hired Harry Edwards and the Detroit College of Law hired Edward Littlejohn. Two years later, the University of Detroit Law School hired Warren Bracey.

Relatively few people of color became lawyers before the 1960s. In 1950, the 1,450 African American lawyers in the country accounted for less than 1 percent of the total 180,461 lawyers.[3] The percentage had not changed a decade later.[4]

In 1964, the 433 enrolled African American law students accounted for less than 1 percent of the law students nationwide, and Hispanic enrollment was even less. In the 1971–72 academic year, after the national efforts described in this chapter, the law schools enrolled 3,744 African American and 1,156 Hispanic students.[5]

In 1970, African American Professor Derrick A. Bell Jr., then a lecturer at Harvard Law School,[6] wrote that before the mid-1960s, "racial prejudice, combined with a continuing lack of educational and economic resources, served to curtail seriously the number of Blacks who aspired to join the legal profession and limited greatly the range of success and accomplishment for

---

3. Edward J. Littlejohn and Donald L. Hobson, "Black Lawyers, Law Practice, and Bar Associations, 1844 to 1970: A Michigan History," *Wayne Law Review* 33 (1987): 1625, 1628. The ABA, contrary to the *Statistical Abstract of the United States: 1960*, puts the total number of lawyers in the United States in 1950 at 221,605. See "ABA National Lawyer Population Survey: Historical Trend in Total National Lawyer Population 1878–2017," https://www.americanbar.org/content/dam/aba/administrative/market_research/Total %20National%20Lawyer%20Population%201878-2017.authcheckdam.pdf.

4. In 1960, the 2,012 Black lawyers and judges represented less than 1 percent of the 205,515 lawyers and judges in the country. They collectively numbered only 3,728 (1.4 percent) in 1970. See ABA Section of Legal Education and Admissions to the Bar, "Legal Education and Professional Development—An Educational Continuum: Report of The Task Force on Law Schools and the Profession: Narrowing the Gap" (American Bar Association, 1992), 25. The report is commonly referred to as the MacCrate Report, named for the chair of the task force.

5. The category of Hispanic students included Mexican American, Puerto Rican, and other Hispanic students. African American J.D. Enrollment, 1971–2010, provided by ABA Section of Legal Education and Admission to the Bar to author and in author's private files.

6. Bell became the first tenured African American professor at Harvard Law School in 1971. In 1980, he became dean at the University of Oregon, returned to Harvard in 1986, but took a leave of absence in protest of Harvard's denial of tenure to two professors of color and resigned in 1992. He then served as a visiting professor at New York University Law School until his death in 2011.

those who somehow overcame these multiple handicaps to law practice." He acknowledged the expansion of job opportunities for Black legal talent in government, industry, and some law firms. The Black students who populated the elite law schools were more militant and presented challenges to the law school faculties.[7] While Wayne Law was not an elite law school, Wayne Law students reflected the general trend.

During the period 1967–70, the elite law schools experienced a range of student protests.[8] In 1969, African American law students at Columbia occupied the law library to press the school to increase its commitment to people of color. At Howard University, law students protested for a month to force faculty to institute pass-fail grading and student participation in law school governance.[9]

ABA's CLEO Program

Following the passage of the Civil Rights Act of 1964 and the Voting Rights Act of 1965, the ABA and Congress started addressing the lack of diversity in the legal profession compared to that in other professions.[10] Among other things, Congress enacted the Higher Education Amendments of 1968[11] to "pro-

---

7. See Stevens, "Law Schools and Law Firms," 551, 585. This study relied on data mainly from law schools at Boston College, the universities of Connecticut, Iowa, Michigan, and Pennsylvania, Stanford University, the University of Southern California, and Yale University.

8. Liberal protesters in those schools clashed with the more radical "left-liberals." See Kalman, *Yale Law School and the Sixties.*

9. "BALSA Stages 'Study-in,' Black Admissions Key Issue," *Columbia Law School News,* May 13, 1969, 1; "Howard Students Seize Law School," *New York Times,* February 19, 1969, A34, cited in Kalman, *Yale Law School and the Sixties,* 339n56.

10. Four decades later, law remained the least diverse of the professions. See https://www.americanbar.org/groups/litigation/committees/jiop/articles/2018/diversity-and-inclusion-in-the-law-challenges-and-initiatives. See also Elizabeth Chambliss, *Miles to Go: Progress of Minorities in the Legal Profession* (American Bar Association, 2005), 6–7, noting that in the twenty-first century, "according to the American Bar Association (ABA), only two professions (the natural sciences and dentistry) have less diversity than law; medicine, accounting, academia, and others do considerably better."

11. P.L. 90–575, 82 Stat. 1014, an act to amend the Higher Education Act of 1965. The

vide low-income, minority, or disadvantaged secondary school students and college students with the information, preparation, and financial assistance needed to gain access to and complete law school study."[12] Congress tasked the ABA's Council on Legal Education Opportunity (CLEO)[13] with establishing programs designed to "provide alternative standards" for law schools to admit minority-group students.

Before the 1960s, state and local law schools had relatively open admissions policies. They admitted students who successfully completed three or four years of college education. Even so, many dropped out or were asked to leave by the end of their first year of law school. From 1960 to 1970, with the growing interest in a legal education, law schools were unable to accommodate all of the students who applied. Most law schools began to require applicants to submit a college transcript, including undergraduate GPA, and LSAT score.

Law schools continued to experience significant attrition among first-year students. Some students withdrew and others were terminated or placed on probation for academic reasons. Many had trouble mastering the analytical skills tested in first-year courses or did not commit the necessary time to their legal studies. The cliché at undergraduate college orientation that "if you look to your left and right, one of you will not be here at the end of the year" applied equally to first-year students at many law schools.

Dean Joiner, a life member of the NAACP, believed that some groups in society did not get their "fair justice." He was active in the American Bar Association[14] when both the ABA and Congress recognized that law schools had

---

Higher Education Act of 1965, part of President Johnson's Great Society, expanded the availability of government-backed student loans and funding for low-income, minority, or disadvantaged secondary school and college students to gain access to the legal profession.

12. http://www2.ed.gov/programs/legal/index.html.
13. CLEO was a nonprofit project of the American Bar Association Fund for Justice and Education. http://www2.ed.gov/programs/legal/eligibility.html.
14. Joiner served on the ABA Committee on Ethics and chaired its Committee on Specialization.

to take action to help diversify the legal profession.[15] In Joiner's first years as Wayne's dean, the law school admitted a more highly credentialed entering class. Notwithstanding the higher factor scores Wayne required for admission, the faculty supported Joiner's goal of increasing the number of entering African American and Hispanic students. Students, including students of color, who would have been admitted in the 1950s because they completed the required years of undergraduate education were being denied admission in the late 1960s if their combined GPA and LSAT factor scores were below the level set by the school's faculty.

In 1968 the law school implemented a program to actively recruit students of color. During the 1968–69 academic year, Professor Arthur Lombard and Tyrone Fahner, assistant to the dean, traveled to colleges in the southern United States, especially the Historically Black Colleges, to recruit students of color. Fahner also organized a minority student recruitment conference at Wayne with thirteen schools in the region.[16]

The CLEO-participating law schools were expected to accept an applicant who successfully completed the CLEO program and exhibited "a special showing about chances of success" in that law school. The CLEO program accepted students who would have been denied admission to a CLEO-participating law school if the school admitted students solely on the basis of the applicant's combined GPA and LSAT score. The CLEO program students competed with other CLEO students. In 1969, Yale and other elite law schools admitted African American students who succeeded in an ABA summer CLEO program.[17]

---

15. Years later, as a federal judge, Joiner ruled, in what was referred to as the "black English" case, that the Ann Arbor school board had to send some local elementary school teachers to a class for "consciousness raising" so that they would be better equipped to teach their students who spoke a dialect used by their Black students. See *Martin Luther King, Jr. Elementary School Children et al. v. Ann Arbor School District Board*, F. Supp. 1371 (1979).

16. See Jaffe, "Minorities Sought," *Advocate* 3 (March 1969); and "Minority Recruitment," *Advocate* 3 (February 1969), WSR002163, Reuther Archives.

17. The Black Law Student Union recruited students and pressed the faculty to admit more African Americans and provide them access to the CLEO Institute (Kalman, *Yale Law School and the Sixties*, 161).

Wayne Law hosted one of the national CLEO Institute programs in the summer of 1969[18] and ended up admitting 17 students from that program. They had college GPAs or LSAT scores lower than those of most of their first-year classmates. With the LSAT score as one predictor of success in the first year of law school, as a group, the CLEO students were predicted to score below their classmates on their first-year examinations.

The final grade in most of Wayne's first-year courses was based entirely on a single year-end examination. The students received very limited feedback during the year on how they were doing in those courses. While they took a practice examination in each substantive course during the fall term and received comments from their professor, a first-year student's performance on his or her practice test was not factored into the final grade in the course. The law school did not have in place any academic support programs for first-year students. While some faculty and law review and moot court students had volunteered to assist the CLEO-admitted students during their first year, the CLEO students succeeded in college and did not recognize that they needed help.

The combination of the faculty's mandatory grading norms and Wayne's recent first-year attrition data predicted that some first-year students would be terminated or placed on academic probation at the end of the 1969–70 academic year. Under the grading norms, professors were *required* to give Es (failing grades) to 5 percent and Ds to 15 percent of the students in each of their first-year courses.[19] In the 1968–69 academic year, more than 25 percent

18. By 1972, Professor Edward Littlejohn, an African American member of the Wayne Law faculty who mentored many of Wayne's African American students, challenged the CLEO program's approach that limited students in that program to individuals who did not meet the admission factors of the participating schools and did not require CLEO students to compete with students admitted under the school's regular admission criteria.

19. First-year students are assigned to particular sections of their required first-year courses. Wayne Law imposes first-year grading norms to provide grading consistency among the multiple sections of the first-year courses. The *Wayne Law Review* automatically invites students to join the review at the end of their first year on the basis of their first-year GPAs.

of first-year students were terminated,[20] and a year earlier, about 15 percent were terminated or placed on probation.[21]

On April 15, 1970, before professors submitted final grades in their first-year courses, students sent a memo to Dean Joiner, questioning the law school's commitment to increase Black lawyers in society and demanding that the law school establish an open-admissions policy for all African American applicants.[22] In his response, Dean Joiner reiterated the law school's commitment to students of color and explained that an open-admissions policy would be inconsistent "with the function of the Law School in training lawyers who can adequately perform for their clients and for their community."[23]

In line with the law school's attrition experience, 13 percent of the first-year students were terminated at the end of the 1969–70 academic year. The CLEO students received some of the required Ds and Es and most were on academic probation or were terminated.

Edwin Taliafaro, a first-year student, led the protesting African American students who demanded that the law school readmit the CLEO students en masse. The predominantly African American Wolverine Law Student Association (WLSA) publicized their grievances within the law school and university, with national CLEO officials, and in the media.[24]

The WLSA claimed that grades submitted for the terminated students "may have been influenced by criteria other than academic ability." They demanded

---

20. Twenty-seven percent of the first-year day students and 29 percent of the first-year evening students were terminated or placed on probation at the end of their first year.

21. Seventeen percent of first-year day students and 12 percent of first-year evening students were terminated or placed on academic probation at the end of that year.

22. The students demanded, for example, that all law school committees include a Black law student and Black lawyer. "Proposals for Change," memo from Wayne Black Law Students to Charles A. Joiner, Dean, Wayne State University Law School, Faculty Administration and Student Body, April 15, 1970, author's personal file.

23. Dean Joiner, "Your Proposal for Change, Dated April 15, 1970," April 17, 1970, author's personal file.

24. For example, the Wolverine Law Student Association of Wayne State University Law School wrote to Dr. Melvin D. Kennedy, Executive Director, Council on Legal Education Opportunity, August 13, 1970, author's personal file.

that the law school review all examinations in which any first-year student received a grade below C+.[25] Associate Dean Donald Gordon reviewed the grades submitted in all of the first-year courses and concluded that the faculty did not engage in any pattern of discrimination against the African American law students.[26]

A larger group of Wayne Law students demanded that the law school readmit all terminated Black students and allow all students "to make their own decisions whether to return to Law School."[27] Dean Joiner sought advice from the school's accrediting body, the ABA Section of Legal Education and Admission to the Bar. In the response, Millard Ruud, consultant to this ABA section, wrote that ABA-accredited law schools must maintain high scholarship standards and "fairness to the student himself requires that the unfit student be eliminated when such unfitness becomes manifest."[28]

The law school's formal appeal process was available to *any* student who was terminated on the basis of first-year grades. Most of the terminated CLEO students appealed and the faculty's Readmission Committee reviewed all of those petitions. On August 25, 1970, Dean Joiner sent an open letter to the Wayne Law students that explained the law school rules governing readmission and the committee's action:

> The law school has made a special study of [each student terminated for academic reasons] in light of all available information, including

---

25. Memo marked "urgent" from Wolverine Law Student Association at Wayne State University Law School to Dean Charles Joiner, Wayne State University School of Law, July 24, 1970, author's personal file.
26. Confidential Memorandum, Donald H. Gordon, Associate Dean, to Charles W. Joiner, Dean, July 24, 1970.
27. The undated letter urged students to refuse to register for fall classes.
28. Millard Ruud to Charles W. Joiner, August 25, 1970: "The need for elimination in a particular school will be determined to a large extent by the degree of selectivity exercised in admitting students." The "student who has performed unsatisfactorily . . . should have the burden of proof to establish the high likelihood that if given a further opportunity he will succeed and that some factor other than lack of capacity, whether in interest or aptitude, explain his failure."

that supplied by the students. . . . This special, individual consideration of each case has led to an offer of re-admission by the Law School of all minority-group students except four. This special action is not discrimination in reverse. It is simply an effort to consider all facts with regard to re-admissions and to make judgments tailored to individual cases . . . [C]ontrary to the demands of a few, we have not and will not readmit en masse.[29]

The protesting students were not satisfied. On August 31, 1970, a group of law students chained the entrances to the law school, preventing ingress and egress and demanding that the law school readmit all terminated students. The faculty and administration refused to take further action, and the students unchained the doors before the law school administration asked the university police to remove them by force.

Dean Joiner received letters accusing the law school of racial bias by readmitting many students of color. In response, Joiner[30] explained that the 13 percent failure rate for the first-year students that year was consistent with prior law school experience, and that in the readmission process that year, the committee did not give more favorable treatment to any particular group of petitioning students. The law school did not act "adversely to the interest of the students because of an ill-conceived act on the part of a few, nor has it acted adversely to the interest of the profession in following normal, well-established, ordinary procedures to determine whether or not students should be re-admitted."[31]

---

29. Charles W. Joiner, Dean, to All Wayne State University Law School Students, August 25, 1970 (with a note on the letter that it was also distributed to the law faculty), author's personal file.

30. The following discussion was based on Dean Joiner's September 3, 1970, letter to Michael T. Timmis Esq., President, Wayne State University Law School Alumni Association, author's personal file.

31. See Harry Salinger, "Flunked Students Were Readmitted," *Detroit News*, August 27, 1970.

Improving First-Year Academic Success

The student protests in the spring and summer of 1970 prompted the faculty to review the school's academic rules that Wayne Law students had complained about for years. The faculty instituted an anonymous grading system[32] and changed the mandatory grading norms for first-year courses. Professors were required to give graded midterm examinations in the yearlong, first-year courses so that final grades were no longer based solely on a single year-end examination. The faculty implemented a supportive services program for first-year students, provided more student input into faculty decision making, and modified the summer program for entering students.[33]

Wayne law students complained that they suffered a competitive disadvantage in the job market against students from other schools in the region because the Wayne grades, on average, were lower. In 1970, the faculty made the grading norms more flexible, allowing professors teaching first-year courses to give a higher percentage of As and Bs and a lower percentage of Ds and Es.[34]

---

32. Students questioned the impartiality of the grading system that required students to write their names on their examinations. To address that concern, the faculty adopted an anonymous grading system in October 1970. "Dean Gordon—Proposal for Anonymity in Grading," Faculty Meeting Minutes, 1970–71, no. 5, October 14, 1970, 1; "Anonymous Grading System," Faculty Meeting Minutes, 1970–71, no. 11, December 16, 1970, 5, WSR000639, box 4, file 16, pp. 139, 161–62, Reuther Archives.

33. See Dean Charles W. Joiner, "From the Dean, UPDATE," *Wayne State University Law School News*, October 19, 1970. See also "Dean Henry—Proposals for a System of Academic Support and Assistance for 1st and 2nd Year Students," and "Dean Berry—Proposed Mid-Term Examinations for First Year Students," Faculty Meeting Minutes, 1970–71, no. 3, September 30, 1970, pp. 1–2, and memos recommending this action, both in WSR000639, box 4, file 16, pp. 133–34, Reuther Archives.

34. "Grading Norms Committee," Faculty Meeting Minutes, 1970–71, no. 11, December 16, 1970, p. 5, WSR000639, box 4, file 16, p. 144, Reuther Archives. The grading norms continued to change as schools in Wayne's region raised their grading norms. For example, in 2012, the first-year norms in required courses were structured as maximums, with a maximum of 30 percent in the A range, a combined maximum of 90 percent of As and Bs, and a maximum of 10 percent Ds and 5 percent Fs. Document provided by Rebecca Hollancid, Registrar, Wayne State University Law School, author's archives.

Wayne professors were no longer required to give Es, regardless of students' performance on their examinations.[35]

The school established a supportive services program for all first-year students. In the fall of 1970, the professors teaching first-year courses hired teaching assistants (upper-class students) for those classes, and the school hired a writing specialist to help students improve their skills. Several professors assisted the readmitted students to help them make progress academically. Peter Sugar ('70) taught legal research and writing to first-year students and established a new program to help first-year students improve their exam-taking skills.[36]

Students wanted a voice in law school governance, including participation in the development of law school policy.[37] The faculty responded. The Student Board of Governors selected students to attend and participate in faculty meetings.[38] Students were added to the faculty's Admissions and Scholarship, Curriculum, and Placement committees, as well as a few others.[39]

Dean Joiner hired Professor Edward J. Littlejohn[40] to help recruit and enroll students of color. Littlejohn had experienced firsthand the obstacles facing many African Americans who sought access to the legal profession. He was raised in his stepfather's "shotgun apartment" leased to workers of the Dodge foundry in Hamtramck. He graduated fifth in his class in high school and while some of his classmates (including children of immigrants) received scholarships to Wayne University, he was not offered any college scholarships. After high school, he worked in a factory manufacturing auto parts and was expected

---

35. Under the 1970 norms, in each first-year class, 10 percent were to receive As, 25 percent Bs, and 45 percent Cs.
36. Sugar became the longest-serving adjunct professor who, with some breaks when he was in business out of state, taught for almost fifty years.
37. See "Clarification of Role of Student-Faculty Committee Members," update, *SBG Law School News*, October 12, 1971.
38. See the students' perspective on this issue in "Faculty Okays Student-Faculty Committees," update, *SBG Law School News*, May 4, 1970.
39. Dean Joiner memo to faculty, April 7, 1970, author's personal files.
40. Edward Littlejohn, interview by the author, November 2, 2014.

to contribute toward the household expenses. When he quit his job to attend Wayne University, he had to leave home. He worked to finance his college education and living expenses but eventually became homeless. At that point, the military seemed the better option. After military service, Littlejohn returned to Detroit, completed his college education, and while working full-time attended the Detroit College of Law's evening program. Littlejohn graduated at the very top of his class and soon thereafter, DCL hired him as its first tenure-track African American professor.

Littlejohn dramatically changed Wayne Law's program to attract, enroll, and graduate students of color. Under the faculty's discretionary admissions policy, the Admissions Committee could admit applicants whose factor scores were below the "automatic admit" cutoff. Under Littlejohn's plan, the Admissions Committee could admit students of color within that discretionary admission pool if their credentials predicted that they were likely to succeed in their first year at Wayne Law.

Littlejohn created a new summer program. All entering first-year students in 1972 could elect to begin their legal studies in the summer and take one or two first-year law courses. All students admitted under the discretionary admission program were strongly encouraged to enroll in the summer school and compete with their other first-year classmates. With these changes, the law school was more successful in admitting, retaining, and graduating a racially diverse student body.

In the 1970s, the law school attracted many African American students. Two of them, Jeffrey Edison and Gad Holland, grew up in different Detroit neighborhoods. Edison was raised in a middle-class family that lived in a racially changing, predominantly Jewish and African American neighborhood of single-family homes in northwest Detroit. A nearby federal government-sanctioned "wall" constructed in 1941 separated African American from White families.[41] Edison attended Macdowell Elementary School,

---

41. In the 1940s, the Federal Housing Authority required the developer in this neighborhood to build a wall separating African American from White homeowners before it would insure mortgages on homes in this area: http://www.npr.org/2012/09/11/160768981/racial

which was about 90 percent Jewish and 10 percent Black when he entered and was about 80 percent Black and 20 percent Jewish when he finished the ninth grade in 1966. A similar racial change occurred during his years at Mumford High School.

Gad Holland was raised in a predominantly African American, high-rise housing complex on the near-east side of Detroit. He attended academically questionable schools and faced pressure to participate in drug-trafficking and other illegal activity. Holland and Edison were in high school when, in July 1967, Detroit erupted in fires in a West Side neighborhood located between them. Edison's remaining White school friends at Mumford High all but disappeared as their families moved to the suburbs. The isolated White families in Holland's neighborhood did not have the resources to consider moving.

In 1969, Edison left Detroit to join his brother at Howard University. Holland's mother moved to Detroit from Morristown, Tennessee, where she attended the local two-year Morristown College and wanted her son to start college there. In 1969, Holland tried Morristown College for a year before he transferred to Howard University, where he met Edison.

Holland and Edison wanted to become lawyers. Admission to law school was competitive when Wayne admitted both of them in 1973. Holland missed Wayne's 1973 summer program because he was completing his Howard bachelor's degree.

Gad Holland and Jeffrey Edison had very different experiences at Wayne Law. Edison was an activist law student. He believed that an African American individual "should work to change [an] . . . oppressive and exploitative, or racist or discriminatory" status quo.[42] Holland attacked law school like he had

---

-regional-divide-still-haunt-detroits-progress. Edison established the Michigan chapter of the National Conference of Black Lawyers (NCBL), viewed at the time as "the legal arm of the black revolution." He became national co-chair of the NCBL. He has received many awards, including the Wolverine Bar Association's Trailblazer Award in 1994; the Detroit Branch, NAACP's Freedom Fighter Award in 1999; and the W.E.B. DuBois Outstanding Leadership Award in 2007. Edison participated in the development of the Wayne County Circuit Court's Restorative Justice Project, designed to prevent recidivism.

42. Jeffrey Edison, interview by the author, June 5, 2015.

attacked college, being self-reliant and studying long hours alone. For Holland, law school was a struggle. While "some students graduate with honors; I was honored to graduate."[43]

Chokwe Lumumba, one of Edison and Holland's first-year classmates, changed his name from Edwin Taliaferro when he became active in the Republic of New Africa (RNA) and other social movements in Detroit. After his first year at Wayne Law in 1969–70, he withdrew and moved to Jackson, Mississippi, where the RNA movement was centered.[44] Lumumba returned to the law school in 1973 to repeat his first year. Lumumba was invited to join the *Wayne Law Review*, which invited students with high first-year grades. He declined the invitation in a fourteen-page letter,[45] explaining in part that if the *Law Review* were designed to improve students' proficiency in writing skills and research techniques, it should invite students in greatest need of improving those skills—those with lower law school grades.

Following graduation, Lumumba and Edison practiced law with the state public defender's office in Detroit. Edison then established his own criminal defense practice, gaining the respect of local judges. Looking back after years of law practice, Edison felt that Wayne Law prepared him and his African American classmates "to become vigorous, disciplined advocates for human rights; [it] prepared us to become freedom fighters." After working at a private law practice in Detroit, Lumumba returned to Jackson in 1988, was elected Jackson's mayor in 2013, and served as mayor until he died.

After graduation, Holland worked for a small law firm and then opened his own practice representing, in part, individuals seeking workmen's compensation benefits or appealing their denials of Social Security disability benefits. He spent many nights until closing in the Wayne law library researching issues in client cases.

---

43. Gad Holland, interview by the author, April 19, 2016.

44. Detroit was the intellectual center for the Republic of New Africa.

45. In the interest of full disclosure, the author was the law school's associate dean during Lumumba's 1973–74 academic year and was mentioned in the letter with comments not intended to be flattering.

Many people of color who graduated during Charles Joiner's deanship created their own career opportunities. One of them, Derrick Humphries ('72), moved to Washington, D.C., and established Humphries and Partners PLLC after serving in a number of legal positions, including as counsel to the Congressional Black Caucus.

Challenging the Admissions Policy

Tension between the faculty and some student groups resurfaced in 1978 when the faculty changed the law school's admissions policy in response to the U.S. Supreme Court decision in the Bakke case.[46] Bakke upheld the right of a public medical school to include race as one of a number of factors in its admissions policy but prohibited racial quotas in admission decisions. The faculty, concerned that its existing admissions policy might not withstand scrutiny under the Bakke test, scheduled a meeting to discuss possible changes. On September 15, 1978, in a meeting open only to faculty and authorized student representatives, the faculty revised the law school admissions program.[47] The Black Legal Alliance, LaLey, other law student organizations, and some local attorneys who were denied admission to the closed meeting claimed that the faculty's vote changing the school's admissions policy in private violated the Michigan Open Meetings Act.

Carlo Martina, who was president of the Student Board of Governors at the time as well as a student member of the law school Admissions Committee, learned about the change during an Admissions Committee meeting. According to Martina, since the students could not obtain the relief they were seeking (discussion of the issue in an open meeting), they applied what they learned in their Wayne classes and brought legal action against the faculty and law school administration.[48]

---

46. *Regents of the University of California v. Bakke*, 438 U.S. 265 (1978).

47. "Law Suit Filed," *Advocate* (November/December 1978): 1.

48. Carlo Martina provided his recollection during the FLAC's 50th anniversary celebration in 2015.

Elizabeth Bunn ('77)[49] and other lawyers filed the lawsuit on behalf of some local attorneys and student organizations. They sought relief against the dean and the faculty to prevent them from implementing the new admissions policy approved in a non-public meeting. Law student John Canzano ('79) provided the research to support the plaintiffs' claims that the faculty vote on the admissions policy was a final decision by a public body subject to the Open Meetings Act. Judge William Cahalan relied on Canzano's research in granting a preliminary injunction to prevent the faculty from implementing the new admissions policy until it was adopted in a meeting open to the public.[50]

The faculty held a public meeting to discuss the previously adopted admissions policy.[51] Preparing for that meeting, the professors discovered that the faculty had relied on faulty data in developing the policy.[52] In the open meeting, the faculty adopted a revised admissions policy praised by the students.

---

49. Elizabeth Bunn was general counsel for Michigan Counsel 25 of the American Federal, State, County and Municipal Employees Union (AFL-CIO) and in 2002 was elected secretary-treasurer (chief financial officer) of the UAW, the highest position a woman held in that organization. Bunn became the organizing director of the AFL-CIO in 2010.

50. According to the Order of January 20, 1979, the law school could not implement the McIntyre-Sedler proposal until there was a hearing on the merits or the admissions policy was adopted in accordance with the Michigan Open Meetings Act (Sec. 10, Michigan Open Meetings Act, MCLA 15.270(5)).

51. Sedler, "In the Event of a Negative Ruling," *Advocate* (October 6, 1977): 9–12; on his opposition to affirmative action on "moral" grounds, see Grano, "Comment on 'King,'" *Advocate* (March 1978): 8–9. Timothy Orlebeke urged that in addressing constitutional issues like those presented in Bakke, it is important to consider the philosophical framework within which constitutional principles like equal protection operate. See Timothy Orlebeke, "How Do—or Should We Decide Bakke?" *Advocate* (November 3 1977): 6–7. See also the exchange between Professor Grano and Chuck Palmer in the *Advocate* (October 6, 1977). Professor John Dolan wrote in the February 1979 edition of the *Advocate* that educators should be preparing "community leaders who will forge public opinion and public policy," and to do that, they should have a "special admissions policy" for "people who suffer economic and educational disadvantage" and not limit that policy only to people of certain races.

52. Contrary to the faculty's intent, the adopted policy would have reduced the total number of students, including students of color, who could be admitted under the school's discretionary admissions policy.

The law school's programs to enroll a racially diverse student body resulted in more students of color graduating, practicing their profession in law and accounting firms, and becoming judges and academics. For example, Marcia Cooke ('77) started practicing law as a staff attorney for Michigan Neighborhood Services, then as deputy public defender with the Legal Aid and Defender Association of Michigan before serving as an assistant U.S. attorney in the Eastern District of Michigan.[53] She was confirmed as a Federal District Court Judge for the Southern District of Florida. Adam Shakoor ('76), Paula Humphries ('79), Leonia and Leona Lloyd ('79), and Norma Dotson Sales ('80) were elected to Detroit's 36th District Court. Marie Inniss ('79) practiced with two Detroit law firms before she joined the law school to lead its Recruitment and Admissions efforts. Charles Williams ('80) served as president of New Detroit and held several positions in Detroit government and with nonprofits.[54]

Some Hispanic graduates became judges. For example, Judge Isidore Torres ('76) served on Detroit's District Court. According to his obituary in the *New York Times*, "as a boy, Isidore Torres owned two pairs of pants: one for school, one for hoeing sugar beet fields outside Bay City, Mich., alongside his mother and siblings." The Torres family "shuttled between Michigan and Texas looking for migrant work, eventually settling in Bay City [Michigan] so the children could receive a steady education."[55]

While some graduates of color created their own successful legal careers, the job opportunities open to them with established law firms remained limited until the overall demand for legal talent increased and Wayne graduates succeeded in jobs previously closed to them.

53. Cooke also served as a Federal Magistrate Judge in the Eastern District of Michigan, in the U.S. Attorney's Office in the Southern District of Florida, and as the Chief Inspector General in the Florida governor's office.
54. New Detroit was born out of the civil unrest in Detroit in 1967. It remains "a coalition of leaders working to achieve racial understanding and racial equity in Metropolitan Detroit." https://www.newdetroit.org/our-history.
55. Stephen Kurczym, "Isidore Torres, Trailblazing Hispanic Judge in Michigan, Dies at 73," *New York Times*, January 29, 2021. Judge Torres died of Covid-19. His brother Abel Torres ('82) was a prosecutor in Bay City.

5

Expanded Job Opportunities

When Dean Charles Joiner resigned in 1972, he left Wayne with a solid foundation for future growth. He changed the faculty and curriculum, encouraged the faculty to get involved in national and state bar activities, and promoted the school and its students with decision makers in Michigan and national law firms and within the ABA.

The composition of the faculty changed over the next ten years. A number of the senior faculty who were neither expected nor encouraged to engage in scholarship and some of whom had a legal practice downtown retired or died. The newer faculty focused their efforts on scholarship and teaching. With the school's increased visibility and reputation, Wayne lost professors hired since 1965 to other schools. David Hood became the inaugural law school dean at the University of Hawaii, and four others moved to schools in California.

Wayne professors were in demand as visitors at other law schools, in large part based on their reputations as excellent teachers. Professor Stephen Schulman was the first of many Wayne professors who taught at the University of Michigan Law School.

The growing demand for a legal education that began in the 1960s continued until the 1982 economic recession. Then applications declined but national enrollment remained fairly constant until the twenty-first century.[1]

Except for the post–World War II economic boom years, the number of active lawyers in the country increased annually by 1 to 3 percent, but during the 1970s, the annual increase ranged from 5 to 7.6 percent. In 1980, the 15.4 percent increase far surpassed the percentage increase in any year before or after 1980.[2]

New law schools opened and existing schools expanded their enrollments and hired more professors. In this period, law schools enrolled more female students and fewer male students.[3]

Donald Gordon, Joiner's associate dean, served as interim dean for a year after Joiner's departure then left for the newly established Hawaii law school with his Wayne colleague and inaugural Hawaii dean David Hood. The Wayne faculty courted Gordon and in 1975 he returned as the school's fourth dean, serving from 1975 to 1980.

Wayne Law benefited from the dramatic increase in female applications nationally in the 1970s, when it enrolled women in numbers well above the national averages. The University of Michigan Law School drew a national student body and limited the number of Michigan residents that they accepted. With Wayne Law's improved reputation in Michigan, the law school attracted many women who wanted to attend a law school in the state and either were not accepted by Michigan Law or for personal reasons preferred a Detroit-area law school.[4]

1. "First Year and Total J.D. Enrollment by Gender 1963–2013," https://www.americanbar .org/groups/legal_education/resources/statistics/statistics-archives.
2. "ABA National Lawyer Population Survey: Historical Trend in Total National Lawyer Population, 1878–2017," https://www.americanbar.org/content/dam/aba/administrative/ market_research/Total%20National%20Lawyer%20Population%201878-2017 .authcheckdam.pdf.
3. Since that recession, except for a few years, the male-female ratio in law school enrollment nationally settled at 55 percent male, 45 percent female.
4. Some women who attended Wayne Law in the 1970s confided to their female classmates and professors that they experienced unwelcome advances and inappropriate comments from their male classmates. When a female student notified the administration that an employee engaged in inappropriate behavior toward her and other women, after a prompt

In 1972, the Wayne State University faculty voted to unionize.[5] President Gullen was comfortable dealing with the faculty through its union. He came to Wayne from the unionized American Motors Company. The law faculty considered filing a petition for removal. It speculated that since the majority of union members were from the lower-salaried liberal arts faculty, the union would promote salary increases for lower-paid professors and, over time, the law school salary scale would compress.[6] Once the Michigan Employment Relations Council (MERC) denied the medical school faculty's request to be removed from the bargaining unit, the law faculty did not pursue removal.

Dean Gordon built on Dean Joiner's efforts to increase the law school's visibility and reputation. He wanted to expand opportunities for faculty and students to teach and study outside of the United States.[7] Gordon established a faculty lecture exchange with the nearby University of Windsor Faculty of Law,[8] as well as a faculty and student exchange program with the University of Warwick in England.[9] In some years, a visiting Warwick exchange student interned with an American law firm or law-related agency. Professor John Mogk was a Visiting Scholar at Warwick and, while there, he worked with Warwick professors who were developing England's energy law.

Dean Donald Gordon, Jerry DuPont, director of the University of Hawaii Law Library, and Georgia Clark, director of the Wayne Law Library, wanted

---

investigation, the law school terminated him in the middle of the term. In the same years, a few female students were involved in personal relationships with their professors that could jeopardize the professor's academic position under current mores.

5. The union selected the American Association of University Professors (AAUP) as its bargaining representative. In subsequent contracts, the faculty's union was the Wayne State University AAUP-AFT Local 6075, jointly affiliated with the AAUP and the American Federation of Teachers (AFT).

6. The salary compression did in fact take place. Many union contracts included across-the-board salary increases that were capped at earnings below those of many law school professors.

7. The exchange programs are discussed in more detail in chapter 7.

8. For example, in 1983, Windsor professor Scott Fairley and Wayne professor Robert Sedler both spoke about the new Canadian Charter of Rights and Freedoms.

9. The Warwick University exchange program gave students the opportunity to study in England and faculty the opportunity to teach and engage in research there.

to preserve aging legal documents and make them accessible to the public. To promote this goal, Wayne, Hawaii, and Harvard universities established the Law Library Microform Consortium (LLMC), a nonprofit cooperative of libraries.

For most of her thirty-five years at Wayne, Georgia Clark served as director of the law library. She provided the leadership to reshape Wayne's library and expand its clientele.[10] During her tenure, the library became a welcoming place not only for all Wayne students and faculty but for lawyers and non-lawyers in the Detroit community.[11] Clark was unique among law library directors. She was not a lawyer and, even more unusual, the law library was not independent of the university library system.[12] Clark led the library's transition into the digital age of information technology.[13] In 2016, Clark became the only person who was not a Wayne Law professor or alumnus to be inducted into the law school's Wall of Fame, the highest non-academic honor granted by the law school.[14]

---

10. Georgia Clark was respected by her staff and the library users. She mentored and nurtured her staff, many of whom left for attractive positions with law firms and other law school libraries. She encouraged her staff to follow her lead—join and become involved in professional law library organizations.

11. "The Arthur Neef Law Library in 2006," *Wayne Lawyer* 23 (Spring 2006): 42.

12. If the library director is not a lawyer, the law school must show that with the director's leadership, the library complied with ABA's law library standards. The relationship between the law school and the Wayne university library system is atypical. The ABA's accreditation standards generally require the law library to be an arm of the law school, not the university library system, and require the library's budget to be determined and administered in the same manner as the law school's budget. See Standards 602 and 603, ABA Section on Legal Education and Admission to the Bar's 2016–2017 Standards and Rules of Procedure for Approval of Law Schools, http://www.americanbar.org/groups/legal_education/resources/standards.html.

13. By 2000, the law school boasted the twenty-third-largest public academic law library in the country. Clark was honored at the law school's 2008 Treasure of Detroit event and retired the same year. The donor plaque outside the library lists a small fraction of the patrons who admired her for the services that she and her staff professionally and graciously provided. In recognition of her extraordinary contributions, the law school commissioned the Georgia Clark cabinet located in the library that displays the faculty's academic work. Clark also created the rare book room in the law library named after her late husband, George Clark.

14. The Miller Family Wayne Law Alumni Wall of Fame Award "is to acknowledge graduates and former faculty and staff of Wayne State University Law School whose

Georgia Clark. (Reprinted with permission of the law school)

Upon Gordon's retirement as dean and in recognition of his decades of extraordinary teaching, Eugene Driker and a group of alumni established the Donald H. Gordon Award for Excellence in Teaching.[15] Professor John Dolan wrote that Dean Gordon valued faculty governance and respected the role of faculty, "even when it made his job more difficult."

The Class of 1980 entered Wayne fifty years after the school opened its doors in September 1927. The class was racially, ethnically, and gender diverse. During their law school years, those students spent time in the library, completing assignments by locating resources from books on the shelves, years before they did that research on their laptops at home. They prepared their papers on typewriters and, while at school, they called home or friends from a public pay phone in the school's basement. Most focused on their law studies, treating law school as their full-time job. Many of those students were strapped financially, skimping on the apartments they rented and the food that they ate. Some members of that class played softball during law school and after graduation continued to meet annually in the Detroit area. The graduates in the Class of 1980 had more employment opportunities than did their near-term successors, who were confronted with a serious economic recession and fewer legal jobs.

In 1980 John Roberts became the law school's fifth dean, serving until 1987. Dean Roberts came from a decanal position at Yale Law School. His goal was to increase the school's national reputation. He recognized the importance of a law school's national reputation even before *U.S. News & World Report* started ranking law schools in 1987, heavily weighting a law school's reputation among professors, practicing lawyers, and judges.[16] To make the salary scale

---

extraordinary professional success and contributions, profound positive influence on Wayne Law, and high degree of character and integrity are recognized by their peers." http://law.wayne.edu/about.

15. Professor Paul Harbrecht was the first recipient of the Gordon teaching award in 1982. When Judge Damon Keith presented Harbrecht with this award, Harbrecht was confined to a wheelchair with amyotrophic lateral sclerosis (Lou Gehrig's disease). See *Wayne Lawyer* 2 (Spring 1982): cover and p. 14.

16. In *U.S. News* rankings, national reputation is weighted 40 percent, consisting of peer reputation score at 25 percent and lawyer/judge reputation score at 15 percent.

for Wayne professors more competitive, Roberts secured university funds to increase salaries for professors susceptible to recruitment by other law schools.

When Roberts was hired, the university authorized him to increase the size of the faculty to 41 full-time professors. Instead, when the Michigan legislature's budget allocation to Wayne dropped during the 1982 recession, the faculty contracted from 39 in 1981 to 34 by 1983.

To increase Wayne's reputation in the legal academic community and among lawyers and judges hiring Wayne graduates, Roberts encouraged professors who clerked for judges to work with Wayne students to obtain judicial clerkships. He was successful. Sixteen students in the Class of 1980 and eighteen students in the Class of 1981 clerked for judges on federal and state courts.[17] In 1983, Wayne graduates clerking for a Federal District Court judge on the Eastern District of Michigan outnumbered the clerks from other law schools. In the Class of 1987, four students received clerkships on the Federal Court of Appeals, four on the Federal District Courts, and three on state Supreme Courts.[18] Some federal judges hired long-term "career" clerks. Kristin Wilcox Dighe ('87) was a career clerk for Judge Rosemary Collyer on the U.S. District Court for the District of Columbia. Then, as Nancy Edmunds, Hilda Gage, and other Wayne graduates became federal and state court judges, they hired clerks from their alma mater.

New Opportunities for Graduates

In the pre-Joiner years, most graduates engaged in law practice representing individuals. The pioneering graduates during the Joiner deanship became transactional lawyers representing business in the corporate law firms. They

---

See https://www.usnews.com/education.

17. In the Class of 1986, eight graduates received clerkships with federal judges and federal magistrates. See "Law School Briefs," *Wayne Lawyer* 5 (Spring 1986): 13. The eight graduates were Lynn Eccleston, Kenneth Chadwell, Joel Gehrke, Kristen Lacrom, Anita Schnee, David Engel, Stephen Tomkowski, and Eric Richards.

18. "Judicial Clerks," *Wayne Lawyer* 6 (Summer 1987): 28.

impressed the lawyers in their firms and, by their success, provided the next generations of Wayne graduates with opportunities in the litigation and corporate departments of those firms. Wayne developed the reputation as a school that educated students who were prepared to practice as new associates in corporate law firms. The graduates were populating prestigious Michigan law firms and becoming leaders in their firms and in the legal community.

As women were representing half of the top Wayne Law graduates, Michigan law firms recognized that if they did not hire Wayne women, they were bypassing half of the most talented graduates. According to Judge Nancy Edmunds, a 1976 summa cum laude graduate, gender was not a barrier for her female classmates to obtain the most sought-after legal jobs. Some women, however, found that after having children, the work available at their law firms changed and their progress toward partnership was slower.[19]

From 1972 until 1981, the U.S. economy was strong, enabling Wayne Law graduates to obtain jobs not previously available to Wayne students. Some practiced as commercial litigators and corporate general counsels, represented wealthy individuals, or entered academia with tenure-track positions in law schools outside Michigan. While graduates could practice as labor lawyers, prosecutors, and defense lawyers before Joiner's deanship, graduates in the post-Joiner years took cases to the highest state and federal courts more frequently than in prior years. Some graduates chose to enter politics, while others chose to represent athletes or become part of the entertainment industry.

Corporate General Counsels

When corporations seek lawyers to serve as their general counsels, they not infrequently look to their "outside" lawyers in the law firms who represent them. As Wayne graduates populated Michigan corporate law firms, corporate clients started recruiting those outside counsels to serve as their general counsels.

---

19. These comments come from men at those firms who witnessed these issues with colleagues and their lawyer spouses.

Many transactional lawyers in the large Michigan law firms became corporate general counsels. The following is illustrative.

David Potts ('69), after practicing for twenty-two years with his Wayne classmates at Carson, Fischer and Potts, joined the Detroit Lions as its general counsel. Susan Greenfield ('75) was general counsel for Palace Sports and Entertainment, the venue where the Detroit Pistons basketball team played for many years.

Wayne provided Alex DeYonker ('75) access to the legal profession. DeYonker's father died when he was two years old, leaving his single mother struggling to raise five children. He found law school very challenging, especially balancing full-time school and work, but found that Wayne Law was the right fit for him. He lived his law school years "with his head down, charging through school." During those years, he was Professor Stephen Schulman's research assistant. Schulman introduced DeYonker to Hugh Maekins, Director of Enforcement at the Michigan Corporate and Securities Bureau, when Maekins was discussing state securities law in his Business Planning course. Maekins hired DeYonker, and DeYonker succeeded Maekins as the bureau's Director of Enforcement.

DeYonker then joined the Warner Norcross and Judd firm in Grand Rapids. According to DeYonker, many Wayne graduates are "a little bit more ambitious" and deeply engaged in their legal practice. A person from a blue-collar family has "a little more intensity." In 2006, DeYonker left Warner to become Spartan Stores' executive vice president, general counsel, and corporate secretary.[20]

Three consecutive managing partners of the Warner Norcross and Judd firm (WNJ) were law school alumni. Alex DeYonker was the firm's managing partner from 2002 to 2005. He was followed by Douglas Wagner ('76), who led the firm for over a decade.[21] Douglas Dozeman ('83) became managing partner in 2016.

---

20. Alex DeYonker, interview by the author, Grand Rapids, April 13, 2016.
21. Wagner was the third Wayne Law graduate when he joined WNJ in 1976. The first Wayne graduate at WNJ was Vernon Saper ('72). Wayne's second graduate to be hired by WNJ, two years after Saper, was Robert Chovanec ('74).

Alex DeYonker, 2002–5.

Doug Wagner 2005–16.

Doug Dozeman, 2016–.

John J. Collins Jr. ('76) and Lynn Hartley ('77) met while attending the law school and married at the end of John's second year (her first). After Wayne, he earned an LL.M. in taxation from the University of Florida and excelled in that program. Instead of accepting Florida's offer to stay and teach for two years, Collins joined the Miller Canfield firm in Detroit and became a partner in a record four and a half years, eclipsing David Joswick's five-and-a-half-year record. He left law practice to serve as Capital Cities' general counsel, then returned to Miller Canfield, and again was lured away as Champion Enterprises' vice president, general counsel, and corporate secretary. From Champion, Collins became general counsel and a managing director at Alix Partners, a business management consulting firm. Collins taught at Wayne Law for many years, including commuting from New York to help start the school's new General Counsel Externship program.[22]

Terry Larkin ('79) was the grandson of immigrants. His parents encouraged their children to pursue higher education. The family moved around the world with his father, a Ford Motor Company executive. Larkin considers himself "fortunate" to have attended Wayne rather than the University of Michigan Law School: "Wayne was better." Law captivated him and he immersed himself in learning critical thinking.[23]

Larkin began his legal career at the Bodman law firm. The firm had 35 lawyers when Larkin joined in 1979 and reached about 150 when he left after 29 years. He had a transactional practice, helping closely held companies go "public" and counseling companies involved in acquisition and merger transactions. In 2008, after Larkin served as an outside counsel for the Lear Corporation, Lear lured him to become their general counsel, vice president, and secretary to the Board

---

22. John Collins, interview by the author, May 27, 2015. In the interest of full disclosure, Collins endowed the Alan Schenk prize in the business planning course. In the externship program, Collins provided students with an unvarnished view of an "in house" law practice: the opportunities, the problems to worry about, and the judgment, balance, and perspective required to practice in a corporate law department.

23. In business planning, he could combine all that he learned in other business courses, coming "as close to real life law practice as we could get in law school."

of Directors. Soon after joining Lear, he became engrossed in guiding his company through an exceptionally short, four-month bankruptcy reorganization.

Larkin explained his transition from representing Lear as outside counsel to becoming its general counsel. As outside counsel, he gave advice on business problems and the client made the decisions. As general counsel, he also provided advice but now had to be careful that he did not usurp senior management's decision-making role.[24]

Aleksandra Miziolek ('80) was attracted to Wayne Law with a scholarship that was important to her and her immigrant parents. She graduated summa cum laude and served as *Wayne Law Review's* editor in chief. She clerked for Chief Federal District Court Judge James Churchill and then joined the Dykema law firm in Detroit. After her exposure to litigation during her clerkship, she decided that she needed more control over the outcomes of her cases and was better suited for a transactional practice. With men dominating her preferred field of mergers and acquisitions, she found that she had to be persistent to secure that work.

Miziolek led a demanding professional life, raised children early in her legal career, and gave time to civic and philanthropic activities. Most women lawyers found that they could not establish their reputation, have children, and be active in charitable work, all at an early stage in their career. The Dykema law firm accommodated women like Miziolek who wanted to have children and maintain a demanding practice. She found that with her "book of business" with clients and her Blackberry, she could nurture her clients and grow with them as she had four children. After thirty-two years of law firm practice, in 2014, Miziolek became the auto supplier Cooper Standard's vice president, general counsel, and secretary.[25]

---

24. Terry Larkin, interview by the author, July 9, 2015. Terry is active in civic and charitable activities. He is involved in several nonprofit and civic organizations and with the concurrence of Lear, he serves as an independent director on the Board of Directors of Kelly Services. One of his charities, Life Directions, was born out of the 1967 Detroit Rebellion. The organization helps Detroit high school students by developing mentors in those schools to help other students avoid violence and crime. Terry serves on the board of the Detroit Regional Chamber of Commerce and is active with the Capuchin Soup Kitchen in Detroit.

25. Aleksandra Miziolek, interview by the author, November 24, 2014. Miziolek also

David Liner's promotion from within a corporation to its general counsel and then to private practice with a corporate law firm was atypical. Liner ('80) joined the Masco Corporation's legal department after graduation and rose to vice president and general counsel in 1997. He left Masco to join the Dykema Gossett law firm in 2001 and then returned to Masco (then Roper Technologies, Inc.) as vice president, general counsel, corporate secretary, and chief compliance officer. He also served as a director of CECO Environmental Corporation, a global energy, environmental, and industrial technology company.

Karen Livingston Wilson ('83) was Citizen Insurance's first African American and first woman in the company's long history to become its vice president, general counsel, and secretary. Jay Colvin ('89) represented high net worth clients with the Bodman law firm in Detroit for twenty-five years before he was tapped to become the Detroit Lions' vice president for legal affairs and general counsel.

One graduate, Jason Hillman ('01), strayed from the typical trajectory of going from partner in a corporate law firm to general counsel of a corporation. Hillman became general counsel only four years after his law school graduation. Hillman, the grandson of immigrants, came to Wayne Law after earning a degree from Michigan State and spending three years in broadcast journalism.[26] He came to Wayne rather than Michigan because he "bombed" the LSAT.

Wayne students do not approach competition, practice, and life with a sense of entitlement. Rather, they work for their successes. Hillman developed an appreciation for his Wayne legal education while a student when his Moot Court team competed against students from elite eastern law schools. In a semifinal round, he faced a Duke Law School team that seemed confident against "that" Wayne team from Detroit. Wayne won. Hillman became Wayne's Moot Court chancellor and looked forward to a postgraduate career as a litigator.

Hillman's attitude, in meetings and negotiations, was that he was "not the smartest person in the room." Many Wayne Law alumni share that humility and

---

served on Cooper Standard's Global Leadership Team.

26. He was a reporter for Pass Sports in Detroit, interviewing players and management personnel with professional baseball, basketball and hockey teams.

strong work ethic, and that may account for their uncanny successes in law and business.

After graduation, Hillman practiced with the Detroit-area Jaffe Law Firm as a real estate transactional lawyer before being offered the general counsel position with the Cleveland Cavaliers. He advised law students to take a broad cross-section of law school courses because "you may find yourself as the vice president and general counsel of the Cleveland Cavaliers Basketball organization four years after graduation, with 90 percent of your work involving contracts and business transactions." The Cavaliers, he said, were taking a chance.

With the Cavaliers, Hillman applied the team's owner and Wayne alumnus Dan Gilbert's adage: "relationships are the basis of all real wealth." For Hillman, "the key in negotiating a contract is the ability to put the signed contract in the file and, because of the relationship that was established in negotiations, the contract remains in the file."[27]

Representing Individual Clients with Accumulated Wealth

As Wayne graduates were representing individuals with accumulated wealth who needed financial, estate-planning, and family counseling, they developed strong reputations in those areas. "High net worth" clients may be individuals with large real estate holdings, owners of privately owned businesses, or officers and shareholders of large, public companies. Three graduates in the mid-1970s among many others, William Edmunds, David Hempstead, and Roger Cook, represented those clients.

William Edmunds ('76) remembers that two of his four first-year law professors were women. He enjoyed the stimulating environment and "fabulous" professors who were not just smart but good teachers—in terms of both the depth of their knowledge and their ability to engender critical thinking. Edmunds and Nancy Garlock met in law school, married, and chose two different career

---

27. Jason Hillman, interview by the author, June 28, 2017.

Judge Nancy Edmunds, Class of 1976. (Photo reproduced with permission of Judge Edmunds)

William Edmunds, Class of 1976. (Photo reproduced with permission of Mr. Edmunds)

paths within the law.[28] The faculty generally limits the highest academic honor, summa cum laude, to one graduate. For the Class of 1976, the faculty awarded two summas and they went to a married couple, Nancy and William Edmunds.

William Edmunds had many job opportunities. He chose a smaller law firm practice and represented real estate operators and individuals who needed assistance in planning their estates. In his thirty-seven years of practice, he enjoyed negotiating as a "David" opposing the "Goliath" firm lawyers. He had a natural talent for teaching, and after retiring from law practice, he tutored students in Detroit elementary schools.

David Hempstead ('75) did not volunteer in law school classes to answer questions raised by his professors ("gunners," as Daniel Gilbert described those classmates). After Hempstead's stellar performance on a Business Planning examination, Professor Schulman asked Hempstead to meet with him. Schulman wanted to meet the top student on his grading sheet whom he did not recognize by name.[29]

Each year some top first-year Wayne Law students apply to transfer to Michigan's law school to finish their legal education, and Michigan regularly accepts a number of them. Hempstead is illustrative of students who want to practice law in Michigan and had not been disadvantaged in job opportunities by staying at Wayne instead of transferring to Michigan. One of his Wayne classmates transferred to Michigan Law. They both joined the relatively small (twenty-two lawyers at the time) Bodman law firm in Detroit after graduation.

Hempstead was the second Wayne graduate to be hired by the Bodman law firm; Albert Wortley ('43) was the first. Hempstead worked his way up in the firm. The tendency of firms to hire individuals like themselves proved beneficial. Hempstead convinced the partners making hiring decisions to hire more new associates from Wayne. The large law firms were reducing the

---

28. Nancy and William Edmunds, interview by the author, February 24, 2015. Marriages among Wayne Law students were not rare. See https://law.wayne.edu/news/husband-and -wife-meet-at-wayne-law-work-together-to-support-alumni-and-students-33072.

29. David Hempstead enjoyed business planning, not just because it was an intellectually stimulating course but because the course attracted other top students.

time their partners spent in training new associates, and the Wayne graduates enjoyed a competitive advantage as associates who were well prepared to practice with less mentoring. Hempstead became counselor and advisor to many high net worth clients, including the Ford family.[30]

Hempstead viewed Wayne Law as "a place where [law firms] could hire talented people." "I always thought that the law school got me where I am. . . . [Wayne] taught me how to work, how to think," and "you have to give back to what was given to you." He has done so.[31]

Roger Cook ('75) worked part-time while earning degrees from Wayne's Monteith College, Wayne Law, and New York University's LL.M. in Taxation program.[32] He spent his legal career at the Honigman law firm, representing clients who needed tax, financial, and estate-planning services. He held a leadership position in the firm's tax and estate-planning practice. Two Wayne alumni in Cook's law firm were leaders in other areas of the firm's practice. Lawrence McLaughlin ('77) rose to chair the firm's real estate department and I. W. (Bill) Winsten ('79) was co-leader of Honigman's Complex Commercial Litigation Practice Group.[33]

Litigation Lawyers Representing Business

Some Wayne graduates in the post-Joiner years chose careers as litigators in corporate law firms. Nancy Edmunds was raised in Detroit, was a Phi Beta Kappa graduate from Cornell University, and earned a master's degree in teaching

---

30. Hempstead has the Ford family permission to disclose their association. Clifford Longley of the original Bodman, Longley firm was Ford's general counsel.
31. David Hempstead, interview by the author, June 1, 2015. Hempstead was inducted into the law school Wall of Fame in 2018.
32. Roger Cook, interview by the author, July 15, 2015. Monteith College provided some of the very talented Wayne Law students from the mid-1960s to the mid-1970s.
33. Winsten was involved with the law school for decades. He was president of the school's alumni association in 1997–98 and chaired the Wayne Law Board of Visitors in 2008–10. In 2004, Winsten was instrumental in establishing the law school online newsletter to communicate with alumni.

from the University of Chicago. She taught public school until she decided to go to law school. A personal commitment kept her living in the Detroit area, and not wanting to commute to Ann Arbor, she decided on Wayne Law. She loved law school, including her service as editor in chief of the law review, and counts some of her classmates and professors among her lifelong friends.

Edmunds clerked for Federal District Court Judge Ralph Freeman before joining the Dykema Gossett law firm, where she practiced as a litigator for fourteen years. In 1992, she was confirmed as a Federal District Court Judge for the Eastern District of Michigan. Judge Edmunds has shown her respect for Wayne graduates by hiring some of them as her law clerks.

Judge Edmunds had a deep commitment to family, community, and her career in the legal profession. She stands out as one of the most ardent boosters of the law school who, through her reputation, enhanced Wayne Law's reputation in the Michigan legal community. She served on law school advisory committees for decades, including as chair of its Board of Visitors.

Kathryn Humphrey was not the prototypical Wayne student in 1977. Her parents were college graduates, and she had attended Wellesley College. While in college, she participated in a theatrical production that focused on feminism and women's issues. She and two other women actors established a touring company and performed on campuses across the country. While living in Michigan, she decided to pursue a legal education and chose Wayne because of its lower tuition.

Humphrey, like Barry Waldman ('69), believes that Wayne students are more willing to adapt to changes in the practice of law. Humphrey shifted from her commercial litigation practice, predominantly products liability claims in the automotive and airline industries, to environmental litigation and alternatives to trials to resolve disputes. Kathryn Humphrey's first child was born after she established her reputation at the law firm, and she spent more time on philanthropic work once her children were in school.[34]

---

34. Kathryn Humphrey, interview by the author, March 10, 2016. Humphrey served on the Legal Aid and Defender board and on Wayne's Board of Visitors.

Law practice became more competitive and the behavior of some lawyers departed from the civility that marked the legal profession in earlier years. The Michigan chapter of the Federal Bar Association found it necessary to single out lawyers who were "civil," and Humphrey received its 2013 Cook-Friedman Civility Award. Humphrey, like Eugene Driker and Nancy Edmunds before her, was devoted to Wayne Law, providing invaluable guidance to law school administrations over many years.[35]

Criminal Law Practices

The law school offered a rich array of courses that prepared students for careers in criminal law. The criminal law and criminal procedure courses, evidence, and others were popular with students interested in careers as litigators. The law school intermittently offered clinics in which students represented clients charged with misdemeanor offenses. Since 1965, Wayne attracted professors in criminal law and procedure with strong academic credentials and U.S. Supreme Court experience. Many were judged by their students as talented teachers.

In the school's early years, when most courses were taught by adjuncts, criminal law was taught by Recorder's Court Judge W. McKay Skillman. Lionel Frankel (1962–66)[36] was the first full-time professor to teach courses in the criminal law curriculum. The faculty hired Edward Wise in 1965[37] and increased its strength in criminal law and procedure in the 1970s with Professors Joseph Grano, Janet Findlater, and LeRoy Lamborn,[38] and again in the

---

35. In 2005–6, she funded the Fellows Program, which was "designed to reward and promote excellence and leadership at the Law School while enhancing intellectual and professional development." "Fellows Program Established," *Wayne Lawyer* 23 (Spring 2006): 8.

36. He left to teach at the University of Utah College of Law.

37. Edward Wise brought the Criminal Law Project with him from New York University. He became a noted scholar in American and comparative criminal law. A few Wayne professors in their early years in teaching were assigned to teach criminal law, even if it was not in their field of expertise.

38. Professors Grano (1975–2001), Findlater (1976–2017), and Lamborn (1971–97) taught at Wayne until they retired. LeRoy Lamborn helped draft the United Nations Declaration of Basic Principles of Justice for Victims of Crime and Abuse of Power.

twenty-first century when students could take courses from Professors Peter Henning,[39] Anthony Dillof,[40] Adele Morrison,[41] William Ortman,[42] and Dean Richard Bierschbach[43] with expertise in criminal law and criminal procedure.

Wayne Law graduates pursued careers in criminal prosecution and defense since the school's establishment, but until the late 1960s, when African American judges were appointed or elected to the criminal court, African American criminal defense lawyers were not routinely assigned cases representing indigent

---

Joshua Dressler (1982–93), who coauthored textbooks and a treatise in criminal law and procedure, taught at two other law schools before he retired. David Moran (2000–2008) left Wayne to join the Innocence Project at the University of Michigan Law School. Blanche Cook (2014–19), whose scholarship included the prosecution of sex traffickers, left Wayne to become the Robert E. Harding Jr. Associate Professor at the University of Kentucky School of Law.

39. Henning worked for the Securities and Exchange Commission and the U.S. Department of Justice before joining the faculty in 1994. He was a respected scholar, authoring or coauthoring leading treatises covering public corruption, criminal federal practice and procedure, and securities crimes. He was a regular contributor to the popular "White Collar Watch" as part of the *New York Times* Deal Book column on corporate and securities law and was interviewed regularly on national and local media about criminal cases in the news. Henning taught white-collar crime, criminal procedure, and securities regulation.

40. Dillof clerked on the 9th Circuit, was special counsel for the American Civil Liberties Union, practiced with the Corporate Counsel office of the New York City Law Department, and taught at Texas Wesleyan before joining the Wayne faculty in 2002. He also taught Torts and Appellate Advocacy. In his spare time, Dillof and Professor Lance Gable were part of a punk rock band that played in local venues. Professor Dillof taught criminal law and procedure, focusing his criminal law scholarship on policies related to the forms of justice that underlie our civil, criminal, and constitutional law systems.

41. Morrison taught at Northern Illinois University School of Law before joining the faculty in 2009. She taught courses in criminal law and family law-related courses and seminars, including domestic violence, and sexuality, gender and the law.

42. Ortman taught criminal law, evidence, administrative law, and a seminar on advanced topics in criminal law and procedure. As a young scholar, he published articles in a number of prestigious journals. Michigan, Pennsylvania, and Stanford law reviews published his early scholarship. Ortman also started accumulating the Upper-Level Professor of the Year awards by his second year at Wayne.

43. Dean Bierschbach had taught criminal law and procedure, including white-collar crime, and was known for his criminal law scholarship that "explores the interplay of criminal justice's institutional and procedural structure with its substantive and regulatory aims." https://law.wayne.edu/profile/gl9503#definition-Biography.

defendants. Also, defendants of color infrequently hired African American criminal defense lawyers before Kenneth Cockrel and Cornelius Pitts changed that dynamic. Abel Torres ('82) became the first Hispanic assistant prosecuting attorney in Bay County, Michigan, was a juvenile court referee, and served as a member of the Bay County Human Relations Commission.

Many students interested in careers in litigation became criminal prosecutors or criminal defense lawyers (street or white-collar offenses). Some came to law school wanting to practice in the field of criminal law and some may have developed the interest after being exposed to the school's professors and courses. Walter Gibbs Jr. ('63) spent his career as a Wayne County prosecutor. Some graduates, who started as prosecutors, switched into private practice as defense lawyers.

Miriam Siefer ('75) served for decades as the chief defender in the Federal Community Defender office in Detroit. Siefer represented high-profile indigent clients like the "underwear bomber" Umar Farouk Abdulmutallab in a case heard by Judge Nancy Edmunds ('76). Abdulmutallab attempted to blow up a Northwest Airlines aircraft on its international flight to Detroit on Christmas Day in 2009.[44] Siefer taught in the law school's civil and criminal clinic, and she retained her connection with Wayne Law as the field placement attorney in the school's criminal justice externship program.

Michael Hagedorn ('69) as co-counsel took a criminal case to the U.S. Supreme Court in 1976.[45] Starting in the twenty-first century, Timothy Baughman ('74) argued *Hudson v. Michigan*.[46] Valerie Newman ('92) and Harold Gurewitz ('70) also took criminal cases to the Supreme Court. Newman

---

44. See Jones, Law Blog, "On Miriam Siefer, the Woman Who Will Represent Abdulmutallab," *Wall Street Journal*, January 4, 2010. Siefer also represented James Nichols, brother of convicted Oklahoma City federal building bomber Terry Nichols.

45. Hagedorn provided legal services to poor people and to Native Americans on reservations for the South Minnesota Regional Legal Services in St. Paul and Leech Lake Reservation Legal Services project. He was co-counsel in *Bryan v. Itasca County, Minnesota*, 426 U.S. 373 (1976).

46. 547 U.S. 586 (2006). The court sided with Baughman, ruling that the evidence obtained when the police violated the "knock and announce" rule could not be excluded.

worked for the State Appellate Defender Office (SATO) in Michigan and argued two cases in the U.S. Supreme Court.[47]

Harold Gurewitz, a frequent speaker in Professor Henning's white-collar crime course, defended high-profile clients like former Detroit mayor Kwame Kilpatrick. Gurewitz took *Carpenter v. United States*,[48] a significant Fourth Amendment privacy case, to the Supreme Court.

Labor Lawyers

Detroit became a center of the labor movement when the UAW was established in 1935. Boaz Siegel became Wayne's first full-time labor law professor in the mid-1940s. Wayne Law developed one of the first LL.M. programs in Labor Law in 1950, with the courses taught largely by practicing lawyers in the evening.

During the Joiner deanship, the faculty started hiring more labor and employment law professors. In 1968, the faculty added William Gould (1968–71). Gould left for the Stanford Law School, where he spent the rest of his academic career.[49] The faculty replaced Gould with Florian (Bart) Bartosic (1971–80), who came to Wayne after practicing as a union-side labor lawyer, including as counsel for the International Brotherhood of Teamsters union. Bartosic helped many students, especially women, obtain jobs in labor law.[50] There followed a series of hires of labor and employment law professors.[51] Kingsley Browne came from a U.S. Supreme Court clerkship and a management-side labor and employment practice in 1989. He and Boaz Siegel were the

---

47. In 2011, she argued *Laffler v. Cooper*, 566 U.S. 156. See "Battler for the wrongly convicted will join Wayne County Prosecutor's Office," *Detroit Free Press*, November 13, 2017. In 2017, she became the director of the Conviction Integrity Unit in the Wayne County Prosecutor's office. That unit is charged with preventing wrongful prosecutions.

48. 138 S. Ct. 2206 (2018). The Supreme Court held that law enforcement must obtain a warrant issued on probable cause before it can obtain cell-site location information.

49. He chaired the National Labor Relations Board from 1994 to 1998.

50. He left Wayne to become dean of the University of California at Davis School of Law.

51. They included Michael Zimmer, David Loeffler, George Feldman, and Dennis Devaney.

longest-serving Wayne labor professors.[52] The law school relied on adjunct professors like Joseph Canfield and John Runyan to teach the J.D. and LL.M. labor law courses, especially in the years when the school had one or no full-time labor law professors.[53]

Wayne Law, according to Mary Ellen (Doby) Gurewitz ('74), was a good training ground for women who wanted to pursue law as a tool for social change. Gurewitz[54] came to law school after enduring gender discrimination in the corporate world. She graduated from the University of Michigan in 1965 with a degree in economics. Some corporate interviewers told her that they just did not hire women. While working as an economic analyst for a local bank, she asked her supervisor why a male colleague was promoted ahead of her. The supervisor, not recognizing that women might seek positions with more responsibility and higher salaries, told her that his wife would not have wanted to move up to those positions.

After graduation, Gurewitz clerked for a federal judge, worked for the National Labor Relations Board's Detroit regional office, and then spent her career representing unions and their members and becoming an expert in election law at the Sachs Waldman law firm. She developed long-term relationships with her predominantly male union clients[55] and found it rewarding to represent "the interests of ordinary people."[56]

---

52. See Kingsley Browne profile at https://law.wayne.edu/profile/aa2846. Browne (1989–present) clerked for Justice White on the U.S. Supreme Court before practicing with a prominent San Francisco law firm as a management-side labor and employment lawyer. His scholarship centered on employment discrimination law and "the legal implications of evolved differences between the sexes." Browne appeared in television interviews, discussing his scholarship on the evolutionary differences between men and women.

53. Canfield taught labor law courses and seminars for decades. He practiced with the regional office of the National Labor Relations Board. Runyan ('72) taught Employment Discrimination as an adjunct for many years.

54. Mary Ellen Gurewitz married Harold Gurewitz ('70).

55. Gurewitz dispels the notion that union leaders prefer to have male lawyers handle their union matters. She represented a wide variety of unions, including the public school teacher's union, the police commanders, and machinists. She also has represented the Democratic Party in Michigan for many years.

56. Mary Ellen Gurewitz, interview by the author, February 2, 2016.

John Canzano ('79) practiced labor and employment law, becoming the managing partner at McKnight, Canzano Smith, Radtke & Brault. Canzano successfully defended the Michigan Prevailing Wage Act that required public school and state construction projects in Michigan to pay union wage rates.

Many graduates established strong reputations as management-side labor lawyers. Thomas Kienbaum ('68) worked with Detroit's Dickinson Wright corporate law firm until he, his wife, Elizabeth Hardy ('84), and several partners and associates formed their own labor and employment law boutique firm in 1997.[57] Kienbaum served as president of the State Bar of Michigan in 1995–96, and Hardy was elected twice to the Wayne State University Board of Governors.

Burnishing the Wayne J.D. before Teaching Law

Regional and state law schools like Wayne State are not major feeder schools for law professors. Elite law schools tend to hire their own graduates or graduates from other elite schools. Before the 1960s, however, Wayne hired two of its own graduates for its full-time faculty. Boaz Siegel ('41) served as law librarian before joining the full-time faculty in 1945. Harold Marchant was hired in 1954.

Law professors who graduated from regional or state schools generally must burnish their degrees with a graduate degree from one of the feeder elite schools. For example, Richard Barber ('55) received a graduate law degree from Yale before he started teaching law full-time. Maurice Kelman ('59) earned an LL.M. from Harvard before joining the Wayne faculty in 1963. Edwin (Webb)

---

57. For more on Kienbaum's early career with the Dickinson Wright firm and his active involvement with the Detroit Bar Association and the Volunteer Lawyer's Program that he spearheaded, see "Alumni Profile: Thomas G. Kienbaum," *Wayne Lawyer* 5 (Fall 1985): 10–11. Kienbaum actively served and promoted his alma mater, including as chair of the school's 2004 Strategic Planning Committee focused on increasing the university funding of the law school, and chair of Wayne Law's Board of Visitors in 2011–12. Elizabeth P. Hardy ('84) served on the Wayne State University Board of Governors (1991–98). https://www.crainsdetroit.com/article/19970428/SUB/704280876/dickinson-partners-launch-firm.

Hecker Jr. ('69) chose academia after earning an LL.M. from Harvard and practicing law in Detroit. He was the Centennial Teaching Professor (receiving many teaching awards) at the University of Kansas Law School.[58]

Some Wayne graduates entered academia after practicing law or completing a judicial clerkship. Two women in the Class of 1975 were the first Wayne Law women to become legal academics and tenured law professors. Joan Mahoney, discussed in chapter 7, was Wayne's eighth dean. Barbara Schwartz started law teaching in Wayne Law's clinical program before teaching for most of her career at the University of Iowa College of Law. Judith Gordon ('81) taught at the University of California-Los Angeles School of Law.[59]

Lawrence Mann ('80) practiced with a local law firm, became a partner in a national law firm, and moved in and out of his academic career at Wayne Law. He entered the predominantly White campus at the University of Michigan in 1967 after graduating from a Detroit high school where the student body was almost 100 percent African American. He felt that many of his Detroit school friends could have done the work at Michigan but never had the chance.

Mann charted a ten-year journey to a college degree deeply involved with the student politics of the time. The antiwar, civil rights, and budding feminism movements were active on college campuses. Mann knew that if he stayed in Michigan and refused induction into the military, he could be sentenced to five years in prison. He left the University of Michigan and transferred his Selective Service file to Northern California. California residency raised other

---

58. William Volz ('75) taught and served as dean of Wayne's business school and was honored as one of Wayne State University's inaugural Distinguished Service Professors. Wayne educated many other individuals who chose academia, both in legal education and other disciplines. For example, in addition to those mentioned elsewhere, Albert Quick ('67) was dean at the University of Toledo Law School; Clark Johnson ('70) was on the Detroit College of Law/Michigan State University faculty; and Jesse Vivian ('83) was an associate professor on the Wayne State University College of Pharmacy and Allied Health.

59. Gordon offered a course titled "The Law and Your Life: Aligning Your Personal Values with the Practice of Law/Fundamentals of Professional Development," and founded LeaderEsQ, LLC, a coaching and training consulting firm. See https://law.ucla.edu/faculty/faculty-profiles/judith-gordon.

issues for a person who had ties to Black political organizations, so he moved to the southeastern United States, where he was a union organizer, worked in a factory, and tested his physical endurance while operating a jackhammer.

Mann applied to law schools in Michigan. Earlier in his life, he had met the activist African American Detroit lawyer Kenneth Cockrel. He respected Detroit lawyers like Cockrel and Justin Ravitz and Recorder's (Criminal) Court Judge Crockett, who were pushing the boundaries of what was acceptable behavior for criminal defense lawyers and judges at the time. Wayne accepted him and Michigan waitlisted him. His uncle in Indianapolis told him to go to Wayne, work hard, and he would be fine.

Mann was older and poorer than his first-year Wayne Law classmates. He was trying to figure out his own future and decided not to get involved in the racial politics at the law school. He remained cloistered and focused on his legal studies. With excellent grades in his first year, he considered transferring to the University of Michigan Law School but decided to stay at Wayne. Several Wayne professors recognized Mann's talent. Arthur Lombard hired him as his teaching assistant for the civil procedure course. Alan Schenk was so impressed with this extraordinary student who asked insightful questions in his taxation class that over forty years later he remembered where Mann sat in that class.

The school had not been successful in attracting African American professors, so some professors urged their colleagues to "groom" one of their own talented students. Mann was encouraged to pursue postgraduate positions that would provide the credentials needed for an academic position at the law school. He clerked for Federal District Court Judge Horace Gilmore. In this "best job he ever had," Mann recalled how different that job was "from running a jackhammer."

After his federal clerkship, Mann joined the Dykema law firm in Detroit in 1982. There, he felt surrounded by successful White Republicans, many of whom he respected and liked. While the Dykema firm had associates and young partners who graduated from Wayne, the firm in those years was largely populated with Harvard and Michigan men. As an African American associate, he felt somewhat isolated and on trial.

The Wayne faculty hired Mann in 1984. In this, his first tour on the law school faculty, Mann found teaching most rewarding. He had the respect of a cross-section of law students who sought his counsel on their legal education and personal issues.

Professor Mann left teaching twice to litigate products liability cases, predominantly in the automobile industry. In 1991, Mann was lured away from academia but in 1994, Dean James Robinson persuaded him to return to the law school full-time and teach, among other courses, Products Liability. He brought that experience, combined with policy, back to the classroom to provide students with a rich understanding of the application of policy to legal practice. In 2004, Bowman and Brooks again pulled Mann back into practice, including years he was the managing partner of the firm's Detroit practice.

Mann retired from practice in 2014, and Dean Jocelyn Benson enticed him back to his love—teaching. As Associate Director of Professional Skills,

Professor Lawrence Mann. (Reprinted with permission)

he mentored students participating in regional and national moot court competitions.[60]

Clark Cunningham started his legal education at the University of Chicago Law School. After earning first-year grades that would have qualified him to join the *Chicago Law Review*, Cunningham transferred to Wayne and lived in the challenging Cass Corridor between downtown and midtown. He engaged in community work while earning his 1981 law degree summa cum laude. Cunningham clerked for Federal Judge Avern Cohn, practiced law in Detroit, and then began his academic career at the University of Michigan Law School and Washington University School of Law. He was appointed as the chaired professor in Law and Ethics at Georgia State University College of Law. Cunningham's Wayne Law coursework and independent study with Professor Grano provided him with the foundation for two of his scholarly articles.

Law Practice with National Firms

By the 1980s, Wayne students were being hired in larger numbers by national law firms. Donald Horowitz ('72) practiced in Detroit, moved to the Securities and Exchange Commission, and then joined the Kaye, Scholer, Fierman, Hays and Handler firm in New York. Raymond Henney ('83) practiced with Ropes & Gray in Boston. Lynn Fleisher ('86) practiced with Sidley Austin, LLP in Chicago and Christine Scarnecchia ('90) with the Mayer Brown firm in Chicago. Edmund Fish ('87) practiced with Weil Gotshal & Manges in Washington, D.C. B. Lynn Walsh ('82) practiced with Hunton & Williams in Atlanta, and Mark Parcella ('86) practiced with Shearman & Sterling in New York.

---

60. Most of the information about Mann is derived from Lawrence Mann, interview by the author, March 23, 2015.

Graduate Law Programs and International LL.M. Students

In 1950, the law school established one of the country's earliest[61] Master of Laws programs in taxation and labor law.[62] Two women, Ruth E. Riddell and Eleanor Stetz Payne, both in the Class of 1952, were among the first students to earn an LL.M. in taxation.[63]

Wayne enhanced the international diversity of the student body by attracting international students who came to earn a Wayne LL.M. Y'au-Tung (Donald) Chang ('69) came from Taiwan without his family. Many Wayne professors and students remember Chang working in the law library to help finance his legal studies. On his return to Taiwan, he wrote books based in part on what he learned at Wayne about American commercial law. Chang rose to the highest ranks in the Taiwan Ministry of Finance.[64]

Dietrich von Boetticher (LL.M. '72) received a Fulbright grant to study in the United States. He came to Wayne for his American LL.M. because Wayne State University and the University of Munich (where he had been studying) had an exchange program in place.[65] Professor Freidrich Juenger mentored him while he was at Wayne. He received among the highest grades in most of his courses at Wayne, and after graduation, gained legal experience with a Detroit corporate law firm.

---

61. New York University, presumably the first law school to grant an LL.M. in taxation, started its program in 1945. http://www.law.nyu.edu/llmjsd/taxation.
62. The Graduate Council and President Henry authorized these two programs on December 29, 1949. See Irwin, "Wayne University—A History," 211.
63. Hanawalt, *A Place of Light*, 285.
64. The author and Y. T. Chang were quite surprised when the author taught in Taiwan's Public Finance Training Institute in Taiwan in the 1990s and, without knowledge of the prior association, the institute paired the author with "a local government official": Y. T. Chang.
65. The author obtained this material during a zoom meeting with Mr. von Boetticher on July 7, 2021. Von Boetticher decided to purchase and train horses. His first horse to enter German horseracing won the German Derby.

Dietrich von Boetticher (LL.M. '72).
(Reproduced with permission)

At Wayne, Dietrich met students from difficult family situations. He found that the Wayne law students had a remarkable attitude about the road to success: a person can, by hard work, achieve success beyond his or her family's station in life. Dietrich decided that he could use his American education and legal experience to achieve professional and financial success in Germany. He credits Wayne with providing him the tools necessary to pursue his career aspirations.

Dietrich von Boetticher returned home and completed his training to practice law in Germany. He opened a solo law practice, and relying on his American credentials, the Wayne LL.M. and his license to practice law in Michigan, he gave lectures to German business groups on the opportunities available for them to establish operations in the United States. Some of those companies became his law firm clients. His law practice grew into the Boetticher Hasse Lohmann partnership of attorneys in Munich. In addition, instead of merely advising clients on making real estate investments, he established a real estate investment firm. He became a principal in the Kan Am Group that sponsored international real estate funds. Dietrich von Boetticher joined other Wayne Law graduates who combined successful careers in law and business.

In the mid-1980s, when employers paid or subsidized the tuition of many graduate students, student enrollment in the predominantly part-time evening LL.M. programs in taxation, labor, and corporate finance averaged about 150 students each semester. When enrollment in those programs declined, the law school tried to increase demand by offering some LL.M. courses at Wayne State's Oakland Center in suburban Detroit. The experiment was not successful and student enrolment in LL.M. courses continued to decline. Wayne Law did not attract many international students seeking a graduate law degree in the United States after the Michigan Supreme Court tightened the bar examination requirements to exclude most international students who did not have a J.D. from an American law school.

Other Careers and Multigenerational Alumni

In addition to alumni who became corporate general counsels, Wayne graduates practiced law in other parts of corporate America. William Wolverton ('75) became director of Strategic Labor Relations at Pepco Holdings, Inc. Norma Macias ('79) joined the UAW-GM Legal Services. Dolores Nunez ('89) practiced with Ford Motor Company. By 1982, Beverly Clark ('72) became the first Native American (Aamjiwnaanng First Nation, Sarnia Reserve) on the Michigan Civil Rights Commission and in 1983 became the first female elected president of the Michigan Trial Lawyers Association (renamed Michigan Association for Justice).

Some graduates decided after law school or after years of practice to pursue their real passions, including the love of architecture and motion picture production. Deborah Hack ('75) practiced tax law and then, after earning another professional degree, practiced as an architect. Gary Hardwick ('85) produced a television series in the late 1990s, wrote books and screenplays, and directed motion pictures. Christa Grix ('94) was a harpist and became executive director of the Plymouth Symphony Orchestra. Joshua Kushnereit ('12) combined law practice with insurance and real estate businesses.

Many father-daughter combinations received their legal education at Wayne. At the expense of not being inclusive, Angela J. Nicita ('83) followed her father, Judge Anthony Nicita ('53); Elaine Niforos ('93) followed her father, Theodore Niforos ('64); and Magistrate Judith Ann Holtz ('69) followed her father, Norman I. Leemon ('42). Diane Menendez Chapin Nilstoft ('82) followed her father, George Menendez ('49). George Menendez was legal advisor to Mexican, Cuban, and Nicaraguan consulates from 1954 to 1976. Joseph Angileri ('84) and his daughter Kylie ('13) are another family duo. A father-daughter judicial team of alumni in Michigan consisted of Oakland County Probate Judge Barry Grant ('60) and his daughter Oakland County Circuit Court Judge Nanci Grant ('89).[66]

The multiple generations of law school graduates were not limited to fathers and daughters. Bryan Waldman ('93) followed his father Barry Waldman ('69). Daniel Findling ('96) was the son of Fred Findling ('56). Eric Gregory ('12) was the son of George Gregory ('80) and Lorraine New ('80).[67] Karen Safran ('94) is a third-generation law school graduate: David Goldman, her grandfather, graduated in the mid-1930s.[68] Her stepfather, Norman Miller, was in the Class of 1969.

Children of Wayne law professors graduated from the law school as well. Professor Wise's son Andrew graduated in 1992; Professor Schenk's son Matthew graduated in 1996; and Professor Grano's son Daniel graduated in 2007.

---

66. "Fathers and Daughters in Law, Nicita Family," *Wayne Lawyer* 11 (1993): 42, 44–46. Magistrate Holtz's family created a scholarship in her father's honor. Norman Leemon, though graduating in May 1942, took advantage of a special rule triggered by the start of U.S. involvement in World War II and took and passed the Michigan bar examination in April 1942.

67. They were night students. During the day, George Gregory worked as an IRS revenue agent and Lorraine New worked for the Office of Personnel Management.

68. Goldman was the law librarian while he was a law student.

6

Enrollment Declines, Tuition Spikes, and Faculty Turnover

This chapter documents how the law school navigated the decline in the national demand for a legal education precipitated by the 1982 economic recession as, concurrently, the Wayne Law tuition started increasing significantly. Wayne graduates benefited from the school's changed reputation and from the growing number of alumni in decision-making positions in major Michigan law firms. In a tight market for lawyers, Wayne Law graduates were still being hired as associates in those firms. Wayne attracted entrepreneurial students who created businesses. The chapter discusses Stephen Ross ('65), who remade a section of New York City, and Dan Gilbert ('87), who remade downtown Detroit. They served as inspiration for future students to consider a career in business. The chapter concludes with a discussion of the school's faculty and curricular changes they made.

Law School Tuition and the 1981–82 Recession

Twice, since the early 1980s, Wayne's law school tuition spiked in response to a significant economic recession. In both cases, applications declined. The first was the 1981–82 recession, during which the Michigan legislature's support for higher education declined. The second was the Great Recession, especially starting in 2008. This chapter covers the first, and chapter 7 discusses the second.

The 1981–82 U.S. economic recession, most severe in the Midwest "Rustbelt," prompted the migration of workers from Michigan and other Midwest states to the southern and western states.[1] While law school applications dropped nationally, enrollment remained fairly constant. This recession severely impacted Michigan's automobile industry.[2] As state tax revenue declined, the Michigan legislature reduced appropriations for higher education. Public universities like Wayne, faced with reduced government support, raised tuition. Wayne Law historically charged low tuition by national standards and compared with tuition charged by the other public and private law schools in Michigan. From 1980 to 1983, however, Wayne Law's in-state tuition increased 41 percent from $2,362 to $3,320.[3] The University of Michigan Law School's in-state 1983 tuition was significantly higher—$4,091.

Applications to law schools in Michigan declined as both tuition increased and the number of lucrative law firm jobs declined. The corporate law firms did not need as many new associates, even when the economy improved. Law schools were competing for highly credentialed applicants by discounting tuition with scholarships.

In October 1985, in response to the faculty's decision to reduce the size of that entering class by 100 from approximately 320 to 220 students (and the resulting drop in law school tuition revenue), Dean Roberts supported the university's

---

1. The 1981–82 recession was severe, with unemployment as high as 10 percent. The Federal Reserve's policies to contain inflation produced soaring interest rates and a dramatic drop in home sales. David Leonhardt, "The Economy Is Bad, but 1982 Was Worse," *New York Times*, January 20, 2009, B1.

2. By late 1982, unemployment was widespread, including in the automobile industry, as the national unemployment rate jumped to 11 percent. The federal funds rate in 1981 was close to 20 percent and the interest rate on ten-year Treasury bonds was above 15 percent. See https://www.federalreservehistory.org/essays/recession-of-1981-82.

3. The law school's tuition increases in the twenty-first century are attributable largely to cuts in the Michigan legislature's funding for higher education. For example, there was an 11 percent cut in aid in 2011. See David Jesse, "Universities Say Funding System Broken, Lawmakers Disagree," *Detroit Free Press*, July 13, 2015.

decision to increase the law school tuition at a rate higher than that of other Wayne colleges.[4] The entering class remained at roughly 240 students from the late 1980s until the Great Recession of 2008.[5]

Enhanced Graduation Requirements, Computerization, and Visibility

A 1981 faculty study revealed that the law school's graduation requirement of eighty hours was below that of other law schools. In addition, the law school allowed law students to take up to four graduate-level, law-related courses outside the law school, reducing the number of law school courses that students needed to graduate. The faculty increased the graduation requirement to the comparable eighty-six credit hours at other regional schools.[6]

Dean John Roberts built on Wayne's rising reputation. With the advent of computer technology, the law school was a pioneer in the application of web-based legal research. In February 1985, the law school purchased a few computers for the faculty secretaries and a few were affixed to mobile carts for the faculty to share. While the legal profession was just learning about web-based legal research technology, Wayne Law was selected by Mead Data Central in 1986 as a partner to test its new legal database that became LEXIS/NEXIS.[7]

---

4. In 1989, the law students presented a well-documented proposal for a loan forgiveness program for students who accepted public service jobs after graduation. The faculty seriously examined the proposal but, as it lacked funding, did not implement it.

5. Enrollment data were provided by the law school registrar Rebecca Hollancid.

6. With the added hours required for graduation, some professors increased the number of credit hours in their current courses. Dean Roberts, report to the president, 9, author's personal files. Ironically, in 2005, faculty research revealed that the law school's semesters (fourteen weeks long) were lengthier than those at other law schools in the region. In December 2005, the faculty changed the length of a semester to thirteen weeks (Faculty Minutes, December 7, 2005). With the increased credit hours required to graduate and in light of the increased complexity in many areas of the law, the faculty increased the credit hours for a number of courses, especially some two-credit courses to three-credit ones.

7. Students and professors had access to a dedicated terminal to research federal tax issues and state legislative and judicial material.

Dean Roberts raised private funds to expand programs designed to increase Wayne Law's visibility nationally. The Honigman Fellows Program brought prominent academics, practicing lawyers, and judges to the law school. The first Fellow was Yale professor Burke Marshall. While Marshall headed the U.S. Justice Department's Civil Rights Division, the Justice Department was actively involved in the 1963 desegregation of the University of Mississippi, and with Marshall's involvement, Congress approved the Civil Rights Act of 1964. Rex Lee, a former U.S. solicitor general in President Nixon's administration and a future president of Brigham Young University, visited Wayne as a Honigman Fellow. Judge Harry Edwards, another Honigman Fellow, was a professor at the University of Michigan Law School before he was confirmed to serve on the United States Court of Appeals for the District of Columbia Circuit.

Dean Roberts invited prominent judges and lawyers as well. In 1982, Judge Patricia Wald, the first woman to serve on the U.S. Court of Appeals for the District of Columbia Circuit, gave the Commencement Address. In 1984, New Zealand deputy prime minister Geoffrey Palmer visited the law school.

In 1982, the Pauline and Ina Cohen ('74) family established the I. Goodman Cohen Trial Advocacy lectureship to enhance the law school program on trial advocacy and to increase the school's visibility to prospective students and the legal community.[8] In the 1980s, the speakers included Edward Stein, a medical malpractice lawyer; Lorna Propes, a highly respected Chicago trial lawyer; and James Seckinger, director of the National Institute of Trial Advocacy.[9] The Cohen lectures continued into the twenty-first century. In 2016, Michigan lawyers Deborah Gordon and Alice Jennings discussed the challenges they faced when bringing actions against employers in employment discrimination cases.

---

8. I. Goodman Cohen was a respected trial lawyer in Michigan. See https://law.wayne.edu/news/lecture-in-trial-advocacy-february-22-32855; James W. McElhaney, "Final Argument—Using the Second Most Effective Form of Persuasion," *Wayne Lawyer* (Fall 1982): 25.

9. In the 1990s, the speakers included Terence MacCarthy, the executive director of the Northern District of Illinois Defender Program, who spoke about the "science of cross-examination." Judge Joan E. Young of the Oakland County Circuit Court gave the thirtieth annual Cohen lecture in 2015.

John Philo and Michael Steinberg discussed planning for public interest litigation. In 2017, Dana Nessel, elected Michigan attorney general in 2018, and Michael Pitt discussed the challenges they faced when litigating high-impact cases.

Richard Barber (the editor in chief of the inaugural issue of the *Wayne Law Review*) and his wife, Elizabeth Schomer, funded grants for interdisciplinary research by professors in the law school and other departments of the university.

Resource Implications of the Decline in Applications and Enrollment

In 1984, the faculty adopted a long-range plan to maintain the credentials of the entering class in the face of declining applications. The faculty assumed that Wayne's reputation was linked in part to student credentials. The 1985 faculty-approved plan called for reducing the entering class by one-third from approximately 320 to 220 students[10] and reducing the number of full-time professors from 32 to 27.

Dean Roberts submitted the plan to President David Adamany and the university administration for approval.[11] President Adamany was a lawyer, was a member of the law faculty, and taught a law school course a few times. He took a hands-on approach to the operation of the law school. He wanted the law school to adopt stronger measures to offset the reduced tuition revenue. He believed that even exceptional teachers should not receive salary increases

---

10. If the law school enrolled 200 students, the 160 students in the first-year day class would be divided into two sections. That left 40 students in the entering evening program.

11. David Adamany served as university president for fifteen years, from 1982 until 1997. The law faculty had a rocky relationship with him. In just one example of this, on August 26, 1988, striking university clerical workers engaged in peaceful picketing on campus. President Adamany authorized their arrest. In response, law school professors, in a letter to the university's Board of Governors, protested the president's action in arresting peaceful protesters as particularly troublesome "in a university setting where the right to free expression of ideas is central to the very being of the institution."

based on merit unless they also engaged in scholarship or professional activity. Adamany wanted the dean to increase the teaching load for professors who did not also engage in a program of continuing scholarship or professional activity. Over objection from some professors, the faculty's 1985 plan included this university-requested differential teaching component, which created ill will within the faculty.[12] The president also wanted the dean to assign some full-time professors to teach in the summer term instead of paying professors as an overload to teach in the summer.

President Adamany rejected the law school's 1985 long-range plan. Dean Roberts did not implement the differential teaching load plan, but the faculty reduced the size of the entering class. Most of the president's other recommendations were not implemented.[13]

Law School Evening Program

In 1982, during this period of reduced national student interest in a legal education, the faculty examined the future of the school's part-time J.D. program. The Detroit City Law School, predecessor of Wayne State University Law School, had opened in 1927 offering an evening-only legal education. The ABA did not fully accredit night-only law schools.[14] In its drive for full ABA accreditation in the mid-1930s, the law school added a day division.

Over the years, many law schools with both full-time day and part-time evening J.D. programs dropped their evening program. For decades, Wayne's

---

12. In 1991, Adamany reiterated his 1985 request that the law school administration implement the system of differential teaching loads.

13. Adamany wanted the dean to assign some faculty to teach law-related courses for undergraduate students. In 2019, the law school established a minor in law program for Wayne undergraduate students, with the core courses taught by Wayne law professors. See https://law.wayne.edu/news/wayne-state-announces-minor-in-law-program-34358.

14. Most students at the Detroit College of Law in 1938 were enrolled in a part-time program. Total DCL enrollment in 1938 was 382 students, with 331 attending afternoon and evening classes. See ABA Section of Legal Education and Admission to the Bar, "Annual Review of Legal Education for 1938" (1939), 19.

Board of Governors[15] and the law faculty, however, treated the evening program as untouchable. It represented part of the school's commitment to provide access to a legal education to students who could not finance that education without working full-time, who did not want to interrupt their current careers, or whose family responsibilities prevented them from attending day classes full-time. Wayne's evening students had consistently accounted for at least one-third of the entering first-year class and, at least since the mid-1960s, the faculty steadfastly maintained the same admission standards and grading norms for both the evening and day programs.[16]

The evening program was expensive to operate, especially with declining enrollment, because the faculty was committed to an evening program that was comparable to the day program. In 1982, with some professors urging the faculty for budgetary reasons to consider terminating the school's evening program, Dean Roberts appointed a student-faculty committee to examine that program. The number of full-time law professors was declining, yet the school was duplicating the courses taught by those professors in the day and evening hours. The committee recommended that the law school phase out the evening program, but the faculty refused by postponing any final decision on the fate of the program.

Wayne's drop in overall applications in the mid-1980s did not immediately reduce the number of entering evening students,[17] but student interest in Wayne's part-time legal education then started to decline. In 1992, the faculty tried to increase the number of part-time students by approving a

---

15. Alumni Eugene Driker and Marilyn Kelly, who served on the Board of Governors, supported the law school's evening program. Kelly earned her J.D. as a part-time evening student.

16. In a 1983 report to Provost Hanson, Dean Roberts reiterated the law school's commitment to identical standards for the day and evening programs. See Faculty Minutes, May 4, 1983. Dean Roberts acknowledged that the law school should offer, every year, all required courses and a long list of other courses. See also Dean John C. Roberts, Dean's Column, *Wayne Lawyer* (Spring 1984): 2.

17. From 1983 to 1986, when total applications to the law school declined from 1,432 to 934, applications to the evening program remained fairly constant.

"combined" day and evening option. Students in the combined program took one of the required first-year courses in the 4 to 6 p.m. time slot. All evening and combined program students could take any day class after they completed their first-year required courses.[18] The combined program did not increase the number of entering part-time students. In the 1992–93 academic year, 81 students entered the part-time J.D. programs. By 1994, the number declined to 64 and by 2017 it dropped to 28 students. The faculty did not reconsider Wayne's commitment to part-time J.D. legal education.

Dean and Professor Turnover during Downsizing

John Reed, succeeding John Roberts, served as dean from 1987 to 1993. He spent most of his career on the Michigan law faculty and was respected by the Michigan bench and bar. Reed taught by example "the ethical standards that we lawyers aspire to."[19] During his years as dean, the law school continued to rely on its reputation of providing well-trained, practice-ready graduates. In 1987, celebrating the law school's sixtieth anniversary and 7,000 graduates, Dean Reed put the law school's accomplishments into perspective: "When our history is within the span of one professional lifetime, it is clear that we are still relatively young." Wayne had developed "a firm foundation on which to build a more distinguished future."[20] In 1988, Wayne graduates passed the Michigan bar examination on their first try by an exceptionally high 92 percent, slightly higher than the University of Michigan Law School's pass rate.

Two alumni served consecutively as dean of Wayne Law. In 1993, James K. Robinson ('68) became Wayne's seventh dean and first alumnus to serve in

---

18. Faculty Meeting Minutes, April 15, 1992.

19. In 2011, the State Bar of Michigan established the John W. Reed Michigan Lawyer Legacy Award to be awarded periodically to "an educator from a Michigan law school whose influence on lawyers has elevated the quality of legal practice." Wayne Professors Robert Sedler and Alan Schenk were honored to receive this award.

20. One issue of the *Wayne Lawyer* was devoted almost exclusively to the law school's sixtieth anniversary. *Wayne Lawyer* 6 (Fall 1987).

that position.[21] Robinson was well-known and respected in the Detroit and Michigan legal communities. The second was Joan Mahoney ('75), who served from 1998 to 2003. Robinson's deanship (1993–98) straddled the years before and after the Detroit College of Law affiliated with Michigan State University. (Dean Robinson and the subsequent deans are discussed mainly in chapter 7 as part of Wayne Law's response to that DCL move to the MSU campus in East Lansing and the resulting competition for law students.)

Wayne law professors have a long history of publishing books. William Burnham (1980–2008) published a book that he and other American law professors used to teach American law in international programs. Robert Abrams (1978–87), an expert in water and environmental law, coauthored casebooks in both fields with Wayne and former Wayne colleagues.[22] During 1993–95, the faculty published twenty books or chapters of books. Most were books focused on their fields of legal expertise. Three books focused on notorious lawyers and a judge. Kevin Tierney published *Darrow: A Biography*; Jane Friedman published *American's First Woman Lawyer: The Biography of Myra Bradwell*; and Robert Glennon published *The Iconoclast as Reformer: Jerome Frank's Impact on American Law*.

For some Wayne law professors, reputations established through scholarship led to opportunities to consult with practicing lawyers and to serve as experts on legal issues in their fields of expertise. Some Wayne professors engaged in law reform efforts with the American and Michigan bar associations and international institutions. For example, Robert Sedler consulted on constitutional and conflict of law issues. Michael McIntyre and Alan Schenk were involved in tax reform. When they joined the faculty, Noah Hall had been consulting on environmental issues and Charles Brower on international arbitrations.

The faculty's decision to dramatically reduce the size of the entering classes led to a reduction in the number of professors. In its hiring practices, Wayne

---

21. See *Wayne Lawyer* 11 (Summer 1993): 4. This issue of *Wayne Lawyer* includes a discussion of Jim's background.

22. Abrams was the law school's interim dean during the 1986–87 academic year.

law professors placed a high premium on a candidate's scholarship and the likelihood that the person would meet the school's scholarship standard for the grant of tenure. The law school's history of hiring prolific scholars was the main reason why many young scholars left Wayne for higher-ranked schools.

Nineteen professors hired before 1982 remained on the faculty beyond 1995 and provided some stability to the faculty. An equal number of professors and a dean retired or became deans at other schools.[23] From 1982 to 1995, six professors left for positions at other law schools. Nine[24] of the fifteen professors the law school hired between those years were on the faculty in 1995. Many of the roughly thirty professors on the faculty in the fall of 1995 were honored for their scholarship and teaching. The university appointed three as distinguished professors. Several were selected by the students as Professor of the Year, with Janet Findlater receiving that recognition eighteen times. Many received the university's President's Award for Excellence in Teaching and/or the law school's Donald H. Gordon Award for Excellence in Teaching.

Preparing Students for Business Practice

Since the late 1960s, the law school had the strong combination of professors and courses for students who wanted to prepare for a career advising businesses or establishing a business themselves. Dean Joiner, respected by the leading lawyers in Michigan, promoted the school and its graduates. He gave corporate law firm partners the confidence to hire Wayne graduates, who had previously been almost completely excluded from those jobs. Michigan's corporate law firms began to hire more Wayne Law graduates because they found that the Wayne-trained associates hired in the late 1960s were talented, had an enviable work ethic, and were very productive.

---

23. Long-serving professors Samuel Shuman, Richard Strichartz, Kenneth Callahan, and Stephen Schulman retired. Arthur Lombard took the deanship at the Detroit College of Law and Dean John Roberts became the dean at DePaul Law School in Chicago.
24. Four of them, Stephen Calkins, Jonathan Weinberg, Kingsley Browne, and Peter Henning, remained teaching at the law school in 2019.

By the 1980s, judging by the number of graduates hired by corporate law firms in Michigan and the Michigan offices of the international accounting firms, the University of Michigan Law School and Wayne Law became the best sources for legal talent for those firms. Those associates encouraged their firms to hire more Wayne graduates, both men and women.

Graduates singled out some Wayne professors as instrumental in preparing them to litigate banking, bankruptcy, and other commercial disputes[25] and represent business clients in corporate, securities, and tax-planning transactions. Stephen Schulman made Wayne his permanent academic home and taught thousands of students corporate and securities law. Peter Henning replaced Schulman in 1994 and Erica Beecher-Monas joined the faculty in 2005.[26] In 2006, Linda Beale and Susan Cancelosi strengthened the tax faculty with their practice law firm experience. They made long-term commitments to the school.[27] Wayne graduates who focused on transactional practices found that the skills learned in Janet Findlater's Contracts course and Vincent Wellman's Contract Drafting courses prepared them to excel in those fields.[28] The early full-time

---

25. The field of commercial law changed when, starting largely in the 1960s, states adopted the UCC to replace laws governing sales, banking, secured transactions, letters of credit, and other areas of commerce. Separate courses covered buyers in other sales transactions, such as the buyers protected under consumer protection laws. In 1970, the faculty moved the material on the sale of goods, covered in Article 2 of the UCC, to the first-year contracts course. The faculty offered separate courses to cover secured transactions, letters of credit, and other provisions of the UCC.

26. Beecher-Monas taught in the areas of corporate law and evidence, although with her background in the sciences, she was respected for her work on scientific evidence, genetics, and behavioral theory.

27. Some professors who taught transactional courses had shorter stays at Wayne. Edward Greene (1967–68), Paul Harbrecht (1974–83), Joel Resnick (1977–82), Margo Lesser (1981–88), Eric Kades (1995–2002), and Harry Hutchison (2002–6) taught taxation, corporation law, and other transactional courses.

28. Wellman joined the faculty in 1981 after he received his J.D. from Yale and his graduate work in philosophy at the University of Michigan. His scholarship centers on the philosophy of law and on contracts and sales under the UCC. Alumni regularly commended Wellman and Findlater for preparing them to draft contracts and litigate contract disputes. In addition to teaching contracts and contract drafting courses, Wellman taught

professors teaching the UCC and bankruptcy courses stayed several years.[29] John Dolan and Laura Bartell spent their academic careers at Wayne teaching commercial and banking law and bankruptcy. Distinguished Professor John Dolan (1975–2015)[30] replaced David Henson in commercial law and banking.[31]

Some of the pioneering students hired by the corporate law firms established careers in bankruptcy and banking. From the Joiner era, Donald Wagner ('68) developed a strong reputation in bankruptcy. Rasul Raheem ('84) spent thirty years as in-house counsel to Michigan National Bank and LaSalle Bank Corp., and as senior vice president and assistant general counsel for Bank of America before moving to private practice with two major Detroit law firms.

---

criminal law, jurisprudence, and legal process. See *https://law.wayne.edu/profile/aa2882#definition-Biography*.

29. Douglass Boshkoff (1959–63) published books in this field and spent the remainder of his teaching career at the University of Indiana, Bloomington, Maurer School of Law. David Henson (1970–75) was active in the ABA and was a well-known commercial lawyer. At Wayne, he was a demanding teacher but deeply interested in the students, whom he helped obtain legal jobs in Michigan and elsewhere. He worked on the revision of the UCC's Article 9 governing secured transactions, where security interests are taken in personal property, and chaired the ABA's Corporation Banking and Business Law Section and Uniform Commercial Code Committee. He left Wayne to spend the remainder of his academy career at the University of California, Hastings College of Law.

30. Dolan joined the faculty in 1975 after a decade of practicing commercial law and developing expertise in banking law. He developed a specialty in letters of credit and his respected *The Law of Letters of Credit* (1984) was translated into Mandarin. He received many teaching awards, including the President's Award for Excellence in Teaching. He also taught a unique collaborative course with a Detroit law firm. Dolan was elected to the selective Wayne State University Academy of Scholars.

31. Bartell practiced law with Shearman & Sterling, specializing in bank financing and bankruptcy, before joining the faculty in 1996. She published books on secured transactions. She taught bankruptcy law and property and created an innovative course, Effective Oral Communication for Lawyers, designed for law students who wanted to improve the speaking skills demanded in law practice. She served on several important national committees in her field. Supreme Court Chief Justice John Roberts appointed Bartell as associate reporter of the Advisory Committee on Bankruptcy Rules to the Judicial Conference of the United States.

Before and during law school, Michael Sarafa ('97),[32] whose family immigrated from northern Iraq to Detroit, gained experience in government working for a member of the Michigan legislature and for Detroit mayor Dennis Archer's administration. As an evening student, Sarafa enjoyed the diversity of Wayne law students. He found that evening students supported each other; they were in the "same boat," and they wanted everyone to succeed. After graduation, he practiced law and in 2006 became president, CEO, and a director of Bank of Michigan.

Deborah Germany and Candice Coats Moore, both in the Class of 2015, chose the corporate firm route. After a few years, Germany went in house with Chrysler and Moore moved to the Dykema firm, in part as a mergers and acquisitions lawyer.

Careers in National Accounting Firms

The large national accounting firms that provided audit services to business clients also had sizable tax departments, populated with certified public accountants, some of whom were lawyers, and with some non-CPA lawyers.

Before the 1970s, the large Michigan law firms had relatively small tax departments. Michigan's large public companies relied heavily on their accounting firms for their tax and audit work and hired law firms in other cities for important tax services. But as smaller Michigan businesses were growing by "going public" and larger companies were growing by acquiring other companies or merging, the resulting tax issues generated significant legal fees, and the large Michigan law firms started hiring more associates to focus on their growing tax practices.

Law schools traditionally did not offer courses that focused on the importance of accounting in many areas of law practice. Harvard professor David Herwitz popularized an accounting for lawyers course to give students without

---

32. This material was obtained during a videotaped interview with Mr. Sarafa in his office on November 18, 2014.

a business background the opportunity to learn the basics of accounting and auditing that business lawyers in particular must know to discuss accounting-related issues with their clients and their accountants. At Wayne, Alan Schenk offered an intensive two-week, pre–fall term accounting for lawyers course to prepare students without a business background to better understand the vocabulary and relevance of accounting before they tackled the second-year business and commercial courses.[33]

Before the Joiner years, Wayne Law graduates interested in a career in tax rarely if ever were hired by the national accounting firms or the corporate law firms. Some graduates established solo practices or small firms that represented individuals and business, with a focus on tax matters. Erwin Rubenstein ('61) established a boutique tax firm that represented taxpayers in litigation with the government. As previously discussed, three African American graduates in the Class of 1965 established a law firm known for its tax expertise.[34]

Starting in the mid-1970s, the national accounting firms began hiring Wayne graduates for their tax departments. Wayne Law graduates, especially those who came to law school with an accounting or business degree, enjoyed successful careers with those firms. Denton Wolf ('76) and John Grant ('79) spent their careers with Deloitte and Touche (later Deloitte). They became leaders in those firms and helped recruit more Wayne Law students.

According to Joseph Angileri ('84), students from the gritty city law school who came from hard-working, blue-collar families brought with them an entrepreneurial approach to their law school business classes, were not risk-averse, and considered career opportunities beyond the traditional law firm practice. Angileri qualified as a certified public accountant (CPA) before start-ing law school. He received job offers upon law school graduation from five of the then eight national accounting firms and from the General Motors tax staff. Angileri settled on Deloitte and established a mergers and acquisition practice in the firm's Detroit office, adding investment bankers to complement the tax

33. Schenk was a certified public accountant before he obtained a law degree.
34. See Patmon, Young, and Kirk firm discussed in chapter 2.

staff. He led two of the firm's national practices as it expanded its investment banking and financial advisory services practices. He left Deloitte to become president of Compuware, a Detroit-based technology company, and brought his problem-solving skills to his new position.[35]

In the previously male-dominated accounting profession, Wayne women established careers in the tax departments of the national accounting firms.[36] Kathleen Williams Newell ('72) worked with the Michigan Department of Treasury and the Ernst & Young accounting firm. Upon retirement from that firm, she established an elder law practice focusing on tax, estate planning, and probate. Lynn Gandhi ('86) blended family and her career as a tax professional with major law and accounting firms and in corporate tax departments. Gandhi and other women, like Mary Ellen Gurewitz and Aleksandra Miziolek before them, gave future female lawyers the confidence to combine family life and demanding careers.

Margaret Shulman ('97), an immigrant from Russia, became an executive director in the national tax group at Ernst & Young. After graduation from Wayne, Aziza (Pratt) Yuldesheva ('06), who was born in Uzbekistan and raised by parents who were university professors in Ukraine, practiced with a Lansing law firm before joining a national accounting firm. She practiced international tax in the Washington National Tax Office and taught in the firm's educational program. Both women added LL.M.s in taxation to their academic credentials.

Ha Dang ('19) attended law school on a student visa and used an internship in the value added tax (VAT) group of the General Motors tax staff and a VAT tutorial at the law school to obtain an offer to join the VAT staff of a national accounting firm in Chicago.

---

35. Joseph Angileri, interview by the author, May 13, 2016. Angileri's daughter Kylie was a 2013 graduate of the law school.
36. For the increase in the number of women practicing in the accounting profession, see https://www.catalyst.org/research/women-in-accounting.

New and Growing Specialty Areas

Wayne graduates continued to practice law in traditional areas representing individuals and businesses, but they also used their legal education to pursue a wide variety of other, emerging areas of law.[37]

Sports and Entertainment Law

The law school relied heavily on adjunct professors to teach sports and entertainment law. For example, Howard Hertz ('76) taught entertainment law and represented authors and entertainers in the music industry, including author Elmore Leonard and entertainer Eminem.[38]

Carl C. Poston III, after receiving his Wayne J.D. in 1982 and a New York University LL.M. in taxation, practiced law with O'Melveny & Myers in Los Angeles and then established Professional Sports Planning in Houston, through which he represented many prominent professional athletes like Charles Woodson and Penny Hardaway. Gregory Reed (LL.M. '79) represented entertainers and public figures like civil rights icon Rosa Parks.

Some graduates found success in the entertainment industry. Gary Hardwick ('85), president of the Student Board of Governors, entertained his law school professors and classmates with his wit and his scripts for the year-end Wayne State Law School Review that poked fun at all of them. After law school graduation, Hardwick worked as the staff writer and then became the executive producer for *In the House*, a television series that aired in the late 1990s. He directed motion pictures as well, including *The Brothers* (2001), *Deliver Us from Eva* (2003), and *Universal Remote* (2007). Hardwick also wrote several books, including *Grind City*, a Danny Cavanaugh Mystery (2016), and *Dear Baby Jesus: Letter to the Savior* (2018).

---

37. Pamela Morgan ('06) established Third Key Solutions, a consulting and cryptographic key management firm that specializes in decentralized digital currencies and asset-tokens.

38. https://law.wayne.edu/news/love-of-music-led-wayne-law-alumnus-to-discover-entertainment-law-33417.

Health, Environment, Intellectual Property, and the Internet

While the size of the entering classes declined from the 1980s, the law school expanded its offerings in growing areas of law practice, including health and environmental law, patent law, and the Internet.

In the twenty-first century the law school added Peter Hammer (2003–present) and Lance Gable (2006–present), whose research and writing included domestic and international health law. Hammer taught and did research on domestic health law and policy.[39] Gable taught public health law, bioethics and the law, and advanced topics in health care seminars.[40] Wayne did not just start offering health-related courses in 2003. In 1969, the law school hired Ralph Slovenko,[41] one of the school's most well-known professors nationally and internationally. Slovenko, a respected expert on forensic psychology, wrote about law and psychiatry and team-taught a course in this field with Wayne medical school psychiatrist Elliot Luby.[42]

Wayne alumni represented claimants and health care facilities in medical malpractice cases. They included Carlos Escurel ('01),[43] who defended medical malpractice claims.

Starting in 1976, the faculty hired a number of professors whose teaching and research focused on environmental and water law.[44] Zygmunt Plater

---

39. Hammer (2003–present) is discussed in connection with his international health care work and his position with the Keith Center for Civil Rights.
40. During 2013–17, Gable was the law school's interim associate dean, associate dean, and interim dean. he served as a lecturer at Georgetown University's School of Foreign Service and as scholar and senior fellow at the Centers for Law and Public's Health, a collaborative of Georgetown and Johns Hopkins.
41. Slovenko (1969–2013) completed psychiatric training at Tulane Medical School and a residency in psychiatry at the Menninger Clinic. With this background in law and psychiatry, he was a respected expert on forensic psychology and served on editorial boards of journals specializing in psychiatry and the law.
42. Jane Friedman (1971–2002) taught law and medicine and was best known for her book *America's First Woman Lawyer: The Biography of Myra Bradwell* (Prometheus, 1993).
43. Carlos Escurel litigated complex medical malpractice claims and premises liability claims and defended physicians before state licensing boards.
44. Before law schools were regularly offering courses on environmental law, Geoffrey Lanning (1969–88) developed a course that focused on environmental law.

(1976–82)[45] taught environmental and property law at Wayne while he was litigating a case to save the snail darter by delaying the construction of the Tennessee Valley Authority's Tellico Dam. Gunther Handl's (1982–96) research centered in part on international environmental law and law of the sea.[46] Robert Abrams (1978–87) overlapped with Professors Plater and Handl. Abrams taught and coauthored casebooks on water and environmental law.[47]

After almost ten years without a full-time environmental law professor, in 2005, the faculty hired Noah Hall from his position with the National Wildlife Federation's Water Resources Program.[48] He created the first Transnational Environmental Law Clinic, focusing on water rights.[49] In that clinic, students examined governmental environmental policy in connection with the Great Lakes Environmental Law Center.

Some Wayne graduates pursued careers in environmental law. Nicolas Schroeck ('07) joined the faculty to direct the Transnational Environmental Law Clinic and served as executive director of the Great Lakes Environmental Law Center. Among many others with legal careers in environmental law, Krishna Dighe ('87) served as senior counsel in the Environmental Crimes Section of the U.S. Department of Justice. Jeffrey Flocken ('94) was the North American regional director of the International Fund for Animal Welfare,

---

45. Plater left Wayne for a position at Boston College Law School.

46. Handl taught environmental law and international law courses at Wayne before moving to Tulane. He was founder and editor in chief of the *Yearbook of International Environmental Law*.

47. *Legal Control of Water Resources* (with Barton Thompson Jr., John Leshy, & Sandra Zellmer, 6th ed., 2018) and *Environmental Law and Policy: Nature Law and Society* (with Zygmunt J. B. Plater, Lisa Heinzerling, David A. Wirth, and Noah D. Hall, 5th ed., 2016). Abrams was interim dean in 1986–87.

48. Hall also served as assistant director of the Minnesota Center for Environmental Advocacy. He focused his research and much of his teaching on environmental and water law, including environmental governance, federalism, and transboundary pollution and resource management.

49. Hall was appointed as an independent prosecutor in the Flint, Michigan, case involving the lead poisoning of household drinking water.

advocating for U.S. and Canadian government involvement in wildlife conservation and animal welfare.[50]

Kathryn White, a patent law expert and registered patent agent, joined the Wayne Law faculty in 1996.[51] White was appointed by the U.S. secretary of commerce to the U.S. Patent and Trademark Office Patent Public Advisory Committee. She also served on the U.S. Department of Agriculture's Plant Variety Protection Office Advisory Board. Wayne Law has a long history of educating engineers and scientists who became patent lawyers, including Ed Fish ('87) and Corey M. Beaubien ('06). Stuart Rattner ('11) assists academics in the commercialization of their research into patents.[52]

Jonathan Weinberg (1988–present), the inaugural Associate Dean for Research and Faculty Development, is a prolific scholar[53] who has taught courses on constitutional law and immigration as well as communications law and the Internet. He also taught a seminar on law and cyberspace. He chaired an ICANN[54] working group to make recommendations on creating more Internet top-level domains.[55] Carol Romej (LL.M. '01) and Coline Battersby ('07) practiced in this field.

---

50. Flocken was an endangered species specialist for the National Wildlife Federation. See https://www.cnn.com/2015/05/19/opinions/trophy-hunting-not-conservation-flocken/index.html. He promoted conservation publicly, such as on the CNN film *Trophy*.

51. Eric M. Dobrusin and Katherine E. White, *Intellectual Property Litigation: Pretrial Practice*, 4th ed. (Walters Kluwer, 2019). White taught contracts and patent law and coauthored a treatise covering pretrial practice in intellectual property litigation. She served as a White House Fellow, as well as a Fulbright Senior Scholar at the Max Planck Institute for Foreign and International Patent, Copyright, and Competition Law in Munich, Germany. She also served on the University of Michigan's Board of Regents.

52. Other alumni who practiced in this field included Eric Dobrusin, Bill Gottschalk, Marc Larelli, Chris Darrow, Nadine Mustafa, Daniella Walters, and Lauren Edelman Willens.

53. See Weinberg's profile at https://law.wayne.edu/profile/aa1903#definition-Biography. He was "a visiting scholar at the University of Tokyo's Institute of Journalism and Communication Studies; . . . a professor in residence at the U.S. Justice Department; [and] a legal scholar in residence at the Federal Communications Commission."

54. ICANN is the Internet Corporation for Assigned Names and Numbers. It administers the Internet domain name system.

55. Weinberg taught constitutional law, communications law, immigration law, administrative law, and seminars covering citizenship and law in cyberspace. He contributed

John Rothchild (2001–present) came to the law school from the Federal Trade Commission's Bureau of Consumer Protection, where he specialized in Internet-based fraud and online compliance issues. Rothchild taught, among other courses, the Law of Electronic Commerce, Copyright Law, Trademarks and Unfair Competition, and International Intellectual Property Law.[56] Anna Buddle ('96), Michelle Visser ('98), and Lauren Willens ('15) practiced with a focus on copyright and trademark issues.

Family Law

Starting in 1966 and continuing for more than fifty years, the law school had four professors who focused their writing and teaching on various aspects of family law, child custody and adoption, domestic violence, LGBT rights, and critical race theory. They were Frederica Lombard, Janet Findlater, Adele Morrison, and Sarah Abramowicz.[57] Each brought a different background and research focus to these areas of the law.

Dean Lombard and Professor Findlater each taught at Wayne for forty years or more. Lombard taught family law and served as associate dean from 1992 to 2005. Findlater, discussed later, focused on family law and domestic violence.

Adele Morrison taught family law and the child, family and the state, and the sex, sexuality and the law seminar in addition to criminal law. Before

---

op-ed pieces on current legal issues in the print media and has served as a panelist on programs and symposia on immigration law and privacy in the digital age. Weinberg's scholarship includes articles on the U.S. Constitution, First Amendment on privacy, on Internet, communications, and administrative law, and on the regulation of broadcasting and other electronic media. His recent Cambridge University Press book covers identity and privacy in the digital world. He also taught a seminar on citizenship, food and drug law, and radio and TV regulation.

56. He coauthored a widely adopted casebook, *Internet Commerce: The Emerging Legal Framework* (Foundation Press, 2005). He also wrote an article on preventing the unauthorized use of copyrighted material. He was the associate dean from 2008 to 2013.

57. Occasionally a member of the faculty who focused on other areas of the law would teach family law. For example, Distinguished Professor John Dolan taught the course once or twice.

entering academia, Morrison practiced with lesbian rights, civil rights, and civil justice organizations, as well as a commission addressing sexual assault.[58]

Sarah Abramowicz taught family law.[59] She wrote about adoption and the history of child custody law. In her research, she also explored the intersection of family law pertaining to children and other legal disciplines, such as contract law.

Many graduates focused their practices on family-related issues. Harvey Baskin ('57) gained notoriety when he represented a father in a highly publicized biracial custody case.[60] Carlo Martina ('79) developed a family law practice, employing multiple approaches for divorcing clients, including the innovative collaborative law. One group of Wayne Law female graduates joined together to create a boutique family law firm. In 1994, four women who graduated in the 1970s and 1980s opened an all-women law firm in Ann Arbor to "look at family as a whole, and do the least damage to the family."[61]

Politics and Representing Government

Some Wayne Law graduates entered politics. To name only a few, Gary Peters ('89) was elected in 2014 to replace Carl Levin in the U.S. Senate. Peters previously served as congressman for Michigan's 14th Congressional District and in the Michigan State Senate. Dennis Hertel ('74) was elected in the early 1980s to the U.S. House of Representatives from Michigan's 14th Congressional District. Lynn Rivers ('92) was elected to the U.S. Congress, representing Michigan's 13th Congressional District and served from 1995 to 2003. Dan DeGrow ('78) served in the Michigan Senate. Virgil Smith Jr. ('72), Gerald Law ('74), and Nick Ciaramitaro ('78) all served in the Michigan House of Representatives.[62]

---

58. Morrison directed Washington University School of Law's Civil Justice Clinic as a visiting professor. Her scholarship focused on critical race theory and LGBT rights.

59. She also taught contracts and law and literature.

60. See *Damaschke v. Damaschke*, 21 Mich App 80, 174 N.W. 2d 608 (1970).

61. See Rebecca Sweet, *Wayne Lawyer* (Winter 1995): 31–32. The organizers were Margaret Nichols ('77), Monika Sachs ('78), Eileen Slank ('86), and Rebecca Sweet ('83).

62. See *Wayne Lawyer* 4 (Spring 1985): 12.

Some alumni preferred to work for people in political office early in their post-law school careers. David Clanton ('69), discussed earlier, worked on Senator Griffin's staff before his appointment to the Federal Tax Commission staff. Linda Gustitus ('75) served on Senator Levin's staff, as staff director of the U.S. Senate Subcommittee on Oversight and several other positions before joining the Levin Center at Wayne Law. Matthew Schenk ('96) served on the staff of a number of public figures and government entities, including chief of staff for Wayne County Executive Robert Ficano and as chief operating officer of the City of Detroit Water Board before establishing a government affairs law practice. Some alumni represented units of government as city attorney or outside counsel. Edward Zelenak ('77) served as city attorney for the cities of Lincoln Park and Southgate, Michigan.

Indian Law and Islamic Law

The law school attracted students from diverse religious, racial, and ethnic backgrounds. Over the years, the faculty taught courses that addressed those differences and how the law affected those communities. Professors taught courses or seminars on civil rights, Jewish law, law and religion, Indian law, and Islamic law.

Kirsten Carlson (2011–present) was one of the few Wayne Law professors engaged in extensive social science research, with much of it focused on Indian law. She received the largest social science grant in the school's history, to serve as the principal investigator on a National Science Foundation Law and Social Science Program grant. In terms of law reform, she focused on possible strategies for Indian nations and indigenous groups to seek the reform of federal law and policy. She taught federal Indian law[63] and legislation.[64] Theresa Pouley

---

63. She also taught civil procedure.

64. Carlson held an adjunct appointment in Wayne's Department of Political Science. She received the Donald H. Gordon Award for Excellence in Teaching and was the students' choice for first-year Professor of the Year. She held a university career development chair, was one of two inaugural Levin Center Research Scholars, and received an Outstanding Junior Faculty Award from the Wayne State Academy of Scholars.

('87) was chief judge of the Tulalip tribal court and President Obama appointed her to the Indian Law and Order Commission. Zach Fallstitch ('06) served on the Michigan Indian Legal Services Board.

In 2020, the law school hired Khaled Beydoun as its first full-time professor to teach Islamic law. Beydoun also served as associate director of Civil Rights and Social Justice at the Damon J. Keith Center for Civil Rights.[65]

Legal Research and Writing Faculty

Legal research and writing are essential skills required for lawyers engaged in litigation or transactional practices. When the law school expanded its Legal Research and Writing (LRW) program in the mid- to late 1960s, practicing lawyers taught the course. The content of the course depended on the instructor and his or her conception of the basic legal skills that new lawyers needed. Starting during the Joiner deanship in 1970, the faculty hired full-time LRW instructors on one-year contracts. LRW instructors spend countless hours with first-year students, acclimating them to the kind of research and writing that they must master to succeed in law school and in the legal profession.

The program expanded and Cheryl Scott (1977–83) served as the first director of the LRW program staffed with full-time instructors. The director established a basic curriculum and wrote research problems. The instructors followed the prescribed curriculum, so that all first-year students were evaluated on the same research and writing skills.

Diana Pratt joined the faculty in 1981 and served as the second director from 1983 to 2007. Pratt authored the LRW book that was used at Wayne and many other law schools.[66] Kristin Theut-Newa joined the faculty in 1999

---

65. He wrote *American Islamophobia: Understanding the Roots and Rise of Fear* (University of California Press, 2018) and is coeditor of *Islamophobia and the Law* (Cambridge University Press, 2020).

66. Pratt published several editions of a book to be used in the course "Legal Writing: A Systematic Approach" (American Casebook Series). In 2007, she received the Thomas

and directed the program for many years.[67] The faculty started hiring LRW instructors on contracts extending beyond a year. Some taught at Wayne for a decade or more, including Kathryn Day and Amy Neville.

Business Opportunities for Entrepreneurial Students

Over the years, Wayne Law attracted entrepreneurial students who pursued opportunities in business. William Davidson ('49) turned a family business into the global Guardian Industries.[68] Stephen Ross ('65) and Dan Gilbert ('87) had outsized impacts on New York City and Detroit.

Stephen Ross ('65) spent his elementary school years living in a two-family house in a middle-class neighborhood of Detroit. He rebelled when his family took him out of Mumford High in the middle of ninth grade to move to Florida. He did not adjust well to Miami Beach, did not apply himself in high school, yet he desperately wanted to attend the University of Michigan. With that goal in mind, after two years of academic success at the University of Florida, he transferred to the University of Michigan and spent his summers with his high school friends in Detroit. After college graduation, he planned to enroll in Michigan's MBA program, but with his draft notice expected, he found the longer law school program more appealing. Being too late to apply to Michigan's law school, in 1962 he enrolled in Wayne Law with his University of Michigan roommate Michael Friedman.

Blackwell award. See https://lawprofessors.typepad.com/legalwriting/2007/08/diana-pratt -nam.html. John Dernbach and Richard Singleton, two of Wayne's LRW faculty, coauthored another legal research and writing book in 1981, *A Practical Guide to Legal Writing and Legal Method* (Rothman, 1981).

67. Michael McFerren served as director in 2007, and Anne Marie Burr directed the program from 2009 until 2013.

68. Hughes Potiker ('52), after practicing law, became a pioneer in the discount entertainment coupon book industry. Michael Timmis ('65) pursued a dual career in law and business. He and his investors established the Talon companies to "turn around" businesses in financial trouble.

Ross remembered his Wayne professors as well-qualified teachers who challenged their students and singled out his tax professor Donald Gordon as "at the top" of that faculty. Ross developed an interest in taxation and, after graduation, earned an LL.M. in taxation from New York University. With very good credentials in the tax field, he sought a position with one of the large Detroit law firms. He had several interviews at one, but he could not break the "Jewish" barrier that existed at some Detroit firms at the time. He practiced in Detroit for two years in the tax department of a national accounting firm, finding his work structuring real estate transactions exciting.

Stephen Ross was a risk-taker. On June 6, 1968, the day after Robert Kennedy was killed, a partner at his firm asked him if he would like to attend a tax seminar in New York City. "The words just came out of my mouth. I think I'd like to go to New York for good." He quit the next day, notwithstanding an offer from his firm to transfer him to its New York office. His mother "thought that he was nuts." This decision, made without much thought, was "the best decision in my life." He wanted a career in business.

After working for one investment banking firm for about a year and a half, he joined Bear Stearns's corporate and finance department. He structured a real estate development program that employed the relatively new federal income tax incentive for government-subsidized housing. When the head of his department criticized his subsidized housing project, Ross had some choice words for him and he left (was fired).

Ross wanted his own real estate company. With his experience in structuring real estate transactions, Ross brought together a group with expertise in real estate development, construction, and syndication. Instead of serving as the person who structures the "deal" and receives a small ownership interest, Ross established his own company to pursue the project. He built a successful New York real estate development company, the Related Companies, LP, from this first low-income housing project.

In this and future business dealings, Ross combined his passion for business with his desire to promote social goals: "Dreams happen by work and grow by passion." Ross had passion in his voice when he discussed his Hudson

Stephen Ross. (Reprinted with permission)

Yards project in Manhattan—the largest urban real estate project undertaken in the United States. It was a massive live-work-play redevelopment project that changed "the center of gravity in the city" and served as "a model of what a sustainable city should be."[69]

Ross's investment in the Miami Dolphins provided another opportunity for him to accomplish a social "good" in line with his business interests. When a Dolphins player claimed that he was bullied and subjected to racial comments within the team, Ross established the Ross Initiative in Sports for Equality (RISE) as a "nonprofit organization dedicated to promoting understanding, respect and equality."[70] With Ross, "do well by doing good" is not a cliché. It is his philosophy that dominates his professional and charitable life. Ross received the ROBIE Lifetime Achievement Award from the Jackie Robinson Foundation for his work promoting "social justice, excellence and human dignity."[71]

Daniel Gilbert credits his father and grandfather with instilling an interest in business in him.[72] After graduating from Michigan State University, Gilbert got his real estate broker's license. To be successful as a broker, Gilbert had to attract customers, so he bought a "For Sale" sign and placed it on the front lawn of his parents' home during the day. The sign included his mobile phone number; when someone called, he tried to interest them in a home for which he was agent.

Gilbert enrolled at Wayne Law because his mother told him that he should become a lawyer, but his passion was not in law, and his class attendance was not exemplary.[73]

---

69. "Our goal is to harness the unifying power of sport to advance race relations and drive social progress." The open plaza in the center will be larger than Trafalgar Square in London.

70. http://www.risetowin.org.

71. The material in this section comes from Stephen Ross, interview by the author, New York City, June 9, 2015.

72. Gilbert says Thomas Peters's books *Passion for Excellence* and *Search for Excellence* influenced his approach to business.

73. In the 1980s, law professors were not required under the ABA accreditation standards to take attendance and to penalize students who failed to attend class regularly. Years later, the ABA emphasized classroom attendance as an essential part of a legal education and

Like Ross, Gilbert was a risk-taker. While a law student in 1985, Gilbert, his brother, and a friend rented space in a suburban Detroit strip mall for the summer and opened a real estate mortgage business. They decided that if the business was successful that summer, they would extend the lease; if not, they would close. Rock Financial, followed by Quicken Loans, the Rocket Companies, and Gilbert's other businesses, grew from that modest beginning.

By 1998, Rock Financial went public, selling 27 percent of the company's shares to public shareholders. Rock Financial (predecessor to Quicken Loans) sold its mortgage business to Intuit,[74] with Gilbert and his management team retained to operate the business. After a couple of years, Gilbert and a group of investors repurchased the Quicken Loans company at a deeply discounted price.

Gilbert built the Rocket Companies, a series of businesses around the Quicken Loans real estate mortgage business. According to Gilbert, his companies motivate "people to achieve things that they never thought that they could." He believes that business managers must be innovative and creative and business owners must be willing to take risks. In his view, a business that remains static is taking the greater risk.

Gilbert's mortgage lending business operated in the Detroit suburbs, but he made the risky business decision to move the business to Detroit when he was having difficulty recruiting talented employees who wanted to work in a vibrant urban area. To attract those employees, he decided that his business had to be in the City. "From day one, there has been a different energy in our business and we never looked back."

---

criticized member schools in reaccreditation reports if the school did not adopt and enforce attendance requirements.

Dan was an A student in the author's taxation class. He remembers that grade since he was so busy creating a business while attending law school that he did not have a lot of those As.

74. A couple weeks later, the new companies of Silicon Valley crashed. Gilbert and his management team continued to manage the company. Ironically Quicken Loans became too large a part of Intuit's business, so for accounting and other reasons, Intuit decided to sell the company back, along with the Quicken Loans name.

Daniel Gilbert addressing Wayne Law students. (Reproduced with permission of the law school)

Dan Gilbert reinvigorated the City of Detroit. He not only moved his employees to the city but provided incentives for them to rent or buy in Detroit. A Gilbert company then acquired a large swath of downtown Detroit commercial properties in order to gain control over the future development of the core city. Gilbert's revitalization of Detroit was described in 2013 as "one of the most ambitious privately financed urban reclamation projects in American history."[75] With Detroit's new vitality, some prospective students applied to Wayne Law because the law school was located within Detroit.

Since the 1980s, many more alumni chose to establish a business rather than represent business. Alyssa Martina ('82) started a publishing company,

---

75. Much of the material in this section is from Daniel Gilbert, interview by the author, Detroit, September 22, 2015. David Segal, "Motor City Missionary," *New York Times*, Sunday Business, April 14, 2013, 1.

Metro Parent Publishing Group, that specialized in family-focused publications. David Galbenski ('93) created Lumen Legal, which supplied legal staffing, contracts outsourcing, and document review on a short-term basis to a variety of companies and law firms.[76]

Eric Ersher ('94) became interested in business at an early age. His father operated a number of businesses during Eric's childhood. After law school, Ersher practiced with a suburban Detroit law firm but soon learned that law practice did not suit him. He and a partner founded Zoup, a chain of restaurants that specialized in one dish—soup—and he built an international franchise business from those Zoup restaurants.

Some Wayne graduates, like Stephanie Hoos, Thomas Cronkright, and Lawrence Duthler, started businesses while continuing to practice law. Hoos ('99) initially worked for the global law firm Mintz, Levin, Cohn, Ferris, Glovsky and Popeo, PC in Manhattan, where she focused on corporate transactional work for large institutional clients. But the demanding life of a new law firm associate was not enough to satisfy her creative interests. After just a few years, Hoos (whose father, E. Lou Hoos, was a 1968 graduate) founded, designed, and marketed her own luxury swimsuit collection on the side.[77] Her designs were included in global runway shows and were routinely featured in top fashion magazines.[78] She left law firm life to join Barry Diller's technology/media conglomerate, IAC, as in-house counsel and relocated to the West Coast to head the legal department for TBWA\Media Arts Lab in Los Angeles.[79]

Thomas Cronkright and Lawrence Duthler,[80] both from the Class of 2000, spent their youth and college years working in their families' small-town

---

76. Lexitas acquired Lumen Legal in 2020.

77. For a story about Stephanie and E. Lou Hoos, see "Stephanie Hoos '99—Contrasting Successes," *Wayne Lawyer* 22 (Spring 2005): 63.

78. Ibid., 65. Her collection was featured in *Elle*, *Harper's Bazaar*, and *Vogue* and on the cover of *WWD* and *Esquire*. Paris Hilton and other celebrities have been photographed wearing her swimsuits.

79. TBWA\Media Arts Lab is a creative agency dedicated to Apple.

80. Material about Cronkright and Duthler was obtained during a video interview with them at their Sun Title headquarters in Grand Rapids, Michigan, on April 14, 2016.

businesses[81] in the Grand Rapids area. Cronkright's grandfather started a hardware store in Cedar Springs. His father and uncle joined the business, but Cronkright recognized the impact Big Box stores were having on small businesses and chose not to join. Duthler's father had an insurance agency and small business consulting practice. He helped his father's clients with bookkeeping and, not surprisingly, he qualified as a CPA before deciding on law school.

Duthler and Cronkright were not accepted by the University of Michigan's law school because their LSAT scores were "not great." They met at a lunch table at Wayne Law just after grades in their first semester were posted. With their common background and mutual success in those classes, they decided to team up. With their stellar performances in their first year, they could have transferred to Michigan Law School, but they decided to stay at Wayne.

They both said that Wayne Law was a perfect fit for them. They thrived with the law school's attention to theory while providing a "practical" legal education. Duthler joined the *Wayne Law Review* and Cronkright the Student Trial Advocacy Program (later renamed Mock Trial). They treated their legal education as a job and spent the next two years preparing detailed outlines in each course and studying together for spring examinations while walking for hours around Kensington Metropark situated between Milford and South Lyon, Michigan. They appreciated Wayne's "billion-dollar degree" and summarized their legal education as "three years of teaching gray." According to Cronkright, "I would never trade the law degree and experience at Wayne for any degree on the planet."

Duthler and Cronkright intended to return to the Grand Rapids area after law school. With their academic records, they had offers from the best law firms in Grand Rapids. They both joined the Warner Norcross firm and then moved to two other Grand Rapids firms. They concentrated their practices on business and venture capital transactions.

They are risk-takers, like Daniel Gilbert and Stephen Ross and many other Wayne alumni. While continuing to practice law, they qualified as real estate

---

81. Duthler worked for BDO Siedman after passing the CPA exam and before starting law school.

brokers, purchased real estate, and started several new businesses, including an automobile dealership and a mortgage brokerage.[82]

Cronkright and Duthler found that pursuing these multiple ventures while practicing law full-time was not working. They decided to focus on one business, Sun Title, the real estate title business that they started in Rockford, Michigan, five years after their law school graduation. They devoted themselves to Sun as they had devoted themselves to succeed at Wayne Law. They identified a need for a title company that focused on providing customer service. Duthler focused on operations, writing the company manual while attracting and retaining employees. Cronkright focused on client relationships—attracting and retaining customers. As business owners, Duthler and Cronkright no longer had to maintain "billable hours." They could "pick the 100 hours a week that they worked in the business." They were involved in economic development in Rockford as well, and also found time to support the Children's Assessment Center, a local charity that counsels children who are victims of sexual assault.

Jeffrey Aronoff ('04) took a leave from his business practice with a Detroit corporate law firm to operate D:hive, a nonprofit that helps individuals identify community resources to live, work, and build a business in the City of Detroit. He returned to law practice and served part-time as director of the law school's Program for Entrepreneurship and Business Law.

In 2016, a group of law students from the classes of 2013 and 2017[83] founded a start-up, Golfler, which relied on a mobile application for golfers to reserve tee times and obtain weather forecasts and, while playing golf, order food, a beverage, or equipment to be delivered from the course's clubhouse to the player on the course.

---

82. They started a company in California to exploit their patent on mobile technology to process title insurance applications.

83. The original participants were Jason Pearsall ('13), Jordan Jones ('13), and Frank Oyelade ('17). See "Alumni, Student Leading Successful Startup App for Golfers," *Wayne Lawyer* 31 (Winter 2016): 10–11.

7

Focusing on Priorities

In the mid-1990s, Wayne Law was thriving. Recent graduates were finding jobs and passing the bar examination. Graduates were recognized in the profession.

In focus groups in the mid-1990s, Wayne law students touted the value and quality of their legal education, their success on the Michigan bar examination, and their opportunities in the postgraduation job market. They recognized the importance of Wayne alumni serving in positions of influence within and outside the legal profession.[1]

In the 1990s, women accounted for about 45 percent of Wayne Law's entering classes, but its 14–16.5 percent minority enrollment was below the 20 percent national average.[2] In the five years between 1992 and 1997, the faculty published 31 books and 141 book chapters and journal articles. In those years, Wayne enrolled between 690 and 760 J.D. students. Wayne attracted many international students qualified as lawyers in their home country who were interested in a Wayne LL.M. to qualify to take the Michigan bar examination.[3]

---

1. This information comes from a 1997 briefing book for new university president Irvin Reid.
2. Data provided by law school registrar Rebecca Hollancid.
3. A memo from Professor William Burnham in March 1996 urged the faculty to establish an LL.M. for Foreign Lawyers. International students stopped coming to Wayne in large

The ABA analyzed the July 1995 bar examination passage rates for 181 law schools, comparing each school with the other law schools in that state. Wayne students performed much better than the average student who took the Michigan bar examination. The ABA also used that standard to compare Wayne's relative rank within Michigan with the relative rankings of law schools in other states. Wayne's relative bar passage rate "ranked 15th in the nation, tied with Columbia, and ahead of Harvard, Yale, Northwestern and many other leading law schools."[4] Wayne student success on the Michigan bar examination continued. Wayne's first-time takers had the highest bar passage rate, 97 percent, on the July 1996 examination, and were tied for the highest passage rate on the February 1997 exam. Twenty-five years later, in the July 2020 bar examination, Wayne Law had the highest overall pass rate (90 percent) in the state.[5]

Women started enrolling in law school in larger numbers, beginning in the 1970s. By the late 1990s, Wayne women were among the leaders in the Michigan bench and bar. In 1997, the Michigan Supreme Court became the first state Supreme Court with women justices in the majority.[6] Three of those four women were Wayne Law alumni: Dorothy Comstock Riley ('49), Patricia Boyle ('63), and Marilyn Kelly ('71), the newest Justice. Justice Riley remarked in 1998, when the law school honored her, that the award "means that you have not forgotten that I belong to you, that we have claims on one another and that we can look forward to sharing our memories and dreams yet to come."[7] Women

---

numbers after a Michigan Supreme Court rule no longer allowed foreign-trained lawyers with only an American LL.M. to take the Michigan bar examination.

4. "Dean's Column," *Wayne Lawyer* 15 (Summer 1997): 2.

5. The pass rate for Wayne's first-time takers was 93 percent, one percentage point behind the University of Michigan. For bar exam statistics, see https://www.courts.michigan.gov/courts/supreme-court/; https://www.courts.michigan.gov/4a5e12/siteassets/committees,-boards-special-initiatves/ble/statistics/exam-statistics-2000-february-2021.pdf.

6. See "Women in the Supreme Court," *Wayne Lawyer* 15 (Summer 1997): 8. This article provides a helpful history of women practicing law and becoming judges on state and federal courts.

7. See "Remarks by Justice Dorothy Comstock Riley," *Wayne Lawyer* (Summer 1998): 13.

continued to take the bench, including Debra Nance ('99) on Michigan's 46th District Court in suburban Detroit.

In 1998, for the first time, women held the presidencies in all three Detroit-area county bar associations, and all three graduated from WSU Law.[8]

First Competitive Challenge in Decades

With the 1995 Detroit College of Law's affiliation with Michigan State University, Wayne's law school faced a challenge to its decades-long status as the law school of choice after the University of Michigan for applicants to a law school in Michigan. DCL's move to the MSU Big 10 campus in East Lansing, with its athletic teams and other campus amenities and its name change to Michigan State University College of Law, increased the school's appeal.

For decades, Michigan State University wanted to add a law school. In 1972, a Michigan legislature Special Joint Committee on Legal Education concluded that there was a need for another public law school in Michigan and that Michigan State University should add a law school focused on public service and interdisciplinary offerings.[9] In 1985, however, Michigan Governor Blanchard's Commission on the Future of Higher Education in Michigan, chaired by James K. Robinson, opposed any publicly funded expansion of advanced degree

---

8. The three bar associations were Detroit, Oakland, and Macomb. They were Detroit Bar president Lisa Sewell DeMoss ('77); Oakland Bar president Kelly Allen ('83); and Macomb Bar president Lori Finazzo ('86). In 2017, fifteen Wayne Law graduates were among the Notable Women Lawyers in Michigan. The women were recognized by Crain Content Studio.

9. That report claimed that the University of Michigan and Wayne State University's public law schools exceeded their optimum educational capacity and that Michigan Supreme Court Justice Thomas Brennan intended to establish a private law school in Lansing. Brennan organized the private Thomas Cooley Law School in Lansing in 1972, which expanded to other locations and in some years with an almost open admissions policy boasted the largest student body in the country. Cooley attracted students from around the country who were not admitted to a law school in their state of residence or had other reasons to attend Cooley. Cooley became affiliated with Western Michigan University but remained legally and financially independent. The affiliation is scheduled to end in 2023.

programs such as law schools at state universities.[10] In 1993, the same James Robinson ('68) became Wayne's seventh dean,[11] and a university report in 1995 detailed why the state did not need a third public law school.

The Detroit College of Law, a freestanding private, not-for-profit law school in downtown Detroit, operated in the shadow of the University of Detroit Law School just two miles from Wayne's law school in Midtown Detroit. The ABA's 1993 Reaccreditation Report on the Detroit College of Law found that the school, largely due to its deficient physical plant, was not in compliance with ABA accreditation standards. In November 1994, DCL publicly announced that it intended to move out of Detroit.[12]

DCL's need for a university affiliation and MSU's desire to add a law school coalesced. In 1995, DCL affiliated with and became largely administered by Michigan State University. By 1997, the Detroit College of Law at Michigan State University moved to a newly constructed law school building on the Michigan State campus in East Lansing and ultimately changed its name to the Michigan State University College of Law (MSU Law).

Comparing Wayne and DCL/MSU, a Princeton Review of law schools, using 1997 data, painted a picture of two quite dissimilar law schools. DCL/MSU's tuition was more than double Wayne's in-state tuition. Graduates from Wayne had an average debt of $27,000, compared to DCL/MSU's $48,000. Ninety-one percent of Wayne Law graduates, compared with DCL/MSU's 79 percent, were working in law-related jobs six months after graduation.

In 1997, despite its move to the MSU campus, DCL/MSU Law remained largely the same school that existed in downtown Detroit.[13] Wayne Law did

---

10. The study was titled "Putting Our Minds Together: New Directions for Michigan Higher Education."

11. See *Wayne Lawyer* 11 (Summer 1993): 4. This issue of the *Wayne Lawyer* includes a discussion of Robinson's background.

12. The planned new Detroit Tigers stadium would take property the DCL students had been using for parking.

13. See generally, "Formalizing a Significant Law Presence at Michigan State University: In Assessment and Support of Establishing a Law College Affiliation between the Detroit College of Law and Michigan State University as Part of a Comprehensive Law Alliance,"

not lose many applicants to the relocated school, and Wayne students still had higher credentials.[14] The large Michigan law firms continued to hire significantly more Wayne than DCL/MSU graduates.

The "establishment" of a second law school in Michigan on a Big 10 campus required Wayne Law to take significant steps to maintain its highly credentialed, racially diverse student body whose graduates received offers for the most attractive legal jobs. DCL/MSU attracted students with its name and location and, charging private school tuition, the newly affiliated school had the resources to provide scholarships to attract desirable students.

Michigan's Proposition 2 made it more difficult for Wayne Law to maintain its commitment to students of color. In 2006, Michigan voters adopted Proposition 2, amending the Michigan Constitution to prohibit public educational institutions from discriminating against or granting preferential treatment to any person or group "on the basis of race, sex, color, ethnicity, or national origin in the operation of public employment, public education, or public contracting."[15]

When it affiliated in 1995, MSU Law described itself as a private, independent "law college academically integrated into MSU" but not financially supported with state funds.[16] If MSU Law was indeed a private law school, the Michigan Constitution's prohibition against public universities giving a preference in admission to applicants on the basis of their race did not apply.

---

report for Michigan State University Academic Council Consultation Completed by the Law Resource Group Membership Attached, January 11, 1995, Reuther Archives.

14. In the years 1996–98, 75 percent of the students who applied to both WSU and MSU chose to attend Wayne's law school. WSU students, with an average LSAT score of 156, were in the 76th percentile nationally. DCL/MSU students, with an average LSAT score of 151, were in the 57th percentile. Wayne students' average GPAs of 3.3 compared to DCL/MSU's 2.95.

15. See Michigan Constitution, Article 1, Section 26 on affirmative action programs.

16. It operated with a combined Board of Trustees, with the DCL board appointing two-thirds and the MSU president and Board of Trustees appointing the other third. The MSU provost was responsible for all academic programs with MSU participation, including the law school. In that way, the university had veto power over major law school decisions such as granting tenure to a law school professor.

Notwithstanding the Michigan legislature's previous opposition to the use of state funds for a law school at MSU, in August, 2020, the MSU College of Law became fully integrated into the university[17] and became subject to Proposition 2.

The Wayne Law faculty, in response to Prop. 2, decided that the "law school should, in good faith, take whatever steps it can, within the letter and the spirit of the law, to encourage minority students to attend Wayne State University Law School."[18] In 2020, the law school instituted a new recruitment program designed to attract students from historically underrepresented racial and socioeconomic backgrounds.[19] The free Damon J. Keith Pre-Law Summer Institute for college juniors and seniors recruited graduates from Detroit public high schools who were committed to pursuing a legal education.[20]

Students of color who enrolled at Wayne went on to pursue public interest law and a range of other careers upon graduation. For example, Heather Thompson ('05), who grew up in the Detroit area and graduated from Spellman College, chose the Peace Corps after graduation, serving with a Red Cross health clinic in Burkina Faso communities that were devastated by the HIV/AIDS epidemic. Thompson's attitude was representative of that of Wayne Law students: "Success is not measured by where you study or what you learn, but by what you do with your knowledge to improve life for others."[21]

17. Guzman, "Michigan State College of Law to Fully Integrate with University," *The State News*, June 24, 2020.
18. See Minutes of Faculty Meeting, Wayne State University Law School, December 6, 2006, p. 2, law school archives.
19. See go.wayne.edu/djk-institute.
20. The program also is open to sophomores in Wayne State and Oakland University's 3+3 program leading to admission to Wayne Law.
21. "Heather Joy Thompson: World Class Volunteer," *Wayne Lawyer* 21 (Spring 2004): 30.

New Building and Visibility Programming

In November 1995, Dean Robinson notified the university that the law school needed resources to compete effectively with MSU Law.[22] Starting in 1996, with the goal to increase the school's "visibility," alumnus Eugene Driker endowed the Driker Forum for Excellence in the Law. Participants in those forums included many nationally recognized lawyers and academics. The forums addressed contemporary issues and carried titles such as "The Future of the Law Firm as an Institution," "The Lost Lawyer," "Judicial Independence," and "Corporate Citizenship and the Law."[23]

One forum was devoted to the ABA's MacCrate report on legal education.[24] The MacCrate report, named after the chair and former ABA president, identified fundamental skills and values that lawyers must possess to engage in a "competent and responsible law practice." The nationally and locally recognized participants[25] in the 1996 Driker forum on the MacCrate report "brought

22. In November 1996, to make Wayne more attractive to applicants who resided outside the Detroit area, Dean Robinson and a group of faculty met with officials from Grand Valley State University in Allendale, twelve miles west of Grand Rapids, to discuss a possible satellite law campus there. Wayne Law did not establish a satellite campus.

23. To illustrate the high caliber of these programs, the principal speakers on the future of the law firm were Geoffrey C. Hazard Jr. of Yale and director of the American Law Institute; Ernest Gellhorn of the Jones Day Los Angeles office; and Lawrence Fox of Drinker Bidde & Reath of Philadelphia. "The Lost Lawyer" was the topic of the 1994 forum, based on Yale Law School dean Tony Kronman's book of the same name. The 1998 forum, "Judicial Independence," included judges, practitioners, and academics. The 2004 forum "Corporate Citizenship and the Law" hosted the General Motors general counsel, an FTC commissioner, executives from the health care and food sectors of the economy, and Senator Carl Levin. The 2007 forum, "Google in Court: Copyright and the Universal Library," discussed the use of digital technology to store and disseminate text, video, and other products of human creativity.

24. "Legal Education and Professional Development—An Educational Continuum, Report of the Task Force on Law Schools and the Profession: Narrowing the Gap." Robert MacCrate was the former president of the New York State Bar Association and former senior partner with the New York law firm Sullivan and Cromwell.

25. The participants included MacCrate, Roberta Ramo, immediate past president of the ABA, and Dean John Sexton of New York University School of Law. The others included Dean Robinson, Detroit mayor and former Michigan Supreme Court Justice Dennis

together for the first time the deans of all five Michigan law schools, a majority of the justices of the Michigan Supreme Court, and many leading lawyers, judges and academics to begin a much-needed examination of legal education in Michigan and an assessment of how the profession's major institutions can join together to improve the quality of training for law students and lawyers alike."[26]

During Robinson's deanship (1993–98), the faculty hired eight professors to replace the seven who, between 1995 and 1997, either elected to take the university's early retirement incentive or accepted faculty positions elsewhere. Long-serving Professors Hetzel, Kelman, Littlejohn, Schulman, and Strichartz retired and two professors moved to other law schools.

According to the ABA's 1996 Reaccreditation Report, the Wayne Law physical plant did not meet the school's current needs. In addition, the school required more classrooms to accommodate seminars and other low-enrollment classes, more space for contemplated future programs, and enhanced technology. The twenty-five-year-old "temporary" annex had to be replaced. In October 1996, the Student Board of Governors supported an increase in the law students' facilities fee in order to help finance a new law building.

Joan Mahoney ('75) succeeded Robinson as the law school's eighth dean and the school's first female dean, serving from 1998 to 2003. Mahoney practiced with a Detroit corporate law firm before she joined the faculty at the University of Missouri at Kansas City Law School. She moved to Western New England College of Law, where she served as its dean.[27] In her five-year plan to compete

---

Archer, Michigan Supreme Court Justice Patricia Boyle ('63), and Thomas Kienbaum ('68).

26. "Third Driker Forum Presents Legal Education Conclave," *Wayne Lawyer* (Winter 1996): 12–14.

27. Mahoney received her bachelor's degree from the University of Chicago in three years but reported that she was denied a fellowship when she enrolled in its master's program in history because "Chicago did not give fellowships to women" in the mid-1960s. Mahoney received her PhD from Cambridge University in 1989. During her deanship, the university decided to centralize the law school development office with the university development. Dean Mahoney opposed that move. She wanted to control the law school's fundraising efforts. The university, despite the faculty report recommending that Mahoney be appointed for a second term as dean, the university did not renew her decanal contract.

with MSU Law, she wanted to publicize Wayne's specialty in intellectual property that *U.S. News & World Report* ranked as twentieth, tied with Harvard.[28]

Before her deanship began, Mahoney was involved in the Campaign for the 21st Century to raise funds for a major law school building to be integrated into the existing two building campus. Chaired by Eugene Driker and then Candyce Abbott,[29] the campaign set a fundraising goal of $12 million and ultimately raised over $20 million, including $2.5 million for the Spencer Partrich Auditorium.[30] The estate of Raymond Krell ('58) provided $2.8 million for scholarships. The law school received a $1.5 million bequest from Betty Maiullo, who thought it important to support the public law school in Detroit.[31]

The faculty's spotty track record of attracting, granting tenure to, and retaining female professors started changing with Joan Mahoney's deanship. Between Mahoney's law school graduation in 1975 and the start of her deanship, the faculty hired eleven women, with about one-third remaining by 1998. During her years on the faculty from 1998 to 2009, the faculty hired thirteen women and seven were still on the faculty in 2009. In 2019, the school's fifteen female professors represented 37.5 percent of the forty full-time tenure and tenure-track professors.[32]

To expand the pool of Wayne Law applicants, the faculty approved a six-year combined bachelor and law degree (instead of seven years) and entered into partnerships for this program with Oakland University and Wayne State's College of Liberal Arts and Sciences.[33]

---

28. See "Law School Five-Year Plan," prepared by the dean's office, April 19, 2000, author's personal files.

29. The other members of the campaign planning group were Garry Carley ('64), Tyrone Fahner ('68), Elliott Hall ('65), Jon Muth ('71), Michael Timmis ('65), and Steven Victor ('50). See *Wayne Lawyer* 16 (Summer 1998): 4.

30. Spencer Partrich was part of the Class of 1964. The groundbreaking took place on June 2, 1999.

31. See *Wayne Lawyer* (Summer 1999).

32. These data for 2019 include the dean and associate dean but do not include the four LRW instructors.

33. See https://law.wayne.edu/news/oakland-university-wayne-law-partnership-offers-fast -track-to-bachelors-plus-law-degree-33552.

Wayne Law needed to be cost-competitive with MSU Law to be able to attracted highly credentialed applicants. In 1995, when WSU Law tuition was $5,880, MSU Law's tuition was more than double at about $13,000. The law school administration and student support for a differential fee to help finance the new law building established a precedent for treating the law school differently in future university tuition decisions. For example, when the faculty reduced the 1998 entering class by 10 percent, the university raised the law school tuition by 11 percent, more than the percentage tuition increases for the university's other colleges.

Dean Mahoney did not oppose law school tuition increases. To fund her five-year plan designed to elevate Wayne's *U.S. News* ranking, she proposed that the law school increase its 1999–2000 tuition to $7,710. Tuition kept increasing, and by the 2019–20 academic year, Wayne Law's annual tuition for entering full-time students was $32,882—still the lowest of any law school in Michigan. MSU Law's comparable tuition was $45,600. This 39 percent differential was significantly less than the 220 percent tuition disparity that existed in 1995.

Frank Wu served as the law school's ninth dean from 2004 to 2008. He was one of the few Asian American law deans. He gained recognition from his book *Yellow: Race in America Beyond Black and White* (2003).[34] In two years

New law buildings as of 2017, with the circular Partrich Auditorium on the left and the Keith Center on the right. (Reproduced with permission of the law school)

34. In December 2005, Dean Wu debated affirmative action with Ward Connerly, a national voice against affirmative action. See "Today at Wayne, Nation Briefs—Wu Debates Connerly in Michigan," December 2, 2005, https://today.wayne.edu/news/2005/12/02/

of his four-year deanship, the university imposed a special $2,000 per year law school tuition increase, with the school receiving in its budget 80 percent of those increases.[35] In 2004, a faculty/staff committee developed a comprehensive scholarship program to attract a highly credentialed, racially diverse student body and to provide assistance to students in financial need. The program was funded with Provost Nancy Barrett's designated university allocations[36] and private donor funds.[37]

Talented Teachers

Students typically are interested in the quality of their professors teaching, not their scholarship. The collective bargaining agreement required the dean and the law school's Salary Committee, in allocating merit salary increases for quality teaching, to consider the Student Evaluation of Teaching (SET) scores.[38]

Over its history, the law school was fortunate to have a large number of professors who, in the students' judgment, were excellent teachers. Already in the twenty-first century, students have honored four professors as Professor of the Year many times: Noah Hall, Christopher Lund, Eric Zacks, and William Ortman. It is too soon to predict if Professor Janet Findlater's record eighteen Professor of the Year awards will ever be broken, but Professor Lund accumulated that award seven times between 2010 and 2020.

The enduring significance of talented teachers may be judged, in part, by alumni reflections on their talented law school professors. During the author's extensive interviews and videotaped sessions with alumni, they singled out six

---

nation-briefs-wu-debates-connerly-in-michigan-12412.

35. Faculty Minutes, April 20, 2005.

36. Barrett provided a $1.5 million scholarship program to be administered by the law school.

37. By comparison, in 1995, the law school awarded only need-based scholarships, giving $600,000 to 350 students. Full-time resident tuition and fees for that academic year were $5,880. Wayne Law's ABA 1995 Annual Questionnaire.

38. Over the years, professors criticized the questions in the SETs, and in 2019, a university committee made changes to some of the questions.

Wayne Law professors up to the year 2000 as exceptional teachers. Professors Cowan, Gordon, and Siegel, who started teaching at Wayne in the 1940s and 1950s, were discussed in an earlier chapter. Stephen Schulman (1966–95), Janet Findlater (1976–2016), and Joseph Grano (1975–2001) continued to inspire Wayne Law students until they retired.

Stephen Schulman was idiosyncratic—loved and beloved by his students. Schulman was a chain smoker[39] and had trouble adjusting to the changing university rules prohibiting smoking, first in the classroom, then in his office, and ultimately within a perimeter around the law school. Terry Larkin spoke effusively about him: "[he was] a very demanding professor, yet showed the warmth that he had in his heart." He loved Wayne State University Law School and cared deeply about "all the students who came through—just a remarkable human being." Larkin recalls Schulman "nervously buttoning and unbuttoning his suit coat with one hand as he rhythmically puffed and removed his cigarette from his mouth with the other."[40]

Schulman received every kind of teaching honor that the students, the law school, and the university awarded in his three decades on the faculty. Peter Sugar ('70) admired Schulman "for his massive intellect and teaching ability."[41] According to Barry Waldman ('69), he was one of the Wayne professors that "loved the art of teaching."[42]

Stephen Schulman taught a series of business-related courses at Wayne, including corporations, securities regulations, and an infamous securities seminar. For thirty years, Schulman team-taught with Alan Schenk a year-long business planning (B.P.) course.[43] Despite his retirement in 1995, Schulman

---

39. Schulman had a sign in his office for many years that read "Yes, I mind your not smoking."

40. Terry Larkin, interview by the author, July 9, 2015.

41. Sugar explained that Eastern Europe was a hotbed of entrepreneurship, so he is not surprised that Wayne Law students whose families came from that background would be attracted to business. Peter Sugar, interview by the author, May 22, 2015.

42. Barry Waldman, interview by the author, May 11, 2016.

43. B.P. combined federal securities regulation, corporate taxation, and the Harvard professor David Herwitz–inspired B.P. course. Herwitz created the course in business

continued to teach B.P. until he suffered a stroke several years later. Many of the leading corporate and tax lawyers in Michigan were alumni of that B.P. course.

According to Tracy Allen ('80), the B.P. course changed her life. Schulman prepared her for the opportunities she received from the Securities and Exchange Commission (SEC) and the National Association of Securities Dealers (NASD). The SEC was offering women the opportunity to be trained as arbitrators and NASD was inviting arbitrators to be trained as mediators. Allen became a professional mediator with an international practice.

When Schulman wrote an article, he parsed every detail until he was satisfied (although he was never really satisfied) with every "turn of phrase," even in footnotes. Alex DeYonker ('75) discussed his experience as Schulman's research assistant: "He trained me how to keep thinking and asking questions. It was demanding. I learned a lot, and some of my research ended up in his meticulous footnotes."[44] Schulman's position as co-reporter for the Michigan Business Corporation Act (MBCA) led to his coauthored *Michigan Corporation Law and Practice Treatise.*

Schulman used his connections with corporate lawyers to assist graduates in obtaining jobs. To name only three, he helped Alex DeYonker ('75) obtain a job with the Michigan Department of Corporations and Securities, Gary Dolan ('80) with Merrill Lynch in New York, and Eric Lark ('91) with Detroit's Kerr Russell & Weber law firm.[45]

Many students in the Class of 1980 had a close relationship with Schulman at the midpoint of his career at Wayne. Kathryn Humphrey joined a dozen of

---

planning, designed to be a capstone, one-semester course for students to apply the material from their corporation and taxation courses by discussing a series of problems that arise in the life of a corporation. Herwitz incorporated excerpts from an article jointly authored by Schulman and Schenk in his business planning casebook.

44. Alex DeYonker, interview by the author, Grand Rapids, April 13, 2016.

45. Eric Lark and others helped establish the Michigan Bar Business Law Section's Stephen H. Schulman Outstanding Business Lawyer Award "to recognize Section members who demonstrate the highest quality of professionalism, foster the highest quality of practice, exemplify service and commitment to the Section and the profession, and promote ethical conduct and collegiality within the practice."

her classmates at a dinner in 2015 during which they reminisced about Professor Schulman, who had died in 2000.[46] The guests at that dinner painted a picture of a respectful, yet friendly relationship between the students and their law professors.

Humphrey experienced Schulman's wry sense of humor firsthand. During a meeting in his office, Schulman suggested that Humphrey try some of his snuff. He instructed her on the protocol of using snuff and, as she inhaled snuff "sufficient for a man his size," Humphrey recalled that "it felt like a red-hot iron was in my head." He joked with her about the snuff for weeks.

Timothy Guerriero, one of the Class of 1980 dinner guests, remembers that Schulman brought notes to his classes, but he did not seem to use them. Schulman was so enthusiastic and deeply knowledgeable about the corporate and securities laws that he could not contain that enthusiasm in the classroom. It was "as if he were present at the creation." Students felt that he had the inside scoop on the cases he discussed. "The faculty thought that they could make something remarkable out of us. 'You are here because you are good; we (the faculty) are going to make you better.' Our teachers had abiding confidence in us, expecting us to excel as lawyers."[47]

Sharla Schipper was unable to attend the 2015 dinner, but her edited letter "It's a scotch" captured her experience in Schulman's evening securities seminar held in his apartment in downtown Detroit:

---

46. The author asked Ms. Humphrey to invite some classmates who knew Schulman more than just as a student in one of his classes. At the videotaped dinner in 2015, the students recalled that a member of the business planning course notified Professor Schulman that some classmates intended to collaborate during the fall 1979 48-hour take-home exam. Schulman and Schenk changed the exam from a take-home to two in-class 6-hour exams on two consecutive days. Thirty-five years later, the dinner guests remembered how distressed they were that a couple of classmates planned to cheat and that their plans resulted in a different kind of examination.

47. Comments of Timothy Guerriero and Kathryn Humphrey during the videotaped dinner in 2015 of members of the Class of 1980. Guerriero practiced corporate law, including with international manufacturing companies, and later taught in the school's corporate counsel externship program.

I was scheduled to take the securities class with Professor Schulman starting in the winter term, 1980. Through the grapevine, I had heard that about half way through the evening session, Professor Schulman would break out the scotch. Refusing to be left out, I set out to become a scotch aficionado. I purchased a bottle of Chivas Regal—not knowing any other kind to purchase.

In the month of December 1979, while studying for classes and exams I would end my evening with a very small sip of scotch. That first sip was a gagger, as I shuddered it down!! A sip slowly became a ¼ shot, then ½ shot and finally I was able to down a shot and then 2—always straight, on the rocks.

January classes started, and true to rumor, the scotch came out an hour or so into the evening class, and I was able to enjoy and imbibe.

Did I learn securities, or did I become a scotch fan? I think I became a scotch snob, thank you Professor Schulman. And I have graduated from Chivas Regal to some nice malts, which I know we would have had fun sharing.

As a result of my scotch adventure, Professor Schulman and I struck up a scotch friendship that continued after law school and a dinner or two. One dinner over scotch shortly before I left Detroit for the west side of the state, we committed to meet up again in 25 years for dinner and scotch. The date, the time and location were all pre-determined. Unfortunately, I did not have that dinner with him. [He died in 2000.]

Professors Schulman and Findlater were colleagues and friends and shared their admiration of Wayne Law students. On April 13, 1979, in the spirit of Billie Jean King and Bobby Riggs's 1973 "match of the sexes," the law students[48] instigated a challenge squash match at the university's Matthaei center. Findlater had played racquetball and Schulman (not known for his athletic prowess) thought that the "proper" game was squash. The loser was to "expose" himself or herself

---

48. The author was not able to identify the instigators with certainty, but they may have included Doyle O'Connor.

Stephen Schulman with his characteristic cigarette in hand, 1966–95. (Reproduced with permission of the law school)

on the court after the match.[49] The outcome was never in doubt—Schulman lost. As the students and faculty watched from the gallery above the court, Schulman left and returned robed, facing Findlater and, with his back to the viewing crowd, flashed briefly. To this day, only Professor Findlater knows what, if anything, Schulman was wearing under that coat. The cartoon announcing the "First Annual, All-Star, Celebrity, Challenge SQUASH MATCH" was drawn by Wayne Law's talented cartoonist Professor Maurice Kelman.

Janet Findlater, Emerita Professor of Law, clerked for Michigan Supreme Court Justice Charles Levin before joining the Wayne faculty in 1976. Remaining on the faculty for forty years,[50] she was the second longest-serving female

---

49. During the match, the players had to take a break so that Schulman could smoke a cigarette.

50. Janet Findlater graduated Order of the Coif from the University of Michigan Law School.

The cartoon announced the squash match between Professors Findlater and Schulman.

professor in the school's history.[51] For many years, she was one of only a hand-ful of tenured or tenure-track women on the faculty. Findlater served as a receptive ear and confidante to students who were experiencing personal and law school–related problems.

Professor Findlater combined scholarship and public service. In her field of domestic violence, she coauthored manuals to train law enforcement offi-cers and educate police officers and welfare workers. In many of her articles, she promoted the collaboration between advocates for victims domestic vio-lence and child protective services. From 1988 to 1998, Findlater served on Michigan's Domestic Violence Prevention and Treatment Board.[52] In 2005, she received the State Bar of Michigan's Champion of Justice Award for her work on family violence and children's issues.

Janet Findlater was selected by Wayne Law students as Professor of the Year more than any professor in the school's history. The Student Board of Gov-ernors conducted the annual student poll to select the Professor of the Year, with the person selected regularly recognized at the law school Commence-ment. When Janet Findlater, who taught contracts, criminal law, and advanced courses, received the award in eighteen of her forty years on the faculty, the Student Board of Governors decided to have students select both a first-year and an upper-level Professor of the Year in order to give other professors an opportunity to receive this student recognition. Thomas Cronkright and many other alumni credit Findlater with their solid background in Contract Law that served them well in practice and business.

Wayne students praised the law school's respected criminal law and pro-cedure scholar Joseph Grano. Distinguished Professor Joseph Grano[53] was on

---

51. Frederica Lombard, with forty-one years on the faculty, was Wayne Law's longest-serving female professor.

52. She was involved, with the Annie E. Casey Foundation, in a self-advocacy program to help youth who "age out" of the foster care system develop a support system so that they can advocate for themselves.

53. The president recommended and the university Board of Governors appointed some Wayne professors as Distinguished Professors, considered by the university to be the high-est academic achievement. In 1984, Professor Grano became the first law professor and

Professor Janet Findlater, 1976–2016. (Reproduced with permission of the law school)

the faculty for twenty-six years. Kathryn Humphrey thought Grano had an exceptional ability to present difficult material to students in a manner that was accessible to them. Grano and Professor Robert Sedler both taught Constitutional Law and, while they had personal views on opposite ends of the political spectrum, those personal views did not intrude into their classes. They approached constitutional interpretation differently. When they taught the same course in the same semester, they traded or team-taught a class to expose students to different approaches to the interpretation of a single constitutional principle or a single Supreme Court decision.

Grano and Michigan Law professor Yale Kamisar frequently debated before the students at both law schools. They had contrasting views on the intersection of constitutional law and criminal procedure. In a tribute to Grano on his retirement, Kamisar wrote in part:

> Conservative law professors need people like Joe Grano. But, we liberal professors need people like him too. He challenges us. He provokes us. He makes us (or at least should make us) rethink our positions. And sometimes, no matter how strongly we felt about an issue at first, the force of his reasoning made us change our position, or at least revise it. This is how Joe educated us all.[54]

Professor Grano's portrait hangs in the law school. Professor Dolan wrote that the portrait captured Grano's "dignity, grace and noble bearing." Grano

---

one of the first five university-wide to be appointed as a Distinguished Professor. The other distinguished professors on the law faculty were Professors Dolan, Schenk, Sedler, and Winter. See https://wayne.edu/facts/2016/faculty-staff/distinguished. Grano also received the Federalist Society award in 1997.

54. Professor Grano retired when his Parkinson's disease prevented hm from teaching or engaging in his scholarship. Professor Sedler's tribute and remarks by Joe (read by Maura) appeared in the *Wayne Lawyer*. See "Our Debt to Joseph Grano," *Wayne Lawyer* 15 (Summer 1997): 22; "A Tribute to Distinguished Professor of Law Joseph D. Grano (1943–2001)," *Wayne Lawyer* 20 (Spring 2002): 15–16; and Yale Kamisar, "Joe Grano: The 'Kid from South Philly' Who Educated Us All," *Wayne Law Review* 46 (Fall 2000).

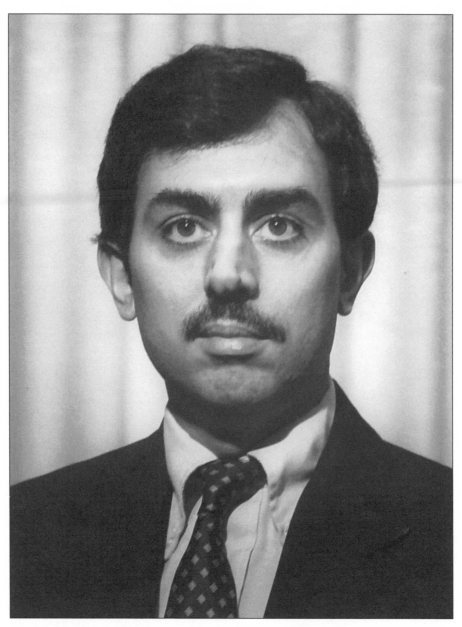

Professor Joseph Grano, 1975–2001. (Reprinted with permission of the law school)

convinced us "that law is not a nihilistic instrument of force and rhetoric, . . . [and made] us feel that nobility and that majesty . . . [that he saw] in the law."[55] In his memory, the Joseph Grano Endowed Scholarship was established and is awarded to an outstanding student in constitutional law or criminal procedure.

---

55. John Dolan, "A Tribute to Distinguished Professor of Law Joseph D. Grano (1943–2001)," *Wayne Lawyer* 20 (Spring 2002): 15.

8

Structural Changes Require Major Adjustments

Robert Ackerman began his four years as the school's tenth dean in 2008, just as the Great Recession was hitting the economy with greater force and, nationally, law school applications were declining. The faculty wanted Wayne Law to maintain its position, along with the University of Michigan Law School, as one of the two top sources of legal talent in Michigan, even if maintaining credentials resulted in a reduction in the size of the entering classes. The faculty therefore maintained admission criteria, and the entering class was down from 220 to 180.[1]

While the full impact of the financial crisis on law schools was not evident at the time, competition for law students increased. As the crisis unfolded, the national as well as local employment opportunities for law school graduates declined. Law firms were balancing the costs of integrating new associates into their practices against recruiting experienced lawyers. Prospective law students were balancing the cost of tuition and lost wages for three years against expected professional income available to repay student loans.

Dean Ackerman focused his energies on the students, their legal education, and their career opportunities. He wanted to emphasize the law school's

1. Faculty Meeting Minutes, April 23, 2008, 1.

strengths in international law, intellectual property, and entrepreneurship. He described Wayne law students as "conscientious, altruistic and mature students" and started publicizing the school as a "center of excellence in public interest and social justice law."[2]

During Dean Ackerman's tenure, the law school hosted high-visibility national personalities in law, including retired Associate Justice Sandra Day O'Connor, former U.S. attorney general Eric H. Holder Jr., and Judge Bruno Simma of the International Court of Justice. Harold Hongju Koh, legal advisor to the U.S. Department of State, gave the 2010 law school commencement address.

To support students pursuing public interest law and assist organizations that provide legal services to underserved communities, in 2009 the law school established Public Interest Law Fellowships (PILFs), awarded either as scholarships or as loan repayment.[3] The PILFs provided opportunities for students to gain practical experience with those organizations.

Aisa Villarosa ('11), a PILF recipient, was impressed with her classmates who were altruistic and passionate about Detroit. In 2009, she, along with classmates Erika Riggs and Julianna Rivera, established the 313 Project.[4] The name was inspired by the three women—Asian American, African American, and Hispanic American—with one cause, the city of Detroit—committed to supporting three charities. Detroit's major telephone area code is 313.

The role of the Wayne Law dean was changing. The dean had been serving as the conduit to the university administration, the face of the school in the profession, in the recruitment of students and professors and in curricular reform. In his first two years as dean, Ackerman concentrated on fundraising for the already planned new wing of the law school to house the Damon J. Keith Center for Civil Rights.[5]

---

2. Robert Ackerman, "Public Interest and Social Justice Law at Wayne Law," *Wayne Lawyer* 27 (Spring 2011): 2.

3. See "Wayne Law Announces Establishment of Public Interest Law Fellowships," February 27, 2009, https://law.wayne.edu/news/wayne-law-announces-establishment-of-public-interest-law-fellowships-32897.

4. "The 313 Project," *Wayne Lawyer* 27 (Spring 2011): 3.

5. The groundbreaking for this building took place on May 17, 2010.

When Benson was appointed dean in 2014, she acknowledged that the work of Dean Ackerman and Associate Dean John Rothchild during their deanships contributed to Wayne's rise in the 2014 *U.S. News & World Report* rankings. Based on 2013 data,[6] Wayne ranked among the top 100 law schools in the country. In addition, Wayne graduates performed better on the Michigan bar examination than those at other Michigan law schools.

The establishment of the Keith Center for Civil Rights was the culmination of Wayne's long history of educating students who became civil rights and civil liberties lawyers. From its first class in 1928, Wayne Law educated individuals like Ernest Goodman who became prominent civil rights lawyers. For example, Dean Robb ('49) came to Detroit from an Illinois farming community to spend a summer working in the Dodge Community House, a faith-based social service organization.[7] He stayed in Michigan and approached his legal studies from his social services background. Robb practiced with the Goodman, Crockett, Eden and Robb firm,[8] the first interracial law firm in Michigan. In the 1950s and 1960s, he served as a "shill" for Black lawyers who wanted to rent office space in Detroit buildings that would not rent directly to Black lawyers. Robb helped recruit lawyers in the northern states to assist Black lawyers in southern towns raise constitutional issues in their criminal and civil rights cases.

In the 1950s, Robb worked with a group of Wayne Law students to establish a Wayne Law chapter of the National Lawyers Guild (NLG), an organization that focused on using the law to address social issues. Bruce Miller ('54) was a member of the Wayne Law chapter of the NLG[9] when the U.S. House of Representatives Un-American Activities Committee (HUAC) was holding

---

6. Faculty Meeting Minutes, March 18, 2014.
7. The Dodge Community House in Hamtramck was one of the Protestant faith-based houses "working with neighbors to help other neighbors to enrich life and build community." http://www.pecose.org/agency-history.
8. Ernest Goodman had practiced with the Sugar law firm, which represented the UAW. Walter Reuther fired the firm when he was elected because the firm supported Reuther's opposition in the election for president of the union.
9. In 1950, report connected the Guild to the Communist Party in the United States. In 1951, the ABA notified law student groups that the guild was a subversive organization.

hearings in Detroit,[10] trying to identify people at the university with ties to the Communist Party. Lorraine Faxon Meisner,[11] a Wayne university student, was subpoenaed and refused to answer whether she was a Communist or a member of the Communist Party.[12] Miller helped organize a 1952 protest, voicing opposition to the university's suspension and then expulsion of Meisner.

Other alumni noted for their work in civil rights (some are discussed elsewhere) included Kenneth Cockrel ('67); Beverly Clark ('72); Michael Pitt ('74); Jeffrey Edison ('75); Deborah LaBelle ('79),[13] Elizabeth Gleicher ('79); and Dana Nessel ('94). John Roy Castillo ('73) was director of the Michigan Department of Civil Rights.[14]

According to Michael Pitt, Wayne Law had a culture of inclusion. The law school welcomed students who had to struggle to get to law school. No student had a status above that of his or her classmates. After practicing employment law with a Detroit firm, Pitt and his spouse, Peggy Pitt, started their own firm litigating predominantly single plaintiff cases involving civil rights, prisoner's rights, and employment law.[15] They passionately encouraged and supported the

---

10. U.S. House of Representatives, Committee on Un-American Activities, "Report on the National Lawyers Guild: Legal Bulwark of the Communist Party," House Report No. 3123 (Washington, DC, 1950).

11. "Wayne University Student Receives Expulsion Notice," *Harvard Crimson*, March 14, 1952, http://www.thecrimson.com/article/1952/3/14/wayne-university-student-receives -expulsion-notice.

12. Bruce Miller's association with these organizations during the McCarthy era created obstacles for him when he tried to gain admission to the bar and sought employment in local labor law firms. To him, labor law "was the fulfilment of his soul."

13. In 2000, LaBelle received a State Bar of Michigan Champion of Justice Award. She brought class action litigation to redress grievances of women prisoners (legal services offices were prohibited from representing prisoners) and to address environmental rights for urban residents. She received numerous awards for her civil and human rights work.

14. In 1994, he was appointed assistant to Detroit mayor Dennis Archer.

15. Michael and Peggy Pitt endowed a Wayne Law scholarship for disabled students and funded a "Public Justice" lecture honoring Dean Robb ('49). Chelsea Fleetham, a recipient of a Pitt-endowed scholarship, had a severe reaction to medication that left her disabled from the neck down. Fleetham graduated in 2014, passed the Michigan bar examination, and operated her own business.

law school's commitment to provide people with disabilities access to a legal education.

Elizabeth Gleicher practiced with the Goodman, Eden, Millender & Bedrosian firm (known for representing clients in civil rights cases) before establishing her own litigation practice, teaching as an adjunct professor at her alma mater, and then taking the bench as a judge on the Michigan Court of Appeals. In 2019, Judge Gleicher was inducted into the law school Wall of Fame.

Before the mid-1970s, gay and lesbian law students kept their sexual preferences private, meeting only in private informal gatherings. In the fall of 1977, when the city of San Francisco elected the openly gay Harvey Milk to the Board of Supervisors, Wayne students organized the Lesbian Law Caucus to support lesbian law students.[16]

Paula Ettelbrick ('84) openly supported gay and lesbian rights at the law school, and she helped organize a human rights conference at the university. Ettelbrick, who was inducted into the law school's Wall of Fame, worked for the Miller Canfield law firm in Michigan before moving to New York and serving in leadership positions with national gay rights organizations.[17] She was the legal director of the Lambda Legal Defense and Education Fund and legislative counsel to the Empire State Pride Agenda. She created a state-level coordinating council, believing that progress in rights for the gay and lesbian communities had to start at the state level. She returned to Wayne to deliver the I. Goodman Cohen lecture in 2005, discussing the need for lawyers to consider not only legal developments but the political and cultural aspects of a gay rights case.[18]

---

16. See *Advocate*, November 3, 1977, 12. The gay and lesbian students established what became the Wayne Outlaws (LGBT).

17. "During her five years as legislative counsel to the Empire State Pride Agenda in New York, from 1994 to 1999, Ms. Ettelbrick was among those urging Mayor Rudolph W. Giuliani to grant domestic partners rights and benefits equal to those of spouses." https://plex.page/Paula_Ettelbrick.

18. Paula Ettelbrick, "More than a Trial: Gay and Lesbian Legal Advocacy," lecture, Wayne State University, March 24, 2005. She taught at a couple of law schools and died at a young age. David W. Dunlap, "Paula L. Ettelbrick, Legal Expert in Gay Rights Movement, Dies at 56," *New York Times*, October 8, 2011.

Dana Nessel practiced as a Wayne County prosecutor for ten years before she and Christopher Kessel established the Nessel and Kessel law firm. She litigated LGBTQ issues, including *Harmon v. Davis*,[19] which established custodial rights for the non-biological parent of a same-sex couple. She represented April DeBoer and Jayne Rowse in *DeBoer v. Snyder*,[20] a case consolidated with others in the Supreme Court as *Obergefell v. Hodges*,[21] which established a same-sex couple's constitutional right to marry. In 2018, Nessel was elected Michigan's attorney general.

Wayne law school's long-term engagement with civil rights was reflected in its faculty and the courses they offered. Significant civil rights cases raise constitutional law issues. Starting in the 1940s, John Glavin (1938–81) taught courses and a seminar on constitutional law. Wayne professors are noted for their scholarship, teaching, and litigation in the field of constitutional law. Maurice Kelman ('59) taught Constitutional Law and Federal Jurisdiction and wrote *The Supreme Court: Judicial Power and Social Change* (1973).[22]

Director of Clinics Erica Eisinger, Professors Jocelyn Benson and Joan Mahoney, and American Civil Liberties Union director Michael Steinberg ('89) all taught civil rights courses.[23] Professor Morrison practiced law with lesbian rights, civil rights, and civil justice organizations.

Three professors clerked for U.S. Supreme Court Justices and infused that experience in their constitutional law, employment law, and criminal law courses. Jonathan Weinberg (1988–present) clerked for Supreme Court Justice

---

19. 489 Mich. 986 (Mich. 2011).
20. *DeBoer v. Snyder*, 772 F.3d 388 (6th Cir. 2014), reversing the District Court's decision in *DeBoer v. Snyder*, 973 F. Supp. 2d 757 (E.D. Mich. 2014). See Wyatt Fore, "DeBoer v. Snyder: A Case Study in Litigation and Social Reform," *Michigan Journal of Gender and Law* 22 (2015): 169.
21. 576 U.S. 644 (2015).
22. The booklet was published as a Xerox Education Publications unit book.
23. Robert Glennon (1973–85) taught constitutional law and criminal procedure, and he wrote a book about Federal Judge Jerome Frank and his legal realism movement. Legal realism relied on empirical evidence as part of its naturalistic approach to law and its impact on American law. Glennon left Wayne for the University of Arizona, where later in his career he became the school's chaired professor of law and public policy.

Thurgood Marshall (1985–86) and for Justice Ruth Bader Ginsburg (1983–84) before she was elevated to the Supreme Court. Kingsley Browne (1989–present) clerked for U.S. Supreme Court Justice Byron White. Dean Richard Bierschbach (2017–present) clerked for U.S. Supreme Court Justice Sandra Day O'Connor.

Wayne Law professors litigated cases in the Supreme Court, including Professors William Burnham, David Moran, and Steven Winter. Burnham (1980–2014) litigated three cases in the U.S. Supreme Court, including *Green v. Mansour*[24] and *Will v. Michigan Department of State Police.*[25] David Moran (2000–2008)[26] persuaded the Supreme Court in *Halbert v. Michigan*[27] to establish an indigent person's right to appointed counsel if the person pleads guilty and then appeals his conviction. In another U.S. Supreme Court case, *Hudson v. Michigan,*[28] Moran lost to alumnus Timothy Baughman ('74). Steven Winter (2002–present),[29] while practicing law, litigated a variety of civil rights cases as an assistant counsel for the NAACP Legal Defense & Educational Fund, Inc. He worked on over a dozen U.S. Supreme Court cases.

---

24. 474 U.S. 64 (1985).

25. 491 U.S. 58 (1989).

26. David Moran left Wayne to establish the Innocence Project at the University of Michigan Law School.

27. *Halbert v. Michigan*, 545 U.S. 605 (2005), holding that Michigan's denial of counsel to an indigent who pled no contest and appealed his conviction violated the equal protection and due process clauses of the Fourteenth Amendment to the U.S. Constitution.

28. 547 U.S. 586 (2006).

29. Steven Winter joined the faculty in 2002 as the Walter S. Gibbs Professor of Constitutional Law and became a distinguished professor in 2017. Before coming to Wayne, he taught on the Brooklyn and Miami law school faculties. Winter's scholarship centers on constitutional law and legal theory. He consulted with a federal agency and an international human rights organization. He authored a book on consumerism and democracy, wrote chapters and contributions on a number of other books, and authored numerous articles on constitutional law and legal theory. He was honored internationally by the Dutch Association of Legal Philosophy as "an outstanding international scholar who has made significant contributions to legal and political theory." See https://law.wayne.edu/profile/an8481. Winter served as a consultant for the Central Intelligence Agency's Strategic Assessments Group and for the Helsinki Watch Committee on its reports on human rights compliance in the United States.

Distinguished Professor Robert Sedler (1977–2021) became the Wayne Law professor most visible in the local media as a commentator on federal constitutional issues. Sedler litigated civil rights and civil liberties issues, including school busing and men's Vietnam-era refusal to submit for military induction. He participated in *Committee to End Racism in Michigan's Child Care System v. Mansou*[30] that successfully challenged the state's denial of biracial and single-sex couple adoptions. He participated in the *Detroit Branch, NAACP v. City of Dearborn* case in the Michigan Court of Appeals,[31] challenging the City of Dearborn's claimed race-based policy to limit its public parks to Dearborn residents.

Robert Sedler assisted his former student Dana Nessel in her U.S. Supreme Court case involving the constitutional rights of same-sex couples to marry. As Michigan's attorney general, Nessel appointed Professor Sedler as a Special Attorney General to advise on constitutional law and civil rights law. Sedler received numerous awards from the NAACP and ACLU and, in 2012, he received the State Bar of Michigan's John W. Reed Michigan Lawyer Legacy Award. The Reed award is presented periodically to a law professor in Michigan "whose influence on lawyers has elevated the quality of legal practice in our state."[32]

Christopher Lund (2009–present), a scholar in the field of law and religion, coauthored the leading casebook, *Religion and the Constitution.*[33] Justin Long (2010–present) taught and wrote in the fields of state constitutionalism and federalism.[34]

Carl Levin, Distinguished Legislator in Residence, served on the Civil Rights Commission, taught a civil rights course at Wayne Law in the early

---

30. The consent decree is 85-CV-74348-DT.

31. 173 Mich. App. 602 (1988).

32. See https://www.michbar.org/programs/reedlaward.

33. In 2017, he received an award from the Law and Religion Section of the American Association of Law Schools for his article "Religion Is Special Enough." He taught constitutional law and a seminar titled "Religious Liberty in the United States." He also taught evidence, torts, and contracts.

34. Long also taught public education law and urban law. He served as the associate director for education law and policy of the Damon J. Keith Center for Civil Rights.

1970s, and chaired the Levin Center at Wayne Law. Justice Kelly, the Distinguished Jurist in Residence and member of the Wayne Board of Governors, taught the seminar Access to Justice, a subject that she focused on while on the Michigan Supreme Court.[35]

Keith Center Established

In 2011, during Robert Ackerman's deanship and as an outgrowth of the Keith Collection of African American legal history, the law school established the Damon J. Keith Center for Civil Rights. The center is a tribute to Judge Damon J. Keith, who served on the Federal Sixth Circuit Court of Appeals and was devoted to civil rights. The center expanded the school's programs on civil rights.

The Honorable Damon J. Keith (LL.M. '56) was the inspiration for the law school's collection of African American legal history. In 1991, Professor Edward Littlejohn created the Damon J. Keith Law Collection,[36] the joint project of the law school and Wayne's College of Urban, Labor and Metropolitan Affairs.[37] "The Collection is dedicated to collecting, preserving, and providing resources pertaining to African American legal history, including the history of prominent African American lawyers, judges, and lawmakers, and others whose service to the community reflects an interest in and commitment to civil rights and social justice."[38]

---

35. Justice Kelly also taught students about litigation in the Michigan courts.

36. Professor Littlejohn wrote about Black lawyers, race law, and cases in Michigan and American history. The *Journal of Law in Society* organized a symposium honoring Littlejohn for his work with race, racism, and the law in March 2016.

37. The collection is housed in the Wayne State University Archives of Labor and Urban Affairs in the Walter P. Reuther Library. The ceremony establishing the collection was held at the university's Community Arts Gallery and was attended by many distinguished guests, including one of Judge Keith's clerks, Professor Lani Guinier (later of Harvard Law School). *Wayne Lawyer* 11 (Fall 1993): 16. The memorandum of understanding entered in February 1996 is titled "The Damon J. Keith Collection, From Concept to Reality: A Collection of African American Legal History."

38. See https://reuther.wayne.edu/taxonomy/term/688. See also "Dean's Column," *Wayne Lawyer* 15 (Winter 1997): 2, 3.

Edward Littlejohn, 1972–1996. (Reprinted with permission of the law school)

Judge Damon J. Keith, 6th Circuit Court of Appeals pictured in the Keith Center building at Wayne Law. (Reproduced with permission of the law school)

The collection established a traveling exhibit: "Marching Toward Justice: The History of the 14th Amendment to the U.S. Constitution." The exhibit documented the government's action promoting justice and equality for some and condoning the enslavement of others.

Judge Keith's devotion to civil rights was evident in his judicial opinions. He served on the U.S. District Court for the Eastern District of Michigan before he was elevated to the Sixth Circuit Court of Appeals. He authored many opinions, affirming civil and other constitutional rights. In *Detroit Free Press v. Ashcroft*,[39] he affirmed Judge Nancy Edmunds's ('76) District Court decision holding that the U.S. Constitution's First Amendment guaranteed

<hr />

39. 303 F.3d 681 (6th Cir. 2002).

the public's access to deportation hearings.[40] In the earlier *Sinclair* case,[41] the U.S. Supreme Court affirmed Judge Keith's decision that the federal government could not engage in the warrantless wiretapping of its citizens, even if undertaken for national security reasons.[42]

Professor Peter Hammer, the A. Alfred Taubman Endowed Chair,[43] is the director of the Keith Center for Civil Rights, which is dedicated to training the next generation of civil rights lawyers, and promotes "the educational, economic and political power of underrepresented communities in urban settings."[44]

The center provides Wayne students with the opportunity to elect courses and clinics related to civil rights and participate in the Keith Center's work on civil rights.[45] Hammer developed and taught courses related to his work with the Keith Center, including "Race, Law and Social Change in Southeast Michigan" and "Re-Imagining Development in Detroit: Institutions, Law & Society." With grants from the Kellogg Foundation and under Hammer's direction, the center established the Detroit Equity Action Lab (DEAL) to "advance the cause of racial equity" and to offer programs that "amplify the voices of DETROITERS and tell STORIES that are not being told."[46]

---

40. See generally on the career of Judge Keith, Peter Hammer and Trevor Coleman, *Crusader for Justice: Federal Judge Damon J. Keith* (Wayne State University Press, 2014). See also the profile of Judge Keith by Professor Littlejohn in *Wayne Lawyer* 12 (Summer 1994).

41. *United States v. U.S. District Court*, 407 U.S. 297 (1972).

42. The law school held a conference on Judge Keith's decisions like *Sinclair*, titled "Judge Keith, the Constitution and National Security: From Sinclair to Haddad." See "An Open-Door Policy for National Security: Judge Damon Keith and the Constitution," *Wayne Lawyer* 21 (Spring 2004): 34.

43. Peter Hammer joined the faculty in 2003 after teaching at the University of Michigan Law School.

44. See law.wayne.edu/keithcenter/index.php; Hammer and Coleman, *Crusader for Justice*.

45. For example, the Civil Rights Clinic assists low-income individuals in civil rights matters arising under state and federal constitutions and laws.

46. A 2018 grant will enable DEAL to engage in original research and offer professional development of community leaders to sustain "a powerful network for social change," build equitable communities in the Detroit region, and work toward the elimination of structural racism. See https://sites.google.com/view/detroitequity/home. See also "Diverse

Capitalizing on Strength in International and Comparative Law

During his tenure as dean, Ackerman continued to focus on projects that would increase the visibility of Wayne Law. Prominent law schools like Harvard, Columbia, Michigan, and others had strong programs in international and comparative law. It was quite unusual for state and regional law schools like Wayne to have a large number of professors with scholarship and expertise in the fields of international and comparative law.

The law school's depth in comparative law started in the 1960s. Edward Wise was Wayne Law's first full-time international or comparative law professor.[47] An expert in criminal law and already a scholar in the field of comparative law, Wise joined the faculty in 1965 and remained until his untimely passing in 2000.[48] Wise was one of the most broad-gauged, well-read scholars in the school's history, with deep knowledge in the fields of literature, history, and philosophy. He, along with Gerhard Mueller of New York University, popularized the field of comparative criminal law in the United States.[49]

Leaders Bringing Perspectives to Detroit Equity Action Lab," *Wayne Lawyer* 30 (Winter 2015): 16.

47. In 1966, Friedrich Juenger was hired to teach courses in the field of international law. Juenger earned his law degree from a German law faculty and had practiced law with the international firm, Baker & McKenzie. Juenger taught and wrote in the fields of international and comparative Law and conflicts of law. Juenger moved to the University of California-Davis Law School later in his career.

48. In 2004, the law school held a symposium in honor of Professor Wise: "International Justice: A Symposium in Honor of Professor Edward M. Wise," *Wayne Lawyer* 21 (Spring 2004): 34. "The forum addressed issues surrounding the international prosecution of state actors participating in international criminal conduct, the role of civil liberties in the war on terrorism, and the development of new international crimes reflecting the cross-border effects of illegal conduct."

49. He served as associate dean from 1986 to 1992 and as acting director of the Center for Legal Studies. See generally, "Faculty in Memoriam: Edward M. Wise," *Wayne Lawyer* 19 (Spring 2001): 26. Wise's scholarship included dozens of articles on domestic and international criminal law, criminal justice, and legal history. See "In Memoriam: Edward M. Wise 1938–2000," *International Criminal Justice Review* 10 (2000): vii.

Some Wayne faculty preferred to fill open teaching positions with professors who satisfied curricular needs, while others favored hiring "the best and the brightest" candidates, independent of their fields of expertise. The "best and the brightest" policy has usually prevailed, expanding the number of professors who have written and taught in the fields of international and comparative law. Starting in 2000 in addition to[50] Brad Roth (1997–present), discussed below, Michael McIntyre (1977–2012),[51] Stephen Calkins (1983–present),[52] and Ralph Slovenko,[53] the faculty hired five more professors who were expert in various aspects of international law. Julia Ya Qin joined the faculty in 2000, Gregory Fox and Peter Hammer in 2003, Paul Dubinsky in 2005, Lance Gable in 2006, and Charles Brower in 2012.[54] By 2019, Wayne had at least ten professors who taught, wrote about, or engaged in law reform in the fields of international or comparative law.[55]

---

50. Professors Linda Beale, Erica Beecher-Monas, Paul Dubinsky, Lance Gable, Alan Schenk, Stephen Winter, and others worked, taught, or engaged in research in the international area. See "Where in the World Are Wayne Law Professors?" *Wayne Lawyer* 26 (Spring 2010): 8–9. Alan Schenk's law reform efforts involved drafting tax legislation for developing countries. He served as a technical advisor for the IMF's law reform work on value R tax in Africa, Asia, and the Caribbean.

51. McIntyre was well-known and authored a major treatise in the field of international taxation. He consulted for years with national governments around the world and was the founding editor of the widely read periodical, *Tax Notes International.*

52. Calkins provides students a unique perspective on antitrust and consumer protection. Calkins served as chief counsel at the Federal Trade Commission in the mid-1990s. He then served as a commissioner on the Competition Authority of Ireland and director of its Mergers Division from 2011 to 2015. The Competition Committee became the Competition and Consumer Protection Commission of Ireland.

53. Ralph Slovenko, a prolific scholar focusing in part on psychiatry and the law, was on the Wayne faculty for forty-four years (1969–2013). The faculty hired Gennady Danilenko (1997–2001), a noted Russian scholar, in 1997. He was a Senior Research Fellow, Institute of State and Law, Russian Academy of Sciences, and wrote extensively in the field of international law, drafting a treaty governing outer space and exploring perestroika and international law.

54. Professors Mogk, Lamborn, Adelman, Burnham, Handel, Calkins, Weinberg, Litman, and Schenk taught and conducted research related to international and comparative law. Professors Dolan and McIntyre wrote books and articles in this area.

55. Lance Gable is also a health care expert. He helped Michigan establish ethical

The farther one travels away from Detroit, the Wayne Law professors in these fields become more well-known for their scholarship, law reform work, and impact on the profession. For example, the late James Crawford, one of the world's most respected academics in public international law who served as judge on the International Court of Justice, told the author how impressed he was that Wayne Law had two so well-known and respected international law scholars—Greg Fox and Brad Roth. He described Roth[56] as the academic, internationally, who in his judgment best bridged the fields of law and political science.[57] Roth mentored a number of his political science students who then continued their education at Wayne Law. Three Wayne Law professors, Greg Fox, Brad Roth, and Paul Dubinsky, coedited *Supreme Law of the Land? Debating the Contemporary Effects of Treaties within the United States Legal System* (Cambridge University Press, 2017).

Paul Dubinsky joined the faculty in 2005 after practicing with the Wilmer Hale law firm, serving as associate director of Yale Law School's International Human Rights Law Clinic and teaching at New York Law School. Dubinsky's scholarship focused on international and comparative law, including transnational litigation, dispute resolution, and treaties.[58]

---

guidelines for the allocation of scarce medical resources during a public health emergency and worked with the World Health Organization to develop course material on Human Rights and Mental Health.

56. Roth joined Wayne's Department of Political Science in 1997, held a joint appointment with the law school and Political Science, and was elected to the Wayne Academy of Scholars. His courses included ones on international law, international protection of human rights, international prosecution of state actors, U.S. foreign relations law, and political theory of public law. He is a prolific scholar, authoring many books. One of his books is *Sovereign Equality and Moral Disagreement* (Oxford University Press, 2011). Some of his scholarship relates to questions of sovereignty, constitutionalism, human rights, and democracy.

57. Judge Crawford was previously the Whewell Professor of International Law at the University of Cambridge. Crawford made these comments to the author while the author was serving as an expert in an international arbitration in England and Crawford was the chair of the arbitration panel.

58. He taught at law schools abroad, and he served in leadership positions in the International Law Association.

Julia Ya Qin earned her law degrees at Peking University in Beijing and at Harvard Law School, clerked for the chief judge on the U.S. Court of International Trade, and practiced with a major American law firm in Hong Kong before joining the faculty in 2000. In addition to teaching international business transactions and international institutions, she offered courses dealing specifically with China.[59] Qin is well-known nationally and internationally for her scholarship on the intersection of China and the World Trade Organization.

Peter Hammer, before he directed the Keith Canter, focused some of his research on international public health and economic development.[60] In his work in Cambodia, Hammer explored the relationship between human rights and economic development.

Charles Brower II, a noted international arbitrator, came to Wayne after fourteen years teaching at the University of Baltimore and University of Mississippi law schools. Brower taught International Commercial Arbitration, International Law, and the Law of Armed Conflict. He served in leadership positions in the American Society of International Law.[61]

Program for International Legal Studies

Ackerman wanted to take advantage of this concentration of Wayne talent in international and comparative law. In 2009, the faculty established the Program

---

59. Qin held a joint appointment for several years with the leading Chinese law faculty at Tsinghua University in Beijing.

60. Hammer has published books and articles dealing with domestic and international health care, including *Change and Continuity at the World Bank: Reforming Paradoxes of Economic Development* (Edward Elgar, 2013). He is the "founding board member and past president of Legal Aid of Cambodia, an organization providing free legal services to Cambodia's poor. He [was] . . . a board member of the Life & Hope Association, an organization in Siem Reap, Cambodia, founded and run by Buddhist monks to address the needs of orphans, vulnerable children and at-risk young women." https://detroiturc.org/peter-hammer-phd-jd.

61. Brower also taught contracts. Brower's scholarship is extensive, including as coeditor of books and the author of numerous chapters of other books on investment arbitration and numerous articles in international and transnational law reviews.

for International Legal Studies (PILS), consolidating the school's programs that addressed international legal issues and foreign legal systems. Professor Gregory Fox[62] directed PILS.[63] In the lecture series for the program, students learned about international law from practitioners in the field who were invited to the law school. During the school year, students attended informal brown-bag lunches at which they discussed legal issues in international law with their professors and practicing lawyers. Through the International Public Interest Law Fellowships,[64] PILS offered summer programs enabling law students to work abroad in a law firm,[65] with a foreign government, or with a nongovernmental entity.[66]

Study Abroad Programs

Wayne, located less than three miles from the Canadian border crossing at the Detroit River, established close ties with the University of Windsor Faculty of Law.[67] In 1987, the State Bar of Michigan and Wayne Law, the University of Detroit Mercy Law, and the University of Windsor Faculty of Law established the Intellectual Property Law Institute (IPLI). Students at the participating law schools could enroll in any IPLI course for credit at their home institution.

---

62. Before entering the teaching profession, Fox practiced with the Hale and Dorr law firm in Boston and was the co-director of New York University Law School's Center for International Studies. While a MacArthur Foundation/Social Science Research Council Fellow in International Peace and Security, he wrote "The Right to Political Participation in International Law." Some of his scholarship focused on the impact of the spread of democracy on the international legal system. See https://law.wayne.edu/profile/an8360.
63. "Proposal to Establish a Program for International Legal Studies," May 8, 2009, was adopted by the faculty.
64. The fellowships have included fellowships in Ghana, Mexico, and the Bahamas.
65. The PILS program sent students to work during the summer with Wilmer Hale (the merged firm) in its London office.
66. The internships with law firms and corporations abroad included work in law firms in Mexico and the United Kingdom and work with Tata Motors in India.
67. In the 1970s, Wayne and the University of Windsor established a faculty lecture series in which a professor from each school would give a talk to faculty and students at the other school.

For over fifty years, Wayne Law participated in faculty and student exchanges with European schools[68] and provided stipends for Wayne students to attend the Hague Academy of International Law in the Netherlands.[69]

The Wayne Law and the University of Warwick, England, exchange program gave Wayne students the opportunity to study in England and Wayne professors the opportunity to teach and engage in research there. Gary Minda ('75) studied there.[70] Professor John Mogk, as a Visiting Fellow at Warwick in 1985–86,[71] engaged in comparative research and worked with Warwick faculty who were developing England's energy law.

Wayne Law established a professor and student exchange program with the University of Utrecht, the Netherlands, in 1978.[72] The relationship produced professional and personal relationships and joint scholarship.[73] When the Utrecht program became inactive, Wayne established a faculty exchange with Maastricht University in the Netherlands. Wayne professors William Burnham and Robert Sedler taught in Russia at the Mari State University law faculty, and Mari State students came to Wayne.

---

68. Wayne welcomed Warwick students like Margaret Childs in 1981 and Kee-Seng Li in 1990. In some years, the law school arranged for Warwick students to intern with an American law firm or law-related agency.

69. A gift from Alwyn Freeman funded the law school's long-standing summer program at The Hague. The Hague Academy is housed in the Peace Palace, where the International Court of Justice is located.

70. Gary Minda is professor emeritus, Brooklyn Law School.

71. Professor Mogk visited at the University of Utrecht in 2001.

72. The fifty-year-old Wayne Law School (at the time) paired with the University of Utrecht, which began issuing law degrees in 1636. Each visiting professor taught a course. Starting in 1992, the Wayne professor taught Introduction to American Law (usually using Wayne Professor William Burnham's book designed for this course) and a course in his or her specialty. The Utrecht visitor at Wayne taught a course on European Union law and structure and a course in his or her specialty. See "Wayne State/Utrecht Exchange," *Wayne Lawyer* 21 (Spring 2004): 6.

73. For example, in 1981, Professor Littlejohn and Visiting Professor Janse de Jonge co-taught a seminar titled "Police Discretion, Its Exercise and Control: A Comparative Approach," and, in 1983, Professor Visser't Hooft from Utrecht taught a course on law, ethics, and technological men.

International Competitions

Wayne teams, mentored by Wayne professors who worked and taught in the international area, excelled in international competitions.[74] In just one example, the Wayne team placed first in the 1982 Niagara Cup International Moot Court competition.

Wayne student performance in the Philip C. Jessup International Moot Court Competition went from impressive to extraordinary. In 1983, Wayne students won the Midwest region in that competition, defeating the University of Michigan, Detroit College of Law, Case Western Reserve, and Duquesne

Jessup team in the 2018 competition ranked sixteenth in the world (*from left:* Aaron Shuman, Layla Zarkesh, Nicole Pitchford, Emad Hamadeh, and Adam Winnie). (Reproduced with permission of the law school.)

---

74. Wayne students excelled in other national competitions. For example, in 1997, Gene Bowen was a finalist in the Scribes competition sponsored by the American Society of Writers on Legal Subjects.

before besting the University of Pittsburgh for the regional championship.[75] Wayne's Jessup team repeated that feat in 1984.

For the fifth time in six years, in 2018 the Wayne team ranked first in the regional Jessup competition. In the White and Case International Rounds, competing with teams from one hundred countries, Wayne's team finished among the top sixteen teams in the world and received many honors.[76]

National Litigation and Transactional Competitions

After their first year of law school, students can select courses that lead to a career in litigation or transactional practice, although many upper-level courses include fields of law that apply to both. Lawyers that practice alone or in small partnerships generally need skills in both areas. The subjects on the bar examinations tend to focus more on courses leading to a litigation practice like torts, evidence, and criminal law and procedure, although corporate and property law, critical in transactional practices, are covered as well.

Wayne students' success went beyond the Jessup competition to a variety of moot court and transactional competitions. The Moot Court National Team won the regional competition and the regional best oralist award in 1979 and 1980.[77] In 1983, Wayne teams won their regional tournaments in the National Student Trial Advocacy Competition and the American Trial Lawyer's Association's Regional Trial Advocacy Contest.[78] The Wayne team of Patricia Lovely

---

75. See "WSU Moot Court Team Advances to National Competition," *Advocate*, issue 3 (April 1983): 1. The successful team included Julie Miller, Thea Marie Sankiewicz, Stephen Gale, Sue Levitt, and Harriet Demetriou.

76. See *Raising the Bar*, a monthly newsletter for Wayne State University Law School alumni and friends, April 2018, https://i.wayne.edu/view/5acd19d09f6e3?utm_source= link&utm_medium=email-5acd19d09f6e3&utm_campaign=Law+-+Raising+the+Bar+ -+April+2018&utm_content=Read+this+email+on+the+Web.

77. Timothy Wilton, "'Practical' Legal Education," *Wayne Lawyer* (Summer 1981): 10. Wayne students also received the best brief award for both sides of that competition.

78. "Trial Advocacy Team Scores Victory," *Advocate* 3 (April 1983): 5.

and Mark Brown reached the semifinal round of the 1985 Regional Frederick Douglass Moot Court Competition.

In 1990, for the second time in five years, Wayne placed first in the National Administrative Law Moot Court Competition.[79] In 2003, Wayne fielded its first National Champion Moot Court team.[80] Wayne hosted the regional National Trial Competition, and Wayne teams participated in the ABA National Appellate Advocacy Competition. In 2017 the Wayne team reached the quarterfinals and in 2019 reached the national finals in the ABA competition.[81]

Transactional competitions were inaugurated and expanded in the twenty-first century. Students started boasting their success in competitions testing skills in negotiating business transactions. In 2014, students, with Professor Eric Zacks's help, established teams for what became the endowed Jaffe Transactional Law Competition.[82] In 2015, under student Justin Hanna's chairmanship, two Wayne teams won honors in the regional competition.[83] In 2021, Wayne hosted the competition held remotely.

Students participated in transactional competitions in the field of sports law. Sarah Gale-Barbantini was the best oralist in the 2011 sports law competition. Rebecca Robichaud of the faculty sponsored the students in an NFL Contract Negotiation Competition. Monique Eubanks and Edwin Piner won the competition in 2019.[84]

---

79. The team that year was Joseph Yanoschik, Jane Quasarano, Michael Dantuma, and James DeLine.

80. See "Moot Court Wins National Championship," *Wayne Lawyer* 21 (Spring 2004): 27.

81. See, for example, "Wayne Law Moot Court Program Ranked among Top 20 of U.S. Law Schools," *Wayne Lawyer* 32 (Fall 2017): 6. The team members were Chris Rambus, Amy Huang, and Jonathan Demers. Members of the 2019 team were Matthew Cassar, Hayley Johnson, and Ahmad Sabbagh.

82. This competition was endowed by the Michigan-based law firm, Jaffe Raitt Heuer and Weiss, with encouragement from Adjunct Professor Peter Sugar.

83. See "Wayne Law Teams Finish Second, Third at regional LawMeet competitions," *Wayne Lawyer* 33 (Spring 2018): 28. The teams included (1) Alexis Havenstein, Nezar Habhab, and Guiliano Mancini; and (2) Linda Mifsud and Elijah Simkins.

84. The NFL Contract Negotiation Competition, in its second year at the law school, provided an opportunity for students to practice negotiation skills in front of practicing attorneys. Students represented either an NFL player or an NFL team and worked to come

Two major factors increased the value of Wayne's Detroit location as a venue for a legal education and served to make Wayne Law more attractive to prospective faculty members. First, in 2010, Dan Gilbert ('87) moved his Quicken Loans operation to the Compuware Building in downtown Detroit,[85] provided incentives for Quicken employees to live in Detroit, and proceeded to invest heavily in making the business district an attractive destination for employees and a magnet for young adults.

Second, Detroit served as a laboratory for law school clinics and experiential learning when, in 2015, the ABA solidified its goal to have law schools offer more skills training by mandating that member schools require students to complete at least six credits of their legal education in skills courses, that is, law school clinics and experiential-learning courses.

Expanding Skills Training

In its first forty years, Wayne Law's location in the City of Detroit was advantageous because the school was accessible to students living within commuting distance in Southeast Michigan, where most of the Michigan population resided. The Detroit location was considered a negative factor by applicants whose families lived in the suburban areas of metropolitan Detroit and other major Michigan cities after the 1967 Rebellion and reports in the local media about Detroit crime and national media publicized the negative news from Detroit. However, Wayne continued to be an attractive option for students lured by low tuition who financed their legal education with part-time or full-time work more readily available in metro Detroit.

Wayne students who excelled academically could compete with graduates of elite law schools for the coveted jobs in the large Michigan law firms.

---

to agreement on a contract for their client. The competition is supervised by Assistant Professor (Clinical) Rebecca Robichaud and sponsored by the law school's Sports and Entertainment Law Society.

85. See https://www.quickenloans.com/press-room/2009/07/13/quicken-loans-move -headquarters-1700-employees-downtown-detroit-mid2010.

In terms of faculty recruitment, Wayne's Detroit location had both advantages and disadvantages. Some faculty candidates refused the faculty's offer because they preferred comparable schools located in California or in other major cities. Wayne was attractive, however, to candidates who wanted suburban housing within commuting distance of the school. Some were drawn to metropolitan Detroit for its reasonable standard of living compared to suburban areas of other major cities. In the twenty-first century, Wayne has been attractive to professors who prefer to live in the City of Detroit or have family ties to the region. In addition, the university has a liberal policy on sabbatical leaves and the law school funds summer research grants and supports faculty travel to professional conferences.

The faculty was slow in following the students' lead in providing hands-on skills training. In 1965, as discussed earlier, Wayne Law students without law school support established the Free Legal Aid Clinic (FLAC) to provide their own skills training by representing underserved individuals with landlord-tenant disputes and family law issues.[86] With their experience in FLAC, many graduates were prompted to represent individuals who otherwise might not have had the resources to hire a lawyer. Michael Pitt ('75) knew from the time he worked in FLAC that he wanted to be a people's lawyer.[87]

In 1969, with Ford Foundation support, an independent Council on Legal Education for Professional Responsibility (CLEPR) made grants to law schools to "open teaching law offices—law clinics—on their campuses, and have faculty

---

86. Local lawyers, on a volunteer basis, offered non-credit tutorials at the law school for interested students to learn about welfare and unemployment rules. For example, in October 1977, students could attend a training session in the law school to learn about welfare law and work in the Welfare Law Clinic that was not formally affiliated with the law school. Students could help unemployed workers obtain benefits under the Michigan Employment Security Act through the Unemployment Insurance Clinic sponsored by the National Lawyers Guild. See *Advocate* 9 (November/December 1978). See also "WLC Update," *Advocate* 9, no. 1 (1978).

87. Pitt's career as a civil rights, prisoner's rights, and employment law lawyer is discussed in chapter 5.

teach students, for academic credit, how to be ethical responsible lawyers while representing underserved people in real cases."[88]

In the late 1960s, law school clinics were experimental and law faculties hesitated to support these experiments. Indeed, the Wayne Law faculty limited the number of credit hours per term that students could earn in "skills" courses.[89] Some Wayne Law professors viewed "skills" training as a move toward a "trade school" legal education.

Historically, law school curricula consisted of doctrinal courses that focused on cases, principles, and policy. Many Wayne professors resisted changes in the school's mixture of doctrinal courses and client-contact clinical programs. Tenure-track professors taught doctrinal courses, and their traditional scholarship that furthered knowledge in a field of law was recognized as more tenure-worthy than articles related to the skills teachable in clinics. Doctrinal courses generally required less course-related faculty time commitments than did clinical courses.

Many law school professors thought that lawyering skills should be acquired in practice, not learned as an essential part of a law school curriculum. In 1969, however, the faculty approved a skills course co-taught by two professors who taught doctrinal courses—a transactional approach to planning business transactions. In 1970, the faculty established a hands-on Clinical Education Advocate Program in which students represented indigent clients in civil and criminal detention cases.[90] However, a group of Wayne Law professors in the 1970s and 1980s opposed the "diversion" of any part of the law school budget for clinical education.[91]

---

88. Elliott Milstein, "Introduction of William Pincus at the CLEPR 40th Anniversary Celebration," *Clinical Law Review* 16 (2009): 21.

89. "CLEPR Program," Law School Minutes, Regular Meeting of the Faculty, 1969–70, No. 17, May 6, 1970, 3, WSR000639, box 4, file 17, Reuther Archives.

90. See "New Clinical Program Offers Students the Real Thing," Update, *Wayne State University Law School News*, January 26, 1970.

91. Wayne also housed the Michigan Legal Services Assistance Project, which provided research support for Michigan's local legal services programs representing low-income or unrepresented clients. The project evaluators from the OEO were so impressed with the

The faculty reluctantly approved new clinics if they were funded with outside grants from the government or foundations. When the funding ended, the faculty dropped the clinic. For example, in 1972, the law school received a federal grant to support an Equal Employment Opportunity Commission (EEOC)[92] Employment Discrimination clinic. Irving Miller from the EEOC directed that clinic.[93] When the funding ended, the law school converted the clinic to a doctrinal course on employment discrimination. For decades, Adjunct Professor John Runyan ('72) taught the evening section of that course.

Professor Timothy Wilton (1977–84) countered the view of many of his colleagues that clinical legal education was "without academic merit." Wilton taught Civil Advocacy and other clinical courses, and he debated with his Wayne colleagues as to whether clinical courses involved substantive academic inquiry and taught students the same analytical tools that they learned in their doctrinal law courses without client involvement. "We teach students to extract from a practice experience the material and immaterial parts, to understand why these parts were important to the result, what effect they had on the process, and to apply that knowledge to new sets of facts."[94]

Miriam Seifer and Marc Goldman taught a criminal advocacy course in the 1978–79 academic year.[95] Barbara (Shaw) Harvey taught a clinic focusing on civil disputes in 1979–82. In 1979, the ABA's Section of Legal Education and Admissions to the Bar issued the Crampton Report, which recommended that law schools expand the role of clinical education in their curricula.[96]

---

quality and success of the program that they recommended that it be used as a model in other states. Confidential letter to Associate Dean Paul Borman, August 25, 1970.

92. The EEOC is a federal agency that enforces federal anti-discrimination laws.

93. Cynthia Gitt directed the clinic during the 1975–76 academic year. There were other full-time directors of the clinic during the years that funding continued. This field now is covered in the Labor Law or Employment Discrimination courses, not clinics.

94. See Wilton, "'Practical' Legal Education," 10.

95. It was a 10 credit-hour course, with 5 graded and 5 pass/no credit. See "Criminal Advocacy Clinic," *Advocate* (November/December 1978): 3.

96. ABA Section of Legal Education and Admissions to the Bar, *Report and Recommendation of the Task Force on Lawyer Competency: The Role of the Law Schools* (1979).

William Burnham (1980–2014)[97] taught a client-contact misdemeanor clinic and trial advocacy[98] and, beginning in 1982, he served as the director of clinical programs. He also helped Wayne students establish a Student Trial Advocacy Program (renamed Mock Trial). By the mid-1980s, the faculty hired more professors to teach doctrinal courses who were skeptical of clinical legal education. With limited enrollment in the existing clinical offerings and tight law school budgets, the faculty abolished most client-contact clinics, leaving Burnham's Trial Advocacy simulation course and the student-run Free Legal Aid Clinic.

The Criminal Appellate Practice (CAP) Clinic was an exception. Established in 1986, the CAP Clinic was staffed for decades by Gail Rodwan from the State Appellate Defender Office (SADO). Students in the CAP Clinic prepared criminal appellate briefs for incarcerated clients.

The ABA continued to press law schools to expand their skills training through clinical programs and externships.[99] In the ABA's 1989 Reaccreditation Report for Wayne Law, the ABA found that Wayne students were not being offered adequate skills training. In 1992, the ABA issued the MacCrate report, criticizing legal education's theoretical approach and calling for more skills training.[100]

---

97. Professor Burnham also taught constitutional law, federal courts, and civil rights litigation.

98. The Criminal Clinic combined "actual case-work and client counseling, like LAC, with the practice-simulation techniques of the Trial Advocacy courses." M. O'Donnell, "The Clinical Experience," *Advocate* 1 (October 1982). William Burnham, phone conversation with the author, July 29, 2016.

99. The ABA Standard 303 on the Law School Curriculum required law schools to "offer a curriculum that requires each student to satisfactorily complete . . . one or more experiential course(s) totalling at least six credit hours. An experiential course is a simulation course, a law clinic, or a field placement."

100. In 1992 the MacCrate report recommended a more practice-oriented, not a theory-oriented, approach to legal education. ABA Section of Legal Education and Admissions to the Bar, *Report of the Task Force on Law Schools and the Profession: Narrowing the Gap* (July 1992).

Tyrone Fahner ('68), who chaired the management committee of the international law firm Mayer Brown, voiced his concern about the "theory-oriented" legal education at schools like Northwestern Law where he earned an LL.M. in criminal law.[101] He found that he benefited more from what he described as Wayne's more "practical" education.

In the mid-1990s, the Wayne students started asking for more skills training to facilitate their transition to practice.[102] Dean James Robinson came from a career in law practice and favored more "real-world" experience. In the academic year 1994–95, Robinson taught a yearlong, one-credit course on lawyering. Professor John Dolan developed a novel Commercial Law Clinic with the involvement and support of a major Detroit law firm. The law school added courses in negotiation and alternative dispute resolution. The law school hired judges and practicing lawyers as adjunct professors to offer more sections of the popular Trial Advocacy course, with Judge Victor Baum teaching his section in his courtroom.

In the twenty-first century, clinical education became an essential part of a law school's curriculum. In 2007, the Carnegie Foundation for the Advancement of Teaching urged more clinical legal education.[103] David Moss, hired in 1998 as assistant director of clinical education, was appointed the director of clinical education in 2007.[104] With Moss's leadership, the law school significantly expanded its clinical education program. He was instrumental in shepherding through the faculty the proposals for additional clinics and the professors to teach them. A reluctant faculty morphed into a faculty supportive

---

101. He served on the Wayne and Northwestern boards.

102. *Advocate*, April/May 1995.

103. The report was William M. Sullivan, Anne Colby, Judith Welch Wegner, Lloyd Bond, and Lee S. Shulman, *Educating Lawyers: Preparation for the Profession of Law* (Jossey-Bass, 2007).

104. Erica Eisinger was the director of the Clinical Program from 1997 to 2007. Moss also taught the disability clinic. The Disability Law Clinic over the years has had some important successes. For example, in 2016 student lawyers prevailed in requiring Medicaid to cover children unable to talk with speech-generating devices. See "Disability Law Clinic Wins Speech-Generating Devices for 3 Children," *Wayne Lawyer* 31 (Winter 2016): 16.

of clinical legal education. As part of that process, the faculty increased its supervision over the student-run Free Legal Aid Clinic.

In 2015, the ABA modified its standards for accreditation of law schools, mandating that students successfully complete one or more courses totaling six credit hours. The law firms, especially after the 2008 economic recession, wanted new associates to be better prepared to work independently, without much mentoring from their partners and senior associates.

The Wayne Law faculty resisted granting equal faculty status to clinical professors, contrary to the national trend and the ABA position on clinical legal education. Wayne hired clinical professors almost exclusively on term contracts without tenure protection.[105] The faculty made an exception when it changed Rachel Settlage's appointment from a contractual employee to a tenure-track professor. In 2019, the faculty went further. It offered all current clinical professors the opportunity to convert their term appointments to tenure-track positions, and all new faculty hired to teach clinics were on a unified tenure track, eliminating the distinction between professors who taught doctrinal courses and those who taught clinics.

Many of the school's earlier skills courses and clinics focused on skills allied with a career as a litigator, including civil and criminal law litigation. The balance changed. Wayne added business-related clinics and experiential learning placements with corporate counsel offices.

Dana (Roach) Thompson (2006–10) developed and directed the Business and Community Law Clinic, in which students represented individuals with new or fledging start-up businesses or nonprofits. The students drafted and filed the documents their clients needed to establish a Limited Liability Company or a for-profit or nonprofit corporation. Under supervision, they also gave advice to business owners on operational issues they encountered during the early organizational phases of their businesses.

---

105. Clinical faculty who were part of the university bargaining unit had the right to vote in faculty meetings, except on hiring, tenure, and promotion. Faculty Meeting Minutes, September 22, 2004.

Lawrence Mann, a Wayne Law tenured professor who left to practice for years as a trial lawyer, returned to the law school in 2014 as the interim director of Clinical Education and associate director of Professional Skills. He assisted law students who were competing in local, regional, and national advocacy tournaments.[106]

Wayne Law attracted both faculty and students interested in immigration law.[107] Rachel Settlage was hired in 2009 to direct the Asylum and Immigration Law Clinic.[108] In that clinic, students represented clients seeking asylum in the United States or the right to remain in the United States. If a client's case proceeded to a hearing stage, the students participated in the Immigration Court hearing.[109] Wayne graduates, in increasing numbers, specialized in immigration law. Settlage served as the director of Clinical Education until she was appointed Associate Dean for Academic Affairs in 2021.

Ruby Robinson ('11), a co-managing attorney for the Michigan Immigrant Rights Center, worked with volunteer attorneys to represent immigrant children in federal foster care. Justin Hanna ('15) and Nora Youkhana ('15) represented members of the Chaldean and other Iraqi communities in Southeast Michigan in their effort to delay the government's announced intent to enforce mass removal orders and deport them without a hearing. Their classmate Farah Al-Khersan represented immigrants through a faith-based organization, Justice for Our Neighbors.[110]

---

106. Mann taught students techniques when appearing before a jury: simplify and enrich the presentation by turning difficult concepts into easy-to-understand ideas.

107. Jonathan Weinberg, with his impressive experience in constitutional law, taught Immigration Law. Before Wayne Law offered an immigration clinic, some alumni established asylum and immigration legal practices. Angelo Paparelli ('76) started representing immigrants; his bicoastal practice was Project for the Mississippi Immigrant Rights Alliance.

108. Settlage practiced with the Asylum Program of Southern Arizona before serving as a clinical fellow with the University of Baltimore School of Law's Immigrant Rights Clinic.

109. When Settlage became the director of all clinical programs in 2017, the faculty hired Sabrina Balgamwalla to direct that clinic.

110. Justice for Our Neighbors is a "faith-driven ministry, welcoming immigrants and refugees into our churches and communities by providing free, high-quality legal services to immigrants who cannot afford a private attorney." See https://www.immigrationadvocates .org/nonprofit/legaldirectory/organization.486633-Justice_For_Our_Neighbors.

Shahad Atiya ('16) emigrated from Iraq to the Detroit area with her family in 2000 when she was twelve years old. After graduation Atiya started her own practice, focusing on immigration and other legal issues facing immigrants, including criminal law and complex cross-border divorce cases.[111] Atiya's classmate Laura Barrera worked in the immigration clinic at the University of Nevada-Las Vegas.[112] Shahar Ben-Josef ('16) served as attorney for the Boston Immigration Court judges.

Detroit provided the resources to offer a wide variety of hands-on clinical experiences that were not readily available at law schools outside a major metropolitan area. For example, Professor Kathryn Smolinski ('11) developed a unique Legal Advocacy for People with Cancer (LAPC) Clinic. Students interviewed and assisted the low-income patients in Detroit's Karmanos Cancer Center with legal issues.

The Patent Procurement Clinic offered Wayne students with the required educational background the opportunity to represent clients seeking a patent before Detroit's satellite U.S. Patent and Trademark Office.

Wayne established a robust externship program (part of the experiential-learning curriculum) in which students obtained supervised legal skills training. In the classroom component, students taking an externship shared experiences with their classmates. Students worked with prosecutors and criminal defense lawyers in the Criminal Justice Externship, with judges in the Judicial Externship, and with staff lawyers in the Public Interest Externship. In the Corporate Counsel Externship, students worked with lawyers in a corporation's legal department. The IRS externship gave students a unique opportunity to observe the administration of the tax laws from within the Chief Counsel's Detroit Area Office.

---

111. Participating in the Jessup International Moot Court Competition, Atiya received honors as the 66th best oralist and her team placed 31st out of 600 teams worldwide. After graduation, Atiya clerked for a special counsel appointed to deal with the Flint water crisis. She also was appointed as a special assistant attorney general on that case.

112. Barrera was the first Fellow in the Edward M. Bernstein & Associates Children's Rights Program at the UNLV law school.

Levin Center at Wayne Law

The law school established a second academic center in 2016: the Levin Center at Wayne Law. Retiring U.S. senator Carl Levin joined the faculty as the Distinguished Legislator in Residence and assumed the chairmanship of the center. In addition to teaching and chairing the Levin Center and practicing law, Senator Levin facilitated a class-action lawsuit emanating from the Flint water crisis. Senator Levin's awards, too numerous to list, include the Federal Bar Association's Wade H. McCree Jr. Award for the Advancement of Social Justice.[113]

Wayne Law students had the opportunity to take courses from Michigan's longest-serving U.S. senator. Senator Levin co-taught a course on legislation and a seminar on international tax avoidance and evasion. He gave students insight into the role of oversight in the legislative process at the federal, state, and local levels.

The Levin Center promoted Senator Levin's passion for congressional oversight as a tool to ensure open government and to hold public officials accountable to high ethical and transparency standards: "The center will build upon Levin's vision and leadership to develop academic coursework, training programs, symposia and research that will ensure future leaders recognize and embrace their role in promoting honest and open government, maintaining the public trust and holding public and private institutions accountable to high ethical and transparency standards."[114]

According to Senator Levin, the center gives students the opportunity to see "how the law meshes with legislative investigations and oversight, through

---

113. According to the law school website, "The Levin Center at Wayne Law educates future attorneys, business leaders, legislators and public servants on their role overseeing public and private institutions and using oversight as an instrument of change. Through academic programming, training and scholarship, the center equips future lawyers, legislators and leaders with an understanding of how effective legislative oversight can lead to significant and meaningful changes in public policy." https://law.wayne.edu/levin-center. Senator Levin co-taught "Tax Policy Seminar: Role and Impact of Congressional Oversight on Abusive Tax Strategies."

114. "Levin Center at Wayne Law Fosters Commitment to Public Service," *Wayne Lawyer* 30 (Summer 2015): 11.

Senator Carl Levin, Distinguished Legislator in Residence. (Reprinted with permission of the law school)

coursework, research, conferences and more."[115] The center awards Wayne students summer internships with U.S. congressional committees, including subcommittees on oversight and investigation. The center also sponsors events on the Wayne campus and in Washington, D.C. In 2018, the Levin Center and the

---

115. See www.law.wayne.edu/levin-center. The center produced tutorials on how to conduct congressional oversight investigations and made them publicly available. See also Carl Levin, *Getting to the Heart of the Matter: My 36 Years in the Senate* (Wayne State University Press, 2021).

Lugar Center[116] co-sponsored a conference commemorating the fortieth anniversary of U.S. senator Frank Church's hearings on the spying by U.S. agencies on American citizens. In 2017, the center hosted the first roundtable of U.S. academics that focused on congressional oversight.[117] The center also funded Research Scholars.[118] In 2021, together with the Keith Center, the Levin Center inaugurated a semester of experiential learning in Washington, D.C.

Wall of Fame

Dean Benson wanted a vehicle for the law school to recognize individuals who had made extraordinary contributions to the school. She worked with Powell Miller to endow an interactive Miller Wall of Fame primarily to honor alumni, faculty, and staff.

Powell Miller ('86) endowed the Wall, which is located in the main entrance to the school. With Miller's legal skills, work ethic, and drive, he took the risk of leaving a comfortable position with a major Michigan law firm, sold his house and car, established his own firm, and succeeded beyond what he envisioned as possible. He filed some of the early class action lawsuits in Michigan that were more commonly brought by larger firms in other major cities. For example, he filed suit against the Intel Corporation for selling defective computer chips and against the Michigan Consolidated Gas Company for exposing families to carbon monoxide. In 2014, he represented the City of Farmington Hills Employee Retirement System against Wells Fargo Bank for losses sustained when the bank invested pension fund assets in risky securities. Miller litigated automobile supply chain disputes and instigated class action lawsuits involving

---

116. The Lugar Center was established by retired U.S. senator Richard Lugar.
117. They examined the state of existing research and developed a national research agenda for oversight.
118. Wayne Law professors Kirsten Carlson and Lance Gable were selected as the inaugural scholars.

shareholder's rights. In 2015, he reached a $970.5 million securities fraud settlement with the insurer AIG.[119]

The Wall of Fame honor is the highest non-academic award presented by Wayne State University Law School.[120] A committee composed of alumni, faculty, and staff annually recommend "graduates and former faculty and staff of Wayne State University Law School whose extraordinary professional success and contributions, profound positive influence on Wayne Law, and high degree of character and integrity are recognized by their peers."[121] Judge Edward Ewell ('85) chaired the committee for years.[122]

In 2016, the first year the award was granted, Wall of Fame inductees were businessmen Daniel Gilbert and Stephen Ross; Federal Judges Damon J. Keith and Nancy Edmunds; lawyers Kenneth Cockrel, Paula Ettelbrick, Eugene Driker, and Jon Muth; Dean Charles Joiner; Professors Janet Findlater, Edward Littlejohn, and Stephen Schulman; and Director of the Neef Law Library Georgia Clark.[123]

Dean Benson Expands Fundraising and Scholarships

Jocelyn Benson, in her scholarship, examined congressional redistricting and in 2010 wrote "State Secretaries of State: Guardians of the Democratic Process." She ran unsuccessfully for Michigan secretary of state in 2010, but as a candidate for public office, she learned firsthand the skills associated with fundraising. In 2014 as dean, she led fundraising efforts not tied to capital improvements. She cultivated two of the law school's most financially successful alumni and, in 2016, Stephen Ross and the Gilbert Family Foundation each pledged $5 million, the two largest gifts in Wayne Law history.

---

119. See R. J. Smith, "The Natural," *Super Lawyers* (2014): 8.

120. https://law.wayne.edu/about/alumni-wall-of-fame-award. See earlier discussion of some of the alumni who received this honor.

121. See www.law.wayne.edu/alumni/wall-of-fame.

122. Judge Ewell served on Michigan's 3rd Judicial Circuit Court in Detroit.

123. In subsequent years, the committee limited the number of inductees to five a year.

Students accepted by Wayne and MSU law schools chose Wayne more frequently. While MSU Law's entering class was substantially larger than Wayne Law's entering class, from 2015 through 2018, of the common acceptances, 216 applicants went to Wayne Law and 197 went to MSU Law. For the 2019 entering class, the overlap data on applicants that applied to Wayne Law and MSU Law showed that 50 enrolled at Wayne and 45 enrolled at MSU.

During the Benson deanship, the law school issued a record number of scholarships to attract highly credentialed students,[124] but that level of aid was not sustainable at a public law school. The scholarship program was restructured to reduce the strain on the law school budget, but the law school had accumulated large deficits from those grants.

In 2016, Benson resigned her deanship to become CEO of the Ross Initiative in Sports for Equality (RISE), a venture designed to improve race relations in sports. In 2018, she was elected Michigan's secretary of state.

Dean Bierschbach: A New Era

Dean Richard Bierschbach joined the law school administration in August 2017 as the school's twelfth dean and with extraordinary credentials. He had a stellar academic background at the University of Michigan Law School before clerking for U.S. Supreme Court Justice Sandra Day O'Connor and D.C. Court of Appeals Judge Randolph. He held high-level positions in the Justice Department, served in leadership positions in the American Bar Association,[125] and practiced with New York law firms. He spent fourteen years on the faculty at Benjamin N. Cardozo School of Law, Yeshiva University, including as vice dean. Dean Bierschbach's scholarship has been published in many of the most prestigious law reviews. He has taught criminal law and procedure, including white-collar crime, and administrative and regulatory law. He received the Pro

---

124. See Faculty Meeting Minutes, October 28, 2014.
125. He co-chaired the ABA Criminal Justice Section's Amicus Practice Committee and served as vice chair of its Administrative Law Section's Criminal Process Subcommittee.

Bono Publico award from the New York City Legal Aid Society for his work on behalf of the society's Juvenile Rights Division.

The law school's commitment to achieve a racially diverse student body included a rocky journey in the 1970s and, as discussed above, was made more difficult with Proposition 2 in 2006, but the commitment remained firm. As Dean Bierschbach said, "attracting a diverse student body requires commitment, focus and a lot of work—it's all hands on deck—and it's essential to bake that reality into every aspect of the institution. . . . You want diversity and inclusion to be evident in every facet of the law school experience, from before admission through graduation and beyond."[126]

The law school's history was already filled with examples of its commitment to provide access to a legal education to immigrants and children of immigrants and individuals from diverse ethnic, racial, and other underrepresented communities.

In the school's formative years, a significant proportion of the student body consisted of students who were children of immigrants from Canada and Western Europe who came to Michigan to work in the automobile plants and children of Jewish immigrants fleeing persecution in Eastern Europe. Starting in the 1960s, the immigrant families came from Poland and other Eastern European countries, seeking better opportunities for their children. In the 1990s, Wayne Law attracted children of immigrants of Chaldean, Muslim, Eastern European, Eastern Indian, and Asian heritage. They thrived and enjoyed successful careers in law and accounting and in high-level corporate positions. The following is a sampling of the graduates from immigrant families in the twenty-first century.

Zeina Baydoun's parents emigrated from southern Lebanon, they divorced when she was young, and her father married a non-Muslim woman. Baydoun ('10) was raised in two different cultures. In middle school, she was "not white enough" and bullied as a Muslim with an unusual name. At Fordson High School in Dearborn, she was "too white."

---

126. "Dean Bierschbach," *Wayne Lawyer* 32 (Fall 2017): 12.

With her mother's encouragement, Baydoun became the first member of her extended family to pursue a professional education, and she found the blend of students in her Wayne Law classes welcoming. According to Baydoun, many families that emigrated from the Middle East possessed an entrepreneurial spirit and wanted to open businesses. She and her family produced and sold an ethnic Fattoush salad dressing, and then purchased and rehabilitated residential and commercial properties.

In many respects, women like Zeina Baydoun were models for more traditional Muslim women who decided to pursue their legal education at Wayne. Zainab Sabbagh Hazimi's ('15) parents emigrated from Beirut in the late 1980s, knowing no English, and lived near other Arab American immigrants in the South End of Dearborn. Her father was employed as an automobile mechanic until he was able to establish his own repair business. Hazimi's parents encouraged their daughters and sons to pursue higher education and both she and her brother Ahmad Sabbagh ('19) chose Wayne Law.

Hazimi wondered if her job opportunities would be affected by her personal decision to wear a hijab. Upon graduation, she received a prestigious clerkship with Federal District Court Judge Sean Cox. After that clerkship, she worked for a major corporate law firm.

Gurinder Singh ('07) was the first in her immigrant Sikh family from India to pursue a professional degree. She experienced some discrimination in public school, in part because her brother, who attended the same school, wore a turban. She was attracted to the business world, having worked in her family's business since high school. While in law school, she sponsored an annual international Punjab dance competition at the State Theatre in Detroit through her event production company.

Singh loved the kind-hearted and passionate law students at Wayne. She participated in the Jessup international competition, finishing second in the Chicago regionals. After law school, she worked on business development with a major Detroit law firm before she joined a technology start-up that designed software to increase business efficiency for companies that expanded internationally.

Aisa Villarosa's parents emigrated from the Philippines, her father in 1958. Villarosa ('11) was the first Wayne Law student to receive the prestigious Skadden Fellowship, awarded nationally to twenty-five to thirty law school graduates.[127] With the fellowship, Villarosa worked with the Michigan Children's Law Center, providing juveniles with court representation.[128] After her fellowship, Villarosa practiced in Oakland, California, with her 313 Project classmates Julianna Rivera and Natalia Santanna and yearned to return to Detroit.

Aziza (Pratt) Yuldesheva came to the United States as a high school exchange student. Yuldesheva ('06) was born in Uzbekistan and raised in Ukraine. She came to Dundee, Michigan, for high school, returned home, and then came back to Michigan on a scholarship from Eastern Michigan University. After college, she worked for three years before enrolling at Wayne Law School.

Yuldesheva's law school experience improved substantially after one of her professors told her that he "saw something special in her ability"—she received an A+ in that course. Yuldesheva thrived in Wayne's Immigration Law clinic and, in her first job after graduation, the law firm gave her the freedom to establish a successful immigration practice. With the encouragement of a Michigan lawyer who was her mentor,[129] she moved to a "Big 4" accounting firm, settled into a career practicing international tax, and taught in Deloitte's educational program. In the previously male-dominated accounting profession, women were becoming the firm leaders. Yuldesheva rose to become a principal in the firm.

Dean Bierschbach came to Wayne with an ambitious multiyear agenda to enhance the school's reputation and its *U.S. News & World Report* ranking. On

---

127. Villarosa was not the only Wayne student to receive a national fellowship. In 2017, Rachel Lerman received the Peggy Browning Summer Fellowship to work with the New Orleans Workers' Center for Racial Justice, an organization supporting workers' rights.

128. Many of her clients were subjected to child abuse and neglect. The center also helped these children obtain social services and assistance during school expulsion hearings.

129. Yuldesheva edited the State Bar of Michigan's *International Lawyer* periodical and became a mentee of a lawyer whose article she edited. When her mentor moved from a law firm to the international accounting firm, he encouraged her to join that firm.

his arrival, he learned that his first job was to put the law school's financial house in order.

When Bierschbach arrived, the law school had been spending more than its budget allocations, including, most notably, the deficit in scholarships. He negotiated a multiyear plan to put the scholarship account back in balance.

Bierschbach embarked on a plan to expand the teaching program to include an undergrade concentration in law and a master's program for non-lawyers to develop some legal background related to their careers in fields like human resources. He recognized that the law school budget had to blend university resources with increased endowments and annual giving.

In 2020, law professors began to teach undergraduate courses leading to a minor in law through Wayne's College of Liberal Arts and Sciences, the Mike Ilitch School of Business, and the School of Social Work.[130] The law school also initiated an online Master of Studies in Law (MSL) degree.[131]

The law school committee work, especially student Admissions, faculty Tenure and Promotion, and committees charged with the development of new programs, was performed by less than the entire faculty. The dean involved more and more professors in these committees.

Dean Bierschbach strongly supported faculty research and scholarship. He created the position of Associate Dean for Research and Faculty Development. Jonathan Weinberg, the inaugural dean, was charged with establishing programs focused on scholarship within the faculty and inviting scholars to the school. Dean Weinberg also coordinated, highlighted, and publicized the accomplishments of the faculty's highly productive scholars. In 2020, Bierschbach secured

---

130. In 1995, during Dean Robinson's tenure, the faculty considered but did not implement a certificate program for non-lawyers, designed to enhance the students' value in their employment.

131. The MSL was "specifically designed to help specialists in human resources expand their knowledge of legal principles and the U.S. legal system." See https://law.wayne.edu/academics/degrees.

funds for the school's first two research scholars—Professors Sanjukta Paul and William Ortman.[132]

U.S. News *Rankings*

In 1997, Dean Robinson and 149 other law school deans wrote a letter to *U.S. News* criticizing its ranking system, which depended on responses from individuals who knew very little about most of the law schools that they were evaluating. Notwithstanding this broad-based criticism that the rankings were misleading and did not provide relevant information to prospective law school applicants,[133] law school applicants continued to use those ratings as a factor in choosing a law school.

U.S. News heavily weights (40 percent) a law school's "reputation" as part of its ranking system.[134] Assuming that Wayne Law's scores on other factors remained unchanged, the school's ranking would increase if the law school had more visibility among the lawyers, judges, and legal academics who were selected to rank law schools.

During Bierschbach's deanship, Wayne's *U.S. News* ranking rose to its highest level in memory. When he arrived in 2017, the 2018 *U.S. News* rankings placed Wayne Law tied for 100.[135] In the 2022 rankings issued in 2021, the school was 72nd.

---

132. In 2017, Sanjukta Paul joined the faculty after clerking for a judge on the 9th Circuit, working as a public interest lawyer on labor and civil rights issues and designing and teaching a clinic focused on litigating workers' rights at the University of California-Los Angeles. Professor Paul taught courses in corporations, labor law, work law, and employment law. Her book *Solidarity in the Shadow of Antitrust* (Cambridge University Press, 2021) covers the intersection of antitrust and labor regulation.

133. The deans did not quarrel with *U.S. News'* policy of gathering extensive data on each law school but strongly objected to the selection of factors and the weight they choose to apply to each of those factors in ranking the nation's law schools.

134. Reputation is part of the Quality Assessment in *U.S. News* rankings. The 40 percent consists of a peer reputation score of 25 percent and the lawyer/judge reputation score of 15 percent. See https://www.usnews.com/education.

135. In 2020, Wayne Law was tied for #83 with the University of San Diego. See https://www.usnews.com/education.

Philanthropy

Bierschbach established a long-term plan to increase philanthropy, and his early efforts were encouraging. In 2018, the law school received a bequest of over $2 million from the estate of Jacqueline Simons Walker ('51), who for years was a judge on California's Worker's Compensation Appeals Board. The university also transferred a major endowment from the general university to the law school.

At a time when competitor schools were publicizing their new chaired professors, Wayne lagged. In 2000, with a gift from the estate of Walter Gibbs ('62),[136] the law school established its first chair. Distinguished Professor Robert Sedler held the Gibbs Chair in Civil Rights and Civil Liberties from 2000 to 2005. Distinguished Professor Winter joined the faculty in 2002 as the Gibbs Chair in Constitutional Law. The second chair was attached to the Keith Center. Professor Peter Hammer, director of the Keith Center, held the A. Alfred Taubman Endowed Chair.

Dean Bierschbach received commitments from Emeritus Professor Edward Littlejohn for the Littlejohn Family Chair to be located in the Keith Center. The John Reed Professorship was funded by alumnus Vincent Foster ('82), chairman and CEO of Main Street Capital Corporation. In 2021, spearheaded by a group of his former students, the law school received commitments for the Alan Schenk Endowed Chair in Tax Law.

Many alumni devoted significant time and effort in leadership positions within the law school and served as resources for the law school deans. They included Eugene Driker, Nancy Edmunds, Thomas Kienbaum, I. W. Winsten, and Kathryn Humphrey. In addition, Candyce Ewing Abbatt ('83) and William Sankbeil ('71) dedicated significant time to their service on the Board of Visitors, Alumni Association, and decanal search committees.

---

136. Gibbs, an assistant prosecutor in Wayne County, left multimillion-dollar bequests to the law school and the Detroit Institute of Arts.

Kathryn Humphrey, Class of 1980. (Reprinted with permission of the law school)

I. W. Winsten, Class of 1979. (Reprinted with permission)

Thomas Kienbaum, Class of 1968. (Reprinted with permission)

Students' Journal for Business

Wayne Law students took the lead in establishing all three of the school's academic journals. In 1954 the law students organized the student-run *Wayne Law Review*. In 1997, the students initiated the *Journal of Law in Society* to evaluate the impact of law within various segments of society. The journal became the scholarly arm of the Keith Center for Civil Rights and published articles emanating from the center's academic symposia.[137] The Wayne Law students were not satisfied with the *Review* and the journal. They wanted a journal for students interested in representing businesses.

In 2010, Eric Zacks brought to the law school his teaching talent and years of experience at Detroit's Honigman law firm advising corporations

---

137. The symposia topics have included "Affirmative Action in College Admissions," "Public Education and Vouchers," and "Reparations: Should We Reimburse for Racism."

and private equity firms.[138] In 2017, Zacks worked with a group of students to persuade the faculty to approve a third student-run journal.[139] Catherine Ferguson was the inaugural editor in chief and Professor Zacks served as faculty advisor. The online, specialized *Journal of Business Law* published "scholarly articles and notes by academics, practitioners and students on a broad range of business law topics affecting the Michigan legal community."[140]

The next chapter in the history of Wayne Law is still to be written.[141] The elements are in place for the law school to be on the cusp of a second leap forward.

For the long term, Wayne Law needs resources to fund a high-quality legal education for a diverse student body in an environment of reduced demand for that education. Wayne Law must obtain resources to compete with the elite law schools for high-credentialed students and recognized faculty scholars to become a significant source of legal talent nationally.

The future of Wayne State University Law School depends on the growing reputation of the school and its graduates in law practice and business in Michigan and nationally. Its status depends on the school's ability to continue to attract a racially, ethnically, and gender-diverse student body of talented, motivated students. The law school needs resources at levels required to operate an elite law school.

Long-term continuity of decanal leadership is necessary for the school to engage in long-range institutional planning and the cultivation of outside financial support.

---

138. The students voted him the upper-level Professor of the Year many times.
139. In 2020, Zacks was appointed as the director of the graduate program.
140. Linda Mifsud, "Wayne Law Adds New Scholarly Journal on Business Law," *Wayne Lawyer* 33 (Spring 2018).
141. Many have been given credit as originating what is commonly accepted as the observation of former *Post* publisher Philip Graham: that newspapers are the "first rough draft of history."

Appendix A

Full-Time Faculty (by start date)

The author has not verified the completeness of the list of full-time faculty, dates of employment, and academic, law school, and university titles and honors.

Name	Title	Full Time
Allan Campbell	Dean	1927–1937
Arthur Neef	Dean	1927–1930 (Part-time Executive Secretary and Instructor) 1930–1935 (Full-time Executive Secretary) 1935–1937 (Asst. Dean) 1937–1967 (Dean) 1945–1967 (Provost) 1953–1964 (Univ. V.P.) 1930–1969 (Prof.)
Carl Whitchurch	Prof.	1935–1963 (Prof.)
Harry Lee Endsley	Prof.	1935–1953 (Prof.)
John E. Glavin	Prof., Assoc. Dean	1938–1940 (Instructor or Adjunct Prof.) 1940–1944 (Asst. Prof.) 1944–1947 (Assoc. Prof.) 1947–1981 (Prof.) 1957–1967 (Assoc. Dean) 1967–1968 (Acting Dean) 1981–1992 (Prof. Emeritus)

Name	Title	Full Time
Boaz Siegel II	Prof.	1941–1952 (Librarian)
		1945–1951 (Assoc. Prof.)
		1952–1972 (Prof.)
		1972–2002 (Prof. Emeritus)
Robert E. Childs	Prof.	1945–1946 (Asst. Prof.)
		1946–1950 (Assoc. Prof.)
		1951–1976 (Prof.)
		1976–1992 (Prof. Emeritus)
William Dickson MacDonald	Asst. Prof.	1946–1948 (Asst. Prof.)
Norbert Dick West	Librarian	1946–1962
Thomas Anthony Cowan	Prof.	1947–1954
George Squire	Asst. Prof.	1949–1953
Melvin Nord	Assoc. Prof., Lecturer	1951–1952, 1956–1957
Harold S. Marchant	Prof.	1954–1955 (Assoc. Prof.)
		1956–1973 (Prof.)
		1973–1982 (Prof. Emeritus)
Samuel Irving Shuman	Prof.	1954–1955 (Asst. Prof.)
		1955–1956 (Assoc. Prof.)
		1957–1982 (Prof.)
Mark Kahn	Asst. Prof. of Economics	1955–1960
Richard Strichartz	Prof.	1956–1959 (Assoc. Prof.)
		1959–1986 (Prof.)
		1986–1995 (Prof. Emeritus)
Benjamin Carlin	Prof.	1957–1974
Donald H. Gordon	Prof., Dean	1957–1958 (Asst. Prof.)
		1958–1961 (Assoc. Prof.)
		1961–1973 (Prof.)
		1970–1973 (Assoc. Dean)
		1975–1990 (Prof.)
		1975–1980 (Dean)
		1990–2011 (Prof. Emeritus)
Douglass George Boshkoff	Assoc. Prof.	1959–1960 (Asst. Prof.)
		1960–1963 (Assoc. Prof.)
Richard Sherwin Miller	Prof.	1959–1963 (Assoc. Prof.)
		1963–1965 (Prof.)
Charles Whitted Quick	Prof.	1959–1966
Bethany J. Ochal	Librarian	1961–1971

Name	Title	Full Time
Lionel H. Frankel	Assoc. Prof.	1962–1963 (Asst. Prof.)
		1963–1966 (Assoc. Prof.)
Donald Barnett King	Assoc. Prof.	1962–1964
Maurice Kelman	Assoc. Prof.	1963–1964 (Asst. Prof.)
		1964–1966 (Assoc. Prof.)
		1970–1996 (Prof.)
		1996–2016 (Prof. Emeritus)
Kenneth Roy Callahan	Prof.	1964–1968 (Assoc. Prof.)
		1968–1992 (Prof.)
		1992–2001 (Prof. Emeritus)
Anthony M. Vernava	Asst. Dean, Prof.	1965–1968 (Assoc. Prof.)
		1968–1970 (Asst. Dean)
		1968–1971 (Prof.)
Edward M. Wise	Prof., Assoc. Dean, Dir. Comparative Criminal Law Project	1965–1968 (Assoc. Prof.)
		1968–2000 (Prof.)
		1983–2000 (Dir. Comp. Crim. Law Project)
		1986–1992 (Assoc. Dean)
Friedrich K. Juenger	Prof.	1966–1968 (Assoc. Prof.)
		1968–1975 (Prof.)
Arthur J. Lombard	Prof., Assoc. Dean	1966–1969 (Assoc. Prof.)
		1969–1987 (Prof.)
		1978–1985 (Assoc. Dean)
Frederica B. Koller Lombard	Prof., Assoc. Dean	1966–1967 (Asst. Prof.)
		1967–1969 (Assoc. Prof.)
		1969–2007 (Prof.)
		1992–2007 (Assoc. Dean)
		2007–2011 (Prof. Emerita)
Peter E. Quint	Asst. Prof.	1965–1967
Alan S. Schenk	Dist. Prof.	1966 (Asst. Prof.)
		1967–1969 (Assoc. Prof.)
		1969–2011 (Prof.)
		1973–1974, 1975–1976 (Assoc. Dean)
		2011–present (Dist. Prof.)
		2019 (inducted into Academy of Scholars)
Stephen H. Schulman	Prof.	1966–1969 (Assoc. Prof.)
		1969–1995 (Prof.)
		1995–2000 (Prof. Emeritus)
Vincent Rinella Jr.	Asst. Prof.	1966–1968 (Asst. Prof.)
Edward Greene	Asst. Prof.	1967–1968

Name	Title	Full Time
Richard W. Bartke	Prof.	1967–1969 (Assoc. Prof.)
		1969–1981 (Prof.)
		1971 (Act. Lib. Dir.)
Robert Feinschreiber	Asst. Prof.	1967–1970
Grant H. Morris	Asst. Dean, Prof.	1967–1969 (Asst. Prof.)
		1968–1970 (Assoc. Prof.)
		1970–1974 (Prof.)
		1971–1973 (Asst. Dean of Academic Affairs)
Robert C. Berry	Prof.	1968–1970
Paul David Borman	Asst. Dean, Prof.	1968–1971 (Assoc. Prof.)
		1968–1973 (Asst. Dean)
		1971–1979 (Prof.)
William Benjamin Gould	Prof.	1968–1971
Charles Joiner	Dean, Prof.	1967–1972
Michael S. Josephson	Prof.	1968–1969 (Asst. Prof.)
		1969–1970 (Assoc. Prof.)
		1971–1974 (Prof.)
John Edward Mogk	Prof.	1968–1971 (Assoc. Prof.)
		1971–present (Prof.)
		2021–present (Dist. Service Prof.)
		1990–1995 (Dir. Graduate Studies)
		2015–present (Chair, Levin Center at Wayne Law Faculty Comm.)
Elwood B. Hain Jr.	Prof.	1969–1972 (Assoc. Prof.)
		1972–1976 (Prof.)
Geoffrey J. Lanning	Prof.	1969–1988 (Prof.)
		1988–2004 (Prof. Emeritus)
Patricia H. Marschall	Assoc. Prof.	1969–1971
Ralph Slovenko	Prof. of Law and Psychiatry	1969–2013 (Prof. of Law and Psychiatry)
		2013– (Prof. Emeritus)
Godfrey Cornelius Henry	Asst. Dean, Assoc. Prof.	1970–1971
Ray David Henson	Prof.	1970–1975
Otto J. Hetzel	Prof. Emeritus	1970–1996 (Prof.)
		1970–1972 (Assoc. Dir. Center for Urban Studies)
		1996–2020 (Prof. Emeritus)
David R. Hood	Assoc. Prof	1970–1973
Elliot D. Luby	Prof. of Law and Psychiatry	1970–1975

Name	Title	Full Time
Florian Bartosic	Prof.	1971–1980 (Prof.)
Morton P. Cohen	Assoc. Prof.	1971–1973
Jane M. Friedman	Prof.	1971–1972 (Asst. Prof.)
		1972–1975 (Assoc. Prof.)
		1975–2002 (Prof.)
Leroy L. Lamborn	Prof. Emeritus	1971–1972 (Assoc. Prof.)
		1972–1997 (Prof.)
		1997–Present (Prof. Emeritus)
Kevin Hugh Tierney	Prof.	1971–1975 (Assoc. Prof.)
		1975–1979 (Prof.)
James Bailey III	Dir. Library	1971–1974
Edward J. Littlejohn	Prof. Emeritus	1972–1976 (Assoc. Prof.)
		1976–1978 (Assoc. Dean)
		1976–1996 (Prof.)
		1996–present (Prof. Emeritus)
Marc Stickgold	Assoc. Prof.	1972–1976
Martin Adelman	Prof. Emeritus	1973–1999 (Prof.)
		1974–1975 (Act. Dean)
		1999–present (Prof. Emeritus)
Georgia A. Clark	Dir. Neef Lib.	1973–1975 (Asst. Dir.)
		1975–1976 (Acting Dir.)
		1976–2008 (Dir. Neef Lib.)
B. J. George Jr.	Prof., Dir. Cntr. for	1971–1976 (Prof.)
	Admin. of Justice	1973–1974 (Interim Dean)
Robert Jerome Glennon Jr.	Prof.	1973–1977 (Assoc. Prof.)
		1977–1985 (Prof.)
Jerold Lax	Assoc. Prof.	1973–1975
Nicholas A. Tomasulo	Visiting Prof.	1973–1975 (Visiting Prof.)
John L Barkai	Assoc. Prof.	1974–1978
Paul Peter Harbrecht	Prof.	1974–1983
Barry L. Zaretsky	Asst. Prof.	1974–1978 (Asst. Prof.)
John F. Dolan	Dist. Prof. Emeritus	1975–1978 (Assoc. Prof.)
		1978–2015 (Prof.)
		2001–2015 (Dist. Prof.)
		2010 (inducted into Academy of Scholars)
		2016–present (Dist. Prof. Emeritus)
Beth Ann Eisler	Assoc. Prof.	1975–1988
Cynthia E. Gitt	Asst. Prof., Dir. Employment Discrimination Clinic	1975–1977 (Assist. Prof.)
		1975–1977 (Dir. Employ. Discrimination Clinic)

Name	Title	Full Time
Denise Carty-Bennia	Asst. Prof.	1975–1977
Joseph Dante Grano	Dist. Prof.	1975–1985 (Prof.) 1985–2001 (Dist. Prof.) 1997 (inducted into Academy of Scholars)
Barbara Klarman	Asst. Dean, Instructor	1975–1976 (Asst. Dean)
Susan R. Martyn	Assoc. Prof., Asst. Dean	1975–1977 (Asst. Dean) 1977–1980 (Asst. Prof.) 1980–1981 (Prof.) 1981 (Emeritus)
Michael J. Zimmer	Assoc. Prof.	1975–1978 (Assoc. Prof)
Janet E. Findlater	Prof. Emeritus	1976–1977 (Asst. Prof.) 1977–2016 (Assoc. Prof.) 2016–present (Prof. Emeritus)
Stuart M. Israel	Assoc. Prof.	1976–1977
Michael J. McIntyre	Prof.	1975–1976 (Visiting Prof.) 1977–2013 (Prof.) 1990 (Board of Governors Faculty Recognition Award for *The International Income Tax Rules of the United States*) 2012 (inducted into Academy of Scholars) 2013 (President's Award for Excellence in Service)
Russell M. Paquette	Asst. Dean	1976–1981
Zygmunt J. B. Plater	Prof.	1976–1978 (Assoc. Prof.) 1978–1982 (Prof.)
Joel Resnick	Assoc. Prof.	1977–1982 (Assoc. Prof.)
Robert Allen Sedler	Dist. Prof.	1977–2000 (Prof.) 2000–2005 (Gibbs Chair in Civil Rights & Civil Liberties) 2000–2021 (Dist. Prof.) 2005 (inducted into Academy of Scholars) 2021–present (Prof. Emeritus)
Timothy Joseph Wilton	Assoc. Prof.	1977–1984
Cheryl Scott Dube	Dir., Legal Research & Writing	1977–1983 (Dir., Legal Research & Writing)
Robert H. Abrams	Prof., Assoc. Dean	1977–1981 (Assoc. Prof.) 1981–2004 (Prof.) 1985–1986 (Assoc. Dean) 1986–1987 (Interim Dean)

Name	Title	Full Time
Jennifer Kate Bankier	Asst Prof.	1979–1982
Steven L. Harris	Assoc. Prof.	1979–1981 (Asst. Prof.)
		1981–1983 (Assoc. Prof.)
Barbara Shaw Harvey	Asst. Prof.	1979–1982
Mary G. Heffernan	Asst. Dean	1979–1981
Steven L. Novinson	Assoc. Prof.	1979–1983 (Asst. Prof.)
		1983–1986 (Assoc.)
William M. Burnham	Prof. Emeritus	1980–1986 (Asst. Prof.)
		1986–1990 (Assoc. Prof.)
		1990–2009 (Prof.)
		2014–present (Prof. Emeritus)
David Loeffler	Assoc. Prof.	1980–1984
John C. Roberts	Dean, Prof.	1980–1986 (Dean)
		1980–1986 (Prof.)
Barbara Bruno	LRW Instructor, Asst. Dean	1980–1982 (LRW Instructor)
		1982–1985 (Asst. Dean, Placement)
Margo K. Rogers Lesser	Asst. Prof.	1981–1988
Mary Margaret Bolda	LRW Instructor	1981–1984
Vincent A. Wellman	Assoc. Prof.	1981–1987 (Asst. Prof.)
		1987–present (Assoc. Prof.)
Diana Pratt	Dir., LRW	1981–1982 (LRW Instructor)
		1983–2007 (Dir. Legal Research & Writing)
Deborah Brouwer	LRW Instructor	1981–1983 (LRW Instructor)
David M. Adamany	Prof., President	1982–2000 (Prof.)
		1982–1997 (President)
		1997–2000 (Pres. Emeritus)
Paul R. Dimond	Prof.	1982–1985
Joshua Dressler	Prof.	1982–1993 (Prof.)
Gunther F. Handl	Prof.	1982–1984 (Assoc. Prof.)
		1984–1996 (Prof.)
Seymour Nayer	LRW Instructor	1982–1985 (LRW Instructor)
Barbara Patek	LRW Instructor	1983–1985 (LRW Instructor)
Melanie LaFave	LRW Instructor	1983–1985 (LRW Instructor)
Marilyn Finkelman	LRW Instructor	1983–1990 (LRW Instructor)
Stephen Calkins	Prof., Assoc. VP for Academic Personnel	1983–1988 (Assoc. Prof.)
		1988–present (Prof.)
		1992–1993 (Interim Dean)
		2008–2011 (Univ. Assoc. VP)
Marta A. Manildi	Asst. Dean, Lecturer	1984–1986

Name	Title	Full Time
Lawrence C. Mann	Assoc. Prof., Assoc. Dir. of Professional Skills	1984–1990 (Asst. Prof.) 1990–1991 (Assoc. Prof.) 1994–2004 (Assoc. Prof.) 2015–2018 (Assoc. Dir, Prof. Skills)
Sandra Gross	LRW Instructor	1984–1995 (LRW Instructor)
Kathryn R. Heidt	Prof.	1985–1994 (Assoc. Prof.) 1994–1995 (Prof.)
Barbara Blumenfeld	LRW Instructor	1985–1990 (LRW Instructor)
John Wesley Reed	Dean & Prof.	1987–1992 (Dean & Prof.) 1992–2018 (Prof. Emeritus)
George Feldman	Asst. Prof.	1988–1995
Marie Scruggs Inniss	Asst. Dean	1988–1993
Michele R. Miller	Dean of Students	1988–2006 (Asst. Dean) 2006–2011 (Dean of Students)
Jonathan T. Weinberg	Prof. & Assoc. Dean for Research and Faculty Development	1988–1993 (Asst. Prof.) 1993–1999 (Assoc. Prof.) 1999–present (Prof.) 2018–present (Assoc. Dean, Research & Faculty Development)
Kingsley R. Browne	Prof.	1989–1997 (Assoc. Prof.) 1997–present (Prof.)
Jessica D. Litman	Prof.	1990–1991 (Assoc. Prof.) 1991–2006 (Prof.)
Florise R. Neville-Ewell	Asst. Prof.	1990–1996
Linda Fowler Sims	Asst. Dean	1993–2008
James K. Robinson	Dean, Prof.	1993–1998 (Dean) 1993–2002 (Prof.)
John Friedl	Assoc. Prof., Dir. Ctr. for Legal Studies	1994–2000 (Assoc. Prof., Dir. Ctr. for Legal Studies)
Peter J. Henning	Prof.	1994–2002 (Assoc. Prof.) 2002–present (Prof.) 2000–2003 (Dir. Grad. Studies)
James D. Robb	Asst. Dean	1994–2002
Zanita E. Fenton	Assoc. Prof.	1995–2001 (Asst. Prof.) 2001–2005 (Assoc. Prof.)
Eric Kades	Assoc. Prof.	1995–2000 (Asst. Prof.) 2000–2002 (Assoc. Prof.)
Laura B. Bartell	Prof.	1996–2005 (Assoc. Prof.) 2005–present (Prof.)

Name	Title	Full Time
Dennis Devaney	Assoc. Prof.	1996–2001 (Assoc. Prof.)
Katherine E. White	Prof.	1996–2002 (Asst. Prof.)
		2002–2007 (Assoc. Prof.)
		2007–present (Prof.)
Gennady M. Danilenko	Prof.	1997–2001 (Prof.)
Brad R. Roth	Prof., Law & Political Science	1997–2001 (Asst. Prof.)
		2001–2011 (Assoc. Prof.)
		2011–present (Prof.)
		2018 (inducted into Academy of Scholars)
Joan Mahoney	Dean, Prof., Prof. Emerita	1998–2003 (Dean)
		1998–2009 (Prof.)
		2009–present (Prof. Emerita)
David R. Moss	Assoc. Prof. (Clinical)	1998–2015 (Assistant Clinical Professor)
		2015–present (Associate Clinical Professor)
		1998–2007 (Asst. Dir. Clinical Education)
		2007–2015 (Dir. Clinical Education)
		2000–present (Dir. Disability Law Clinic)
Christopher J. Peters	Assoc. Prof.	1998–2002 (Asst. Prof.)2002–2009 (Assoc. Prof.)
Amy Neville	LRW Instructor	1999–present (LRW Instructor)
Kristin Theut-Newa	Dir., LRW; LRW Instructor	1999–present (LRW Instructor)
		2014–2016 (Interim Dir., LRW)
		2016–present (Dir., LRW)
Erica M. Eisinger	Dir. Clin. Educ., Assoc. Prof. Clinical	2000–2007 (Assoc. Prof. Clinical)
		2000–2007 (Dir. Clinical Ed.)
David Andrew Moran	Assoc. Prof.	2000–2006 (Asst. Prof.)
		2006–2008 (Assoc. Prof.)
Julia Ya Qin	Prof.	2000–2006 (Asst. Prof.)
		2006–2010 (Assoc. Prof.)
		2010–present (Prof.)
		2014–2016 (Joint Appt. Tsinghua Univ. School of Law)
John A. Rothchild	Prof.; Faculty Director, Master of Studies in Law Prog.	2001–present (Assoc. Prof; tenure in 2007)
		2008–2013 (Assoc. Dean)
		2020–present (Prof.)
		2020–present (Fac. Dir. Master of Studies in Law Prog.)
Ellen J. Dannin	Prof.	2002–2006
Anthony M. Dillof	Prof.	2002–2018 (Assoc. Prof.)
		2018–present (Prof.)

Name	Title	Full Time
Harry G. Hutchison	Prof.	2002–2006
Steven L. Winter	Walter S. Gibbs Dist. Prof. of Const'l Law	2002–present (Gibbs Prof. of Const. Law) 2002–2006 (Dir. Center for Legal Studies) 2017–present (Dist. Prof.) 2021 (inducted into Academy of Scholars)
Gregory H. Fox	Prof., Dir. Prog. for Intl. Legal Studies	2002–2003 (Visiting Prof.) 2003–2009 (Assoc. Prof.) 2009–present (Prof.) 2009–present (Dir. Prog. for Intl. Legal Studies)
Peter Joseph Hammer	Prof.; A. Alfred Taubman Endowed Chair; Dir. Damon J. Keith Center for Civil Rights	2003–2005 (Assoc. Prof.) 2005–present (Prof.) 2009–present (Dir. Damon J. Keith Center for Civil Rights) 2018–present (A. Alfred Taubman Endowed Chair)
Bethany Berger	Asst. Prof.	2004–2006
Frank H. Wu	Dean, Prof.	2004–2008 (Dean) 2004–2009 (Prof.)
Erica Beecher-Monas	Prof.	2005–2017
Jocelyn Michelle Benson	Assoc. Prof.; Dean	2005–2010 (Asst. Prof.) 2010–2020 (Assoc. Prof.) 2012–2014 (Interim Dean) 2014–2016 (Dean) 2016–2017 (Dir., Levin Center at Wayne Law)
Paul R. Dubinsky	Prof.	2005–2017 (Assoc. Prof.) 2011–2015 (Dir. of Grad Studies) 2017–present (Prof.)
Noah D. Hall	Prof.	2005–2010 (Asst. Prof.) 2010–2017 (Assoc. Prof.) 2017–present (Prof.) 2014–2015 (Assoc. Dean. Student Affairs)
Lisa Rucus Mikalonis	Lecturer, Asst. Dean	2005–2006 (Asst. Dean)
Dana (Roach) Thompson	Asst. Prof. Clinical	2006–2010
Derek E. Bambauer	Asst. Prof.	2006–2008
Linda M. Beale	Prof.; Dir. Graduate Studies	2006–2009 (Assoc. Prof.) 2009–present (Prof) 2008–2010, 2017–2020 (Dir. Grad. Studies)

Name	Title	Full Time
Susan E. Cancelosi	Assoc. Dean., Assoc. Prof.	2006–2012 (Assist. Prof.) 2012–present (Assoc. Prof.) 2016–2017 (Interim Assoc. Dean) 2017–2020 (Assoc. Dean)
Steven M. Davidoff	Asst. Prof.	2006–2008
Lance Adam Gable	Assoc. Prof.	2006–2012 (Asst. Prof.) 2012–2020 (Assoc. Prof.) 2021–present (Prof.) 2013–2014 (Interim Assoc. Dean) 2014–2016 (Assoc. Dean) 2016–2017 (Interim Dean) 2021–present (Dir., Minor in Law Prog.)
Krystal M. Gardner	Asst. Dean, Career Services	2006–present (Asst. Dean, Career Services)
Anne Burr	Dir., LRW Program	2007–2014 (Dir., LRW Prog.)
Clara McCarthy	LRW Instructor	2007–2013 (LRW Instructor)
Sarah Abramowicz	Assoc. Prof.	2007–2014 (Asst. Prof.) 2014–present (Assoc. Prof.)
Ericka Matthews-Jackson	Asst. Dean, Admissions	2008–2016 (Asst. Dean, Admissions)
Anne Burr	Instructor & Dir., LRW Prog.	2008–2010 (LRW Instructor) 2010–2014 Dir., LRW Prog.
Robert M. Ackerman	Prof.	2008–2012 (Dean) 2008–present (Prof.) 2017–present (Dir. Levin Center at Wayne Law)
Christopher C. Lund	Prof.	2009–2013 (Asst. Prof.) 2013–2017 (Assoc. Prof.) 2017–present (Prof.)
Adele M. Morrison	Assoc. Prof.	2009–2020 (Assoc. Prof.)
Aaron Perzanowski	Asst. Prof.	2009–2012
Rachel Settlage	Assoc. Prof., Dir. Clinical Education; Assoc. Dean for Academic Affairs	2009–2012 (Clin. Asst. Prof.) 2012–2017 (Asst. Prof.) 2017–present (Assoc. Prof.) 2017–2020 (Dir. Clin. Ed.) 2021–present (Assoc. Dean for Academic Affairs)
Virginia C. Thomas	Dir. Neef Library	2009–present
Kathryn Day	LRW Instructor	2009–present (LRW Instructor)
Brandon Hofmeister	Asst. Prof.	2010–2013

Name	Title	Full Time
Justin Long	Assoc. Prof.	2010–2015 (Asst. Prof.) 2015–present (Assoc. Prof.) 2011–2012 (Assoc. Dir. for Education Law & Policy, Damon J. Keith Center for Civil Rights)
Eric Zacks	Assoc. Prof., Dir., LL.M. Program	2010–2016 (Asst. Prof), 2016–present (Assoc. Prof.) 2021–present (Dir., LL.M. Program)
Kirsten Matoy Carlson	Assoc. Prof.; Adjunct Assoc. Prof. Political Science	2011–2016 (Asst. Prof.), 2016–2020 (Assoc. Prof.) 2016–present (Adjunct Assoc. Prof. Political Science) 2021–present (Prof.)
Charles H. Brower II	Prof.	2012–present
Marilyn Kelly	Dist. Jurist in Residence	2013–present (Distinguished Jurist in Residence) 1997–2013 (Justice, Michigan Supreme Court) 2015–present (WSU Board of Governors)
Kathryn M. Smolinski	Asst. Prof. Clinical Dir. Legal Advocacy for People with Cancer Clinic	2013–present (Asst. Prof. Clinical) 2013–present (Dir. Legal Advocacy for People with Cancer Clinic)
Blanche B. Cook	Assoc. Prof.	2014–2019 (Asst. Prof.) 2019–2020 (Assoc. Prof.)
Carl Levin	Dist. Legislator in Residence, chair, Levin Center at Wayne Law	2015–2021 (Distinguished Legislator in Residence) 1979–2015 (U.S. Senator, Michigan) 2015–2021 (chair, Levin Center at Wayne Law)
Nicolas Schroeck	Asst. Prof., Clinical	2015–2018 (Asst. Prof. Clinical) 2015–2018 (Dir. Transnational Environmental Law Clinic)
Eric C. Williams	Asst. Prof. Clinical	2015–2016 (Asst. Prof. Clinical) 2015–2016 (Dir., Business and Community Law Clinic)
William Ortman	Assoc. Prof.; Edward M. Wise Research Scholar	2016–2020 (Asst. Prof.) 2021–present (Assoc. Prof.) 2021–present (Edward M. Wise Research Scholar)
Richard Bierschbach	Dean, Prof.	2017–present (Dean) 2017–present (Prof.)

Name	Title	Full Time
Sanjukta Paul	Asst. Prof.; Romano Stancroft Research Scholar	2017–present (Asst. Prof.) 2021–present (Romano Stancroft Research Scholar)
Sabrina Balgamwalla	Asst. Prof.; Dir., Asylum and Immigration Law Clinic	2021–present (Asst. Prof.) 2017–2020 (Asst. Prof. Clinical) 2017–present (Director of the Asylum and Immigration Law Clinic)
Anne Choike	Asst. Prof. Clinical; Dir., Business and Community Law Clinic	2017–present (Asst. Prof. Clinical) 2017–present (Director of the Business and Community Law Clinic)
Rebecca Robichaud	Clin. Asst. Prof., Dir. Clinical Education; Asst. Dir., Externship Programs	2012–2013 (adjunct, Asylum and Immigration Law Clinic) 2017–present (Asst. Prof. Clinical) 2017–2020 (Asst. Dir., Externship Programs) 2021–present (Dir. Clinical Education)
Khaled Beydoun	Assoc. Prof.; Assoc. Dir. of Civil Rights & Social Justice, Damon J. Keith Center for Civil Rights	2020–present (Assoc. Prof.) 2020–present (Assoc. Dir. of Civil Rights and Social Justice, Damon J. Keith Center for Civil Rights)
Heather Walker-McCabe	Assoc. Prof. of Law and Social Work	2020–present (Assoc. Prof. of Law and Social Work)
Daniel Ellman	Asst. Prof (Clinical), Dir. Externship Programs	2020–present (Asst. Prof. [Clinical]), Dir. Externship Programs
Hillel Nadler	Asst. Prof.	2021–present (Asst. Prof.)
Jamila Jefferson Jones	Assoc. Prof.	2021–present (Assoc. Prof.)
Nancy C. Cantalupo	Asst. Prof.	2021–present (Asst. Prof.)

Appendix B

Law School Deans

Allan Campbell, 1927–1937

Arthur Neef, 1937–1967

Charles Joiner, 1967–1972

Donald Gordon, 1975–1980

John Roberts, 1980–1987

John Reed, 1987–1993

James K. Robinson, 1993–1998   Joan Mahoney, 1998–2004   Frank Wu, 2004–2008.
                                                                      (Photo by Jim Block)

Robert Ackerman, 2008–2012   Jocelyn Benson, 2012–2016   Richard Bierschbach, 2016–

Appendix C

Wayne University Presidents since 1934

In 1933, a number of colleges administered by the Detroit Board of Education were organized as a university and designated as the Colleges of the City of Detroit. In 1934, the name Wayne University was adopted. Wayne University transitioned into a state university during a transition period 1957–1959. See https://wayne.edu/about/history.

Frank Cody (1934–1942)

Warren E. Bow (1942–1945)

David D. Henry (1945–1952)

Clarence B. Hilberry (1952–1965)

William Rae Keast (1965–1971)

George E. Gullen Jr. (1971–1978)

Thomas Bonner (1978–1982)

David Adamany (1982–1997)

Irvin Reid (1997–2009)

Jay Noren (2009–2010)

Allan Gilmour (2011–2013)

M. Roy Wilson (2013–present)

Index

Page numbers in *italics* refer to images.

University of Michigan Law
    Department, 13
University of Michigan Law
    School, 21, 67, 92, 135, 154
University of Utrecht, 224
University of Warwick, England,
    119, 224
University of Windsor Faculty of
    Law, 119
U.S. News & World Report, 209,
    244–45, 246
U.S. Office of Economic
    Opportunity (OEO), 50, 90
U.S. Supreme Court, 212–14

Van Goethem, Betty, 74n16
Vanzetti, Bartolomeo, 16n21
Vernava, Anthony, 74, 75, 255
Victor, Steven, 193n29
Vietnam War, 46–47, 71–72
Villarosa, Aisa, 208, 244
Visser, Michelle, 172
Visser't Hooft, Willem, 224n73
Vivian, Jesse, 144n58
Vlaich, Mildred, 52
Volz, William, 144n58
von Boetticher, Dietrich, 148–50

Wagner, Annice, 62
Wagner, Donald, 164
Wagner, Douglas, 125, *127*
Wald, Patricia, 156
Waldman, Barry, 83, 89–90, 137,
    151, 196
Waldman, Bryan, 151
Walker, Jacqueline Simons, 247
Walker, Stanton, 47, 48
Walker-McCabe, Heather, 265
Wall of Fame, 239–40
Walsh, B. Lynn, 147
Walters, Daniella, 171n52
Warner Norcross and Judd, 125
Warren, Earl, 69–70
Wayne Law Journal, 41. See also
    Wayne Law Review
Wayne Law Review, 40–46,
    55–56, 112, 250
Wayne's College of Urban, Labor
    and Metropolitan Affairs,
    215
Wayne State University,
    unionization of, 119

Wayne State University Board
    of Governors, 143, 159,
    202n53, 215
Wayne State University Law
    School. *See also* Detroit
    City Law School (DCLS);
    Wayne University Law
    School
    ABA Reaccreditation Report
    (1959) on, 67–69
    ABA Reaccreditation Report
    (1989) on, 232
    ABA Reaccreditation Report
    (1996) on, 192
    academic journals at, 250–51
    admission standards for, 31
    attrition of CLEO students at,
    101–7
    barriers broken by women,
    90–97
    Bierschbach as dean of,
    241–47
    chairs and professorships, 218,
    246, 247
    challenges to admission policy
    of, 113–15
    changes under Joiner, 73–74
    changing role of deans at, 208
    combined degree program,
    193
    comparative law at, 219–22
    competition for applicants, 7
    computerized legal research,
    155
    Damon J. Keith Center for
    Civil Rights established at,
    215–18
    DCL/MSU as competition for,
    187–90
    DCLS renamed, 23
    deans and professors, turnover
    of, 160–62
    deans of, 267–68
    during Depression and WWII,
    27–30
    diversity in enrollment at,
    5, 7–8, 25–26, 51–55, 97,
    99–101, 113–15, 189–90,
    242
    employment opportunities.
    See employment of Wayne
    graduates

    enhanced graduation
    requirements,
    computerization, and
    visibility at, 155–57
    enrollment in, 7–8, 31–32. *See
    also* diversity in enrollment
    evening program at, 158–60
    exchange programs, 224
    expansion of fundraising and
    scholarships at, 240–41
    externship program
    established at, 236
    faculty expansion at, 75–82
    Free Legal Aid Clinic
    established at, 46–50, 229
    full-time faculty of, 253–65
    future of, 251
    grading system at, 104–5,
    108–9
    graduate law programs at,
    148–50
    graduates hired as faculty
    at, 143
    improved employment
    opportunities for graduates
    of, 82–89
    improving first-year academic
    success at, 108–13
    inclusive culture of, 210–11
    increased visibility for, 191–95
    and international
    competitions, 225–26
    international law at, 219–23
    international students at,
    148–50, 185
    Legal Research and Writing
    (LRW) program at, 175–76
    Levin Center at, 237–39
    Master of Studies in Law
    (MSL) degree, 245
    minor in law program,
    158n13, 208, 245
    mission, public interest as,
    9, 208
    Moot Court at, 39–40
    multigenerational alumni
    from, 151
    and national litigation and
    transactional competitions,
    226–28
    new administration of, 71–73
    new law campus for, 69–71